D1049634

ISO 9000

- Motivating the People
- Mastering the Process
- Achieving Registration!

ISO 9000

• Motivating the People
• Mastering the Process
• Achieving Registration!

David Stevenson Huyink

Craig Westover

Burr Ridge, Illinois
New York, New York

This publication is designed to provide accurate and authoritative information in regard to the subject matter covered. It is sold with the understanding that neither the author or the publisher is engaged in rendering legal, accounting, or other professional service. If legal advice or other expert assistance is required, the services of a competent professional person should be sought.

From a Declaration of Principles jointly adopted by a Committee of the American Bar Association and a Committee of Publishers.

Sponsoring editor: Jean Marie Geracie
Project editor: Rita McMullen
Production manager: Laurie Kersch
Interior designer: Laurie Entringer
Cover designer: Tim Kaage
Art manager: Kim Meriwether
Compositor: Precision Typographers
Typeface: 11/13 Palatino
Printer: The Book Press, Inc.

Library of Congress Cataloging-in-Publication Data

Huyink, David Stevenson.
ISO 9000 : motivating the people, mastering the process, achieving registration / David Stevenson Huyink, Craig Westover.
p. cm.
Includes index.
ISBN 0-7863-0115-5
1. Quality control—Standards. 2. Total quality management. 3. Manufactures—Quality control—Standards. I. Westover, Craig. II. Title.
TS156.H895 1994
658.5′62′0218—dc20 93-50172

Printed in the United States of America
2 3 4 5 6 7 8 9 0 BP 1 0 9 8 7 6 5

DEDICATION

To my wife and best friend, Michelle, for all of the support you give me continually and for assuming many of my other responsibilities during the writing of this book.

To my children, Elizabeth, Amy, Rebekah, and Michael, for giving up time you deserved from me so I could produce this work.

To my parents, Hub and Eloise, for teaching me many things, especially to persevere in the face of great challenges.

David Stevenson Huyink
Network Systems Corporation

But one experience is more daunting than writing a book, and that is living with a person who is writing a book. This work is more a testament to the perseverance of my wife, Tam, and my children, Blair and Tyler, than it is to any effort on my part—this dedication a very meager way of expressing my gratitude.

Craig Westover
AT&T Global Information Systems

Foreword

What is ISO 9000 registration and why is it so important? This registration is not simply a quality mark to satisfy customers. It represents cultural change in our prevailing system of management. Prevailing management practices draw from outdated quality systems based largely on inspection. ISO 9000 defines a better system resting on control of processes. *ISO 9000: Motivating the People, Mastering the Process, Achieving Registration!* will provide you with the fundamental knowledge necessary to achieve an effective implementation of ISO 9000. As you read it, you will easily relate the information contained in the book to your own company, and you will begin to understand the importance of the standard and why you must proceed toward registration.

Companies registered to an ISO 9000 standard must have in place a defined and documented quality system that will be evaluated by a disinterested third party. Periodic surveillance audits (two to three each year) will continue while the registration is in force. By purchasing from registered companies, customers will be assured that the processes producing their products meet strict international quality requirements. Companies seeking registration will be compelled to get control of their quality systems and improve them.

ISO 9000 is a win-win proposition. It works as well for a hospital as it does for a manufacturing company. If we wish to compete in the world market, we must change our system of individual adversarial competition and allow people the freedom to cooperate. The ISO 9000 standards require cooperation and the breaking down of barriers between staff areas. They represent a giant step toward world-class quality. That this step must be taken is all too obvious.

Any organization seeking to improve its quality system needs to understand the difficult path ahead. Huyink and Westover have written a book that will provide anyone with the foundation necessary to obtain ISO 9000 registration. As the director of Quality System Assessments for Unisys Corporation, I led the effort to obtain registration of 25 major design, manufacturing, and distribution facilities. As a registered lead assessor of quality systems, I have conducted more than 60 facility assessments and hundreds of internal audits. The information contained in this book is right on the mark. For companies wishing to conduct internal ISO 9000 auditor and ISO 9000 project team training, I recommend they consider using this book as a text. The examples, lessons learned, and comments provided will be especially appreciated by the reader.

Phillip E. Miller, Ph.D.
Director of Quality System Assessments
Unisys Corporation

Preface

In their book, *Quality on Trial,* authors Roger and Maynard Howe and Dee Gaeddert relate the apocryphal story of the Pentagon policy analyst who was called to present before the Joint Chiefs of Staff. The analyst was to present the strategy for dealing with enemy submarine activity in the North Atlantic.

"Gentlemen," he addressed the Joint Chiefs, "I believe we have found the solution to your problem. We heat the waters of the North Atlantic to just below 212 degrees Fahrenheit. At that ambient water temperature, the atmosphere inside the submarines will be unbearable. They will have no choice but to surface. When they do, they will be easy targets for our anti-submarine aircraft."

The Joint Chiefs sat in stunned silence. They glanced quizzically at one another until all eyes finally came to rest on the chief of naval operations. Clearing his throat rather vigorously, the chief addressed the speaker. "And how, sir, do you propose we heat the North Atlantic to 212 degrees?"

"Admiral," responded the bureaucrat, "my job is strategy and policy. The details of implementation I leave to you."[1]

That story carries special meaning for us. When our management officially adopted a strategy of registration to ISO 9001, it did so with the unmitigated confidence of those whose job is strategy and policy; implementation of a quality system that fulfilled the intention of the standard was left to us. Our first reaction was not unlike the surprised admiral's unspoken thought—"How are we going to get this done?"

It is here, however, that the similarity between the heat-the-North-Atlantic story and the real world ends. Heating the North Atlantic is nonsensical and therein lies the humor of the story. Registration to ISO 9000 quality system standards is not only possible, it is arguably essential to remain competitive in the global marketplace—and therein lies the reason it is deadly serious business. And take this point as given: as the ISO 9000 management representative for your organization or as a person involved with a specific aspect of your organization's quality system, well . . .

implementation of an ISO 9000-compliant quality system is up to you.

This book is written for you—the ISO 9000 management representative (as required by the standards) who is charged with managing the ISO 9000 registration project, the executive who understands the importance of ISO 9000 registration and who is sponsoring the registration effort, the line manager who is coordinating quality system activities in his or her functional area, and the individual contributor who realizes that ultimately he or she has the greatest impact on the smooth functioning of the organization's quality system. *ISO 9000: Motivating the People, Mastering the Process, Achieving Registration!* is a book about implementation, not theory. It answers the question "How are we going to get this [ISO 9000 registration] done?"

Let us set some expectations. *ISO 9000: Motivating the People, Mastering the Process, Achieving Registration!* is not a one-stop guide to the detailed specifics of the various standards that make up the ISO 9000 series. Excellent sources of that information—books and seminars—abound. It is not a rehash of the importance or rationale for the standards. It is not yet another high-concept look at the content of the ISO 9000 series. Although each of these areas is necessarily addressed, the primary purpose of *ISO 9000: Motivating the People, Mastering the Process, Achieving Registration!* is to present ISO 9000 registration in an organizational context. *ISO 9000: Motivating the People, Mastering the Process, Achieving Registration!* is divided into four sections that correspond to the four distinct phases of a successful ISO 9000 registration project: getting started, managing the compliance of the quality system, managing the actual ISO 9000 registration project, and managing the maintenance of an ISO 9000-compliant quality system.

Section I, entitled, "How Are We Going to Get This Done?" will help you overcome the organizational inertia every company must overcome when facing a major undertaking. This section will help you get the ISO 9000 project moving in the right direction right from the start. You'll learn ways to overcome the natural resistance to change found in all companies. You'll learn how to put together a registration plan that considers the critical success factors necessary and sufficient to overcome cultural barriers to ISO 9000 registration. And you'll learn techniques that will help you present your ISO 9000 registration project plan to management in a way that will gain not only their approval of the plan, but their commitment to the project.

The second section, "Ensuring ISO 9000 Compliance of the Quality System," helps you through the implementation phase of the ISO 9000 registration project. It will show you what needs to be done to make your organization's quality system compliant with the criteria of the appropriate ISO 9000 standard. You'll learn how to put together a team of individuals to implement the ISO 9000 registration project plan, determine your quality system's initial state relative to the ISO 9000 standards, bring your system into compliance with the standards, and ensure continuing compliance.

The third section, "The ISO 9000 Registration Process," helps you through the actual ISO 9000 registration process from choosing a registration assessment agency to the details of hosting an on site assessment visit. You'll learn how to prepare for a preregistration assessment visit and how to determine your organization's readiness to be assessed. This section will also prepare you for the actual registration assessment, including preparing the people in your company for the assessment visit. You'll gain insight into how an actual registration assessment visit works.

The fourth and final section, "Final Thoughts on ISO 9000," touches on three distinct topics of specialized interest. The first chapter in this section will help you maintain your quality system once your organization is ISO 9000 registered. Although our experience (and many of the examples you will find in this book) is based on ISO 9000 registration within a large organization, we have tapped the wisdom of others to discuss special implications of the ISO 9000 registration project for smaller companies in Chapter 14. Finally, we have compiled several of the more common questions that have been presented to us after our successful registration efforts along with our responses to those questions in Chapter 15. Depending on your level of knowledge of ISO 9000, you may find it helpful to use Chapter 15 as a basic primer on ISO 9000 and read Chapter 15 before going through the linear steps of ISO 9000 registration.

In short, *ISO 9000: Motivating the People, Mastering the Process, Achieving Registration!* is the book we needed, but didn't have, when implementation of our organization's ISO 9000 registration effort was left to us. It discusses the planned elements of our ISO 9000 registration effort that worked, those that weren't effective or were outright mistakes, and with the perfect vision of hindsight, identifies those fortunate accidents that weren't planned but proved beneficial to our registration project.

ISO 9000: Motivating the People, Mastering the Process, Achieving Registration! takes our experience and organizes it into a ready reference for use in implementing your ISO 9000 registration project. Each chapter discusses important and useful principles and techniques applicable to a particular phase of the registration project. Where appropriate, we conclude each chapter with examples of how we applied those principles at our division of AT&T/NCR, the Network Products Division.[2]

The obvious question you should have at this point is "Why should I have confidence in the methodology put forth in this book?" Like us, you no doubt are bombarded with quality literature in general and ISO 9000 literature specifically. What gives us such confidence in the techniques we are presenting? Let us set the stage for our division's ISO 9000 registration effort.

NCR Network Products Division embarked on ISO 9000 registration in late 1989 by becoming acquainted with the standard and benchmarking other organizations at various stages of the registration process. In January of 1990 at the annual strategic planning retreat, our boss, the division director of quality assurance, first positioned registration to ISO 9001 as an organizational goal. The project formally got underway in June of 1990. We were registered to ISO 9001 by the British Standards Institution (BSI) after our first registration assessment in August of 1991—one assessment and four months *ahead* of our in-your-wildest-dreams schedule. And we accomplished this in an atmosphere that, at best, might be described as "somewhat unsettled." During the period from January 1990 to registration in August of 1991, our division

- had three division vice presidents and two directors of quality assurance;
- was converted from an integrated business unit within NCR to an engineering and manufacturing division with separate business units (each using a discrete set of processes and procedures);

- operated for almost a year with no formal organizational structure or charter;
- went through several reductions in the size of the workforce;
- physically moved our engineering organization and our manufacturing facility six weeks before the August registration assessment.

Given that environment, we have to conclude that it was something more than technical understanding of the ISO 9000 standard that enabled us to achieve registration. That "something more"—the planning, the managing, the motivating and informing, the preparing of the organization for a registration assessment—is what you will take away from this book and apply to your own ISO 9000 registration effort. It is your answer when your organization asks the question "How are we going to get this done?"

Acknowledgments

Success has been defined as coming to those who are smart enough to have an idea, dumb enough to act on it, and lucky enough to survive. We did some smart things in our ISO 9000 registration effort, more than a few dumb ones, but if there was any luck involved in our ISO 9000 project, it was the luck of being fortunate to work with some truly outstanding people.

At the celebration we held after our division was registered to ISO 9001, our ISO 9000 project champion noted that the difference between a hunk of coal and a diamond is one of pressure. Under pressure, common coal turns to precious diamond. Under the pressure of business reorganization and ISO 9000 registration project deadlines, the people of NCR Network Products Division shined brighter than any diamond. People took the ISO 9000 registration effort personally, working many extra hours and giving the project their hearts and minds as well as their hands.

We cannot begin to acknowledge all of the people who contributed to the effort of ISO 9000 registration or in one way or another offered a comment or suggestion that found its way into the methodology described in this book. However, as we look back on the project, there are certain people whose contribution to the project and the book must be acknowledged. These individuals are: Dave Anderson, Suzie Babich, Jim Bach, Jo Bailen, Pete Berntson, John Celio, Bill Erlick, Wendy Farbelow, Wilt Feider, Marc Frie, Tom Fulks, Ron Groenke, Tom Hannah, Bob Hayes, Neil Henderson, Mike Hodges, Bill Holz, Bill Jennings, Dave Jensen, Bill Jwanouskos, Al Karsnia, Joe Klukas, Cindy Kriha, Renate Lemke, Dave Loomis (and his ''educated'' notebook), Kathleen Losekamp, Tom Maletich, Lynn Masica, Ken McCauley, Steve Melena, Howard Morgan, Denny Parker, Dan Pigott, Tom Quintavalle, Jackie Reed, Kim Regenhard, Chuck Riley, Kathy Rogowski, Kirsten Skjerbek, Rick Stuhr, Kris Schoen, Roger Vake, Roger Weingarth, John Whaley, Harlan Zurn, Judy Zwanka, and Jeanne Zwicki, with a very special thank you to Mavonne Prokop.

Having acknowledged the contributions of those who contributed to our ISO 9000 registration effort, we also realize that people of this character exist in all organizations, including yours. *ISO 9000: Motivating the People, Mastering the Process, Achieving Registration!* will provide you with a guide for bringing out the best in those people, for efficiently and effectively structuring their efforts, and for successfully achieving ISO 9000 registration for your organization.

David Stevenson Huyink
Craig Westover

Contents

SECTION

I

HOW ARE WE GOING TO GET THIS DONE?

Chapter One

Why All the Excitement about ISO 9000?

Challenges can be stepping stones or stumbling blocks. It's just a matter of how you view them.

Unknown

The ISO 9000 series of quality system standards came quietly into the world in 1987. For a few years, it remained a relatively unknown quantity. However, as the decade changed, ISO 9000 and quality system management suddenly became hot topics in the business world.

Today, magazine articles on quality system management abound, with both general business and quality-oriented publications devoting the major portions of issues to ISO 9000. Advertisements for ISO 9000-related products and service jump from their pages. New publications have been founded specifically to address ISO 9000 requirements. Seminars have sprung out of nowhere. Consulting firms have added ISO 9000 to their repertoire of offerings. New consulting firms specializing in ISO 9000 are hanging out their shingles. Entire tracks and workshops at quality conferences are dedicated to discussion of ISO 9000. Colleges offer courses in ISO 9000 auditing.

Why all the excitement? What is it about the ISO 9000 standards that is creating all the interest? Is ISO 9000 some "quantum theory" of quality? Does it define a set of criteria so profound that it is the holy grail of the quest for quality? If not, what then accounts for the sudden rise in ISO 9000 interest?

THE PURPOSE OF THIS CHAPTER

As a driver of the ISO 9000 registration project in your organization, you require two types of basic knowledge to ensure the success of the registration effort. The first is factual information.[1] As the de facto in-company expert on ISO 9000, you will be asked myriad questions about ISO 9000—questions that can be answered with factual responses. However, facts are often perceived differently by different people.

Thus, the second type of basic knowledge you require to ensure the success of your ISO 9000 project is a general understanding of how ISO 9000 is likely to be perceived by different departments within your organization and by different types of people within those departments.

In this chapter, we'll address both types of knowledge: (1) basic facts about ISO 9000—where the standards come from and why they are important—and (2) the impact ISO 9000 is likely to have on different departments within your organization and on different types of people working within those departments. Armed with both types of knowledge, you will be able to effectively position ISO 9000 with the people of your organization. You will have a framework for positioning ISO 9000 within the cultural context of your organization.

THE NEED FOR STANDARDS

One of the first questions that invariably crops up concerning ISO 9000 is the conceptual question of why quality system standards are necessary at all. After all, humankind has gotten along for centuries without ISO 9000. So why all of a sudden is there all this excitement? The reason can be summed up in a single word—*change.*

From the first voyages of the ancient Phoenicians, the recorded history of humankind has been a history of international commerce. The opportunity to profit from international commerce drove much of the world's early exploration. It drove Marco Polo to China, Columbus in search of a new route to the East, and Matthew Perry to Japan. However, while international commerce was once quite literally an exchange of goods unique to one part of the world for goods unique to another, today international commerce has taken on a quite different look. In today's global economy, "international commerce" more often than not means direct competition among companies selling the same or similar products throughout the world—everything from automobiles to computers to appliances to clothing. On a business-to-business level, companies in one part of the world have a choice of suppliers from around the world.

To maintain some semblance of assurance that scattered suppliers have the ability to deliver consistent quality products, businesses have developed sophisticated supplier management systems that require suppliers to demonstrate that ability. Although conducting the necessary supplier surveys is costly for these businesses, it is deemed worth the price in prevention of quality problems. Suppliers in this scenario also see costs rise as they struggle to respond to variations in their customers' quality system requirements—some of which may be conflicting. One customer will have one set of requirements, a second customer will have another, and a government agency might well have a third set of do's, don'ts, and what if's. For large companies, this is an expensive burden. For smaller suppliers, meeting the multiple requirements of their several customers is at times an impossible task.

The ISO 9000 standards help solve this problem. As the number of companies that accept the ISO 9000 standards as a basis for judging their suppliers' quality systems grows, the problem of having to address multiple and differing customer requirements diminishes. The ISO 9000 standards are *international* standards that provide a means of supplier management for any business, whether its supplier is on the other side of the street or on the other side of the world.

Thus, if your company is going to compete in today's global marketplace, it must be prepared to be judged by standards recognized around the world.

ORIGIN OF THE ISO 9000 STANDARDS

ISO standards are the concern of the International Organization for Standardization. Founded in 1946 and based in Geneva, Switzerland, the organization is, as its name states, an *international* organization. Members of the International Organization for Standardization are standards organizations of the member countries. A *standards organization* is that organization within a country, usually but not always a government agency, responsible for establishing and maintaining standards for the country. Examples of the kinds of standards maintained by these agencies are product standards, safety standards, and more recently, quality system standards. The United States is represented by the American National Standards Institute (ANSI).

While technical people in your company may be familiar with ISO technical standards, many other people who will be affected by the ISO 9000 quality system standards may be unfamiliar with the International Organization for Standardization. As a driver of the ISO 9000 registration project for your company, you must be prepared to answer questions about this international organization in a manner that communicates credibility and addresses perceptions created by a piecemeal understanding of it.

For example, a common misconception about the International Organization for Standardization is that it is a *European* organization. Although it is headquartered in Geneva, it is no more a European organization than the United Nations is a United States organization because it is headquartered in New York. This point is emphasized because many falsely believe that the ISO 9000 standards are only European standards, when, in fact, the ISO 9000 standards are recognized and adopted around the world.

The ISO 9000 standards, approved in 1987 by ISO Technical Committee 176, were based largely on the then effective British BS 5750 quality system standards. The original set of five documents published as the ISO 9000 series contained two guidelines and three standards to be used in contractual agreements. These documents are as follows:

ISO 9000: A guideline for determining which contractual standard to use.

ISO 9001: The contractual standard for companies that design and service what they manufacture.

ISO 9002: The contractual standard for companies that manufacture, but do not design what they manufacture.

ISO 9003: The contractual standard for companies that assemble and test products designed and manufactured elsewhere.

ISO 9004: A guideline for a quality system somewhat more comprehensive than those described in the contractual standards.

Companies seek to register to ISO 9001, ISO 9002, or ISO 9003. *Registration* means that a company has had its quality system (the procedures by which it builds products or provides services) assessed by an independent third party (sometimes an arm of a country's standards organization) which has concluded that the quality system meets the criteria set forth in the appropriate standard.

As a driver of the ISO 9000 registration project, your task is to select the ISO 9000 standard that applies to the business of your company and develop a plan to ensure that your organization's quality system meets the criteria set forth in that standard. You will then arrange and coordinate the activities required to have your quality system registered with a third-party assessment agency recognized in those parts of the world where you do business.

Third-party assessment, where your organization contracts with an independent assessment agency to assess your quality system and, upon compliance with a specific ISO 9000 standard, register your quality system in a registry of compliant companies, is one of three ways in which the ISO 9000 standards can affect a company.

A company may elect to forgo registration in favor of a self-application of the ISO 9000 standards. In this case, the company does a *first-party assessment* and declares compliance with the standard. This strategy is effective only to the degree that customers and marketplaces are willing to accept self-declaration as adequate.

A company may also find itself assessed against the ISO 9000 standards by current or potential customers. In this case, the customer performs a *second-party assessment.* The customer performs its own assessment of its supplier's quality system using the ISO 9000 criteria as a guideline and makes its own determination of the supplier's ability to deliver products or services of consistent quality. Of course, the results of the assessment only apply to one customer, and the supplier may have to undergo similar assessments by other customers.

Because it is perceived by many customers as more objectively valid than first-party assessment and more cost-effective than second-party assessment, third-party assessment and registration to ISO 9000 is the most beneficial choice for both customers and suppliers, and it is the main focus of this book.

The benefit to customers of having their suppliers registered to

ISO 9000 by an independent third party is that they do not have to maintain a large staff to perform supplier assessments. The benefit to suppliers of third-party ISO 9000 registration is that they do not have to comply with multiple and conflicting quality system requirements of their several customers, but as ISO 9000 standards gain acceptance, they can focus their efforts on improving their quality systems in a manner that meets one set of internationally recognized standards. For these reasons, the ISO 9000 standards, although not the ''quantum theory'' of quality, are a very practical solution to the problem of assessing quality systems in a global economy.

Having elected to pursue third-party assessment and registration, you must first determine to which of the three ISO 9000 contractual standards your organization will seek registration: ISO 9000 *Quality Management and Quality Assurance Standards—Guidelines for Selection and Use,* 1987, a publication of the ISO (see Figure 2–1), can help you determine the appropriate standard that applies to your organization. However, that determination is not the end of your decision responsibilities.

Companies may, and sometimes do, register to a standard whose scope is less than what the company actually does. For example, a company that designs, manufactures, and services its products may decide to become registered to ISO 9002, which covers manufacturing but not design/development. It is often easier, faster, and less expensive to make a division of a large organization, like manufacturing, compliant with ISO 9002 than it is to extend compliance to the rest of the company.

Although cost may sometimes be an issue, in our experience, companies that design products but comply only with the ISO 9002 standard frequently do so because they do not have confidence in their ability to bring their design/development functions under control. It is also our experience that when a company *underregisters,* it runs the risk of sending a message to its customers by what it leaves out of the scope of registration. Most companies in that position use ISO 9002 registration as a stepping stone to ISO 9001 registration and full coverage of the scope of what they do.

In addition to the initial ISO 9000 series, the ISO has published other documents as guidelines to implementing these standards outside of the manufacturing arena, specifically software development, process, and service industries. These documents are referenced in Chapter 2.

ADOPTION OF THE ISO 9000 STANDARDS

Since they were issued, the ISO 9000 standards have been adopted as national standards by nearly every industrial country in the world. In some cases, such as Australia, *adoption* carries the force of legislation. In other cases, such as the European Community, ISO 9000 is not a legal requirement to do business, but compliance with ISO 9000 greatly facilitates the process of doing business with member countries.

The ISO 9000 standards are published in several languages. Each country that has adopted them has given the ISO 9000 standards their own titles and numbering systems. For example, in the United States, the ISO 9000 standards are called the Q9000 (formerly Q90) standards published jointly by the American National Standards Institute and the American Society for Quality Control, while in Great Britain they are called the BS 5750 standards. The European Economic Community has adopted ISO 9000 under the rubric the EN 29000 standards. Other countries have other designations.

The important point is that there are no functional differences between the ISO 9000 standards published by the International Organization for Standardization and the versions published by individual countries. The only differences are idiomatic and language-specific. For example, the US standards use the word *organization* with a ''z'' while the British BS 5750 standards use the word *organisation* with an ''s.'' Other than those types of discrepancies, the two standards are contextually equivalent.

Although there are no functional differences among the different governmental adoptions of the ISO 9000 standards, there are *significant political differences that will affect your choice of a third-party assessor with whom to apply for registration of your quality system.* There are cases where a governmental organization restricts the trading of certain products contingent upon the registration of a supplier's quality system to a *specific* adoption of the standards. In those cases, selecting the third-party agency becomes a significant decision. If you find your company in this situation, you must select a third-party registration agency whose *registration is recognized in countries where your company conducts significant business.*

For example, for reasons of health and safety or strategic importance, the European Economic Community (EEC) has targeted certain products to be regulated under recent directives. An implantable medical device is a case in point. Because the EEC views assuring quality system compliance with acceptable standards as important, they have referenced the EN 29000 standards (ISO 9000) in various directives. As these directives take effect, a company to which the quality system compliance portions of the directives apply must be registered to EN 29001 (ISO 9001) or EN 29002 (ISO 9002), *and not to some country's adoption of the standard,* to legally ship its regulated products to the EEC.

The political significance of this registration requirement is that the EEC *alone* determines which third-party agencies can grant registration to the EN 29000 standards. As of this date, only certain third-party agencies within the EEC can grant EN 29000 registration. Dialogue has begun between the EEC and nonmember countries (like the United States) that lays the groundwork for mutual recognition of accreditation of third-party agencies for the purpose of allowing third-party agencies in nonmember countries to grant registration to EN 29000 standards, but no timetable has been agreed upon. There are currently Memoranda of Understanding (MOU) between third-party agencies themselves. These have been set up so that a company may use a local third-party agency and jointly be granted registration by some foreign agency with which the local agency has an MOU. The EEC has not, however, recognized the validity of such MOU agreements relative to regulated products.

Because the issues surrounding governmental requirements for ISO 9000 registration are changing and are therefore confusing, you need to keep track of what these governmental decisions mean to your company. To determine whether the legislation of some external government affects the exporting of your company's product, contact the government agency in your country that deals with international trade, for example, the US Department of Commerce. When selecting a third-party assessment agency, ensure that the agency you select can register your company to a standard accepted by your marketplace countries.

ISO 9000 AND THE QUALITY JOURNEY

Although ISO 9000 is gaining a wider following daily, we should note that not all reaction to ISO 9000 is positive. Some suppliers resent being required to register to an ISO 9000 standard as a condition of doing business with a customer. The standards are viewed as stumbling blocks by suppliers that see them as another layer of bureaucracy that gets in the way of doing "real" business. Others object that the standards are not stringent enough. They believe that companies should be required to adhere to more comprehensive guidelines such as those reflected in the Malcolm Baldrige Award or Deming Prize criteria. You will find both these attitudes prevalent in your organization.

Although such arguments raise interesting questions and can lead to many hours of interesting discussion, there comes a time to stop talking and start doing. It the premise of this book that ISO 9000, when viewed as a stepping stone to improved product quality through improving a company's quality system, is an excellent tool for both improving the way a company does business today and for driving a company towards total quality management[2] in the future. The business of business *is* business, and to fulfill its intent of being a basis for contractual agreement between supplier and customer, ISO 9000 must first be recognized by individual companies as an integral part of doing business and as a tool for providing competitive advantage.

To that end, to lead your organization's ISO 9000 registration project, you must have more than just a factual understanding of ISO 9000. You must understand the impact the effort to become registered to ISO 9000 will have on your organization and its people. In the following sections, we'll look at those two issues—first, the potential impact of ISO 9000 on departments that make up your organization, and second, the potential impact on individuals within those departments.

EFFECTS OF ISO 9000 ON COMPANY FUNCTIONS

Although ISO 9000 is generating generally positive interest in the business world, the announcement that your organization is seeking ISO 9000 registration is likely to cause excitement of a different kind—apprehension. For many organizations, outside inspection and registration of its quality system will be perceived as a judgment on the way it conducts its business. This is an unsettling circumstance for a company's employees and the resulting apprehension can be an impediment to achieving ISO 9000 registration. What's more, the degree to which ISO 9000 will affect a company varies by organization within that company. Although each company is unique, some generalizations can be made about the impact of ISO 9000 on departments within a company.

Manufacturing

Manufacturing functions are typically the least disrupted by the ISO 9000 requirements because, in general, manufacturing organizations in most companies already meet many of the requirements of the standards. That is not to say there is no work to be done in documenting certain functions previously undocumented. However, in most organizations, manufacturing has led the way in quality improvement, often out of necessity. Manufacturing is at the end of the delivery chain in a company. It is often pressured to deliver quality products on time, even in the absence of adequate forecasting or while coping with product quality problems that got "thrown over the wall" from other organizations. Because quality-related issues have been passed along until they can be passed no further, manufacturing has had to react to such issues and improve their quality system for the sake of the rest of the company.

We recognize that this statement is an obvious generality and that it is certainly not true for all organizations. Nonetheless, our experience and our involvement with multiple companies pursuing ISO 9000 registration have uncovered but few exceptions to manufacturing's quality leadership—which is why some companies register to ISO 9002 when they clearly perform the design/

development as well as the manufacturing function. ISO 9000 representatives from these companies justify this strategy by explaining that at the time the decision was made to seek ISO 9000 registration, their companies' manufacturing organizations were already nearly compliant with the ISO 9000 standards. In practice, their biggest effort was to properly document already existing procedures. Not so for their companies' design/development functions.

Design/Development

Many organizations embarking on ISO 9000 registration will find that, compared to manufacturing, there has not been much systematic improvement effort applied to the design/development function. Designers operate under a different set of constraints than manufacturing personnel. They are very deadline driven and often are working on projects that may be 12 to 18 months or more in duration. To design/development engineers, an ISO 9000 registration project is but another project piled on top of everything else they have to do in addition to getting the future of the company out the door. Design/development organizations are typically not chartered with improving their processes. Problems that escape undetected by the design/development organization are either caught and corrected by manufacturing or are handled by a *continuation* function whose responsibility it is to make engineering changes to products with latent defects.

Designers' creative efforts are targeted at *product* improvements, not *process* improvements. For this reason, some designers look at the documenting of processes or procedures, such as required by ISO 9001, as an attempt to stifle their creativity. If the ISO 9001 standard were voluminous and prescriptive, this fear might be well-founded. However, ISO 9001 says very little about the design/development process itself. The ISO 9001 standard deals with design/development input, design/development output, and design/development changes, but does not prescribe a specific design/development methodology. ISO 9001 specifically does not prohibit creative thinking.

Again, we recognize the above statements are generalities, and like us, readers can no doubt point to examples of organizations with highly refined design/development processes. However, even in these organizations, the ISO 9000 champion must recognize that people's mindsets vary from organization to organization. As a general rule, designers will be suspicious of ISO 9000 and protective of their creative processes. Their reaction to changes in their working environment is not aberrant behavior, but typical of any of us asked to change a comfortable status quo.

An important function of the ISO 9000 champion is to "sell" change—to develop win-win strategies so that the ISO 9000 registration project provides benefits for the functional areas in the company. Creating an ISO 9000 compliant quality system within a company's design/development organization can be the most difficult part of an ISO 9000 registration project because design/development organizations typically require more changes in behavior than any other function.

Service

Out of necessity, the service function is well defined in most companies. Like the manufacturing organization, the service organization may require a documentation effort to achieve ISO 9000 registration, but usually requires little if any changes in behavior, with one notable exception. A common problem in the service area is that service people often circumvent documented processes and/or procedures that get in the way of doing what is "right for the customer." While this is admirable behavior and clearly the correct thing to do from the customer's perspective, consistently circumventing documented processes rather than changing them ultimately results in inconsistent service to customers. This is the reason ISO 9000 assessors look at both a company's documented processes and the behaviors of people within the organization in determining whether or not to register a company to ISO 9000. It is also why documented processes and procedures must accurately reflect the behavior of people in the organization.

Marketing/Sales

Although the marketing/sales function is not immediately perceived as a major player in the actual development and implementation of your organization's quality system, ISO 9000 registration will have an impact on the marketing and sales of your company's products and/or services. The degree of that positive impact will vary depending upon the degree of involvement of the marketing/sales organization in the ISO 9000 registration process.

In the best of all possible worlds, marketing/sales would instinctively see the advantage of ISO 9000 registration. Marketers would realize the competitive advantage of a registered quality system. Successful ISO 9000 registration would be used to position the company as an organization that understands and markets quality products and services. ISO 9000 would be seen as a stepping stone to improve quality products and true customer focus.

Unfortunately, marketing/sales, which is so often driven by a quarterly outlook, may not intuitively see the long-term potential advantage of ISO 9000. Many marketing/sales people do not see the significance of the ISO 9000 standard as a *selling* tool. If your organization is registered to an ISO 9000 standard and your competition is not, you can market your company's registration as symbolic of its superior quality focus. Conversely, if your competition is registered to ISO 9000 and you are not, you may find yourself at a competitive disadvantage in the eyes of your marketplace.

Part of your ISO 9000 registration strategy must include demonstrating the business benefits of registration to the marketing/sales organization. Sooner or later, someone will ask you the question "How does ISO 9000 registration effect our bottom line?" That person will likely come from marketing/sales or executive management.

Executive Management

Executives are concerned with business issues. They want to know how expenditures translate into revenue growth, return on investment, market share gain, or other quantifiable objectives. From their perspective, ISO 9000 has relevance only if it affects areas critical to the business. Are important customers asking about or requiring that you have ISO 9000 registration plans? Do you sell significant amounts of your product in parts of the world where the standards are being enforced? Are competitors in your industry pursuing registration?

If these overt pressures are missing, you will have to create them. ''Create'' here is not used to imply that you should fabricate a reason to seek ISO 9000 registration that is not founded in the realities of your business. Rather, it means you must justify ISO 9000 registration by drawing logical conclusions and extrapolating from your current business situation. For example, important customers in your industry may not be asking about ISO 9000, but they are in other industries. Is it logical to assume that your industry will soon follow suit? Although this question requires that you draw a conclusion, if the conclusion is a logical consequence of trends in your marketplace, in essence you will have created a compelling need for ISO 9000 registration. In fact, you will be ahead of the game because you anticipated rather than reacted to the need.

In the final analysis, your company's decision to pursue ISO 9000 registration and your schedule for registration must be driven by the market. Immediate pressures from the environment require a relatively short schedule and consequently a greater concentration of resources to achieve timely ISO 9000 registration. Anticipating, rather than reacting to, the need for ISO 9000 registration, will allow a longer schedule and a more protracted expenditure of resources. However, in either case, no decision will be made to pursue ISO 9000 registration unless there is a business need. You must position ISO 9000 registration not in terms of the benefits you might perceive it has for the business, but in terms perceived as benefits by executive management. Benefits are quantifiable business results.

Sales and revenue are the strongest motivators for management, but also powerful are operating metrics like reduction or elimination of waste, productivity improvement, yield increases, and reduced cycle times. The key point is that to enlist the support of executive management, you must build a business case for ISO 9000 registration.

The General Employee Population

The ISO 9000 registration project will challenge the way an organization does business. Processes and procedures will change, and cultural change will be demanded of the organization as well. Obviously, change affects people differently. As a driver of the ISO

9000 project, you will become a change agent in your company. As was the case in presenting the ISO 9000 story to executive management, when presenting the story to the individual contributors in your organization, you will have to position ISO 9000 registration in terms of benefits they understand and appreciate. Employee and management concerns are not necessarily one and the same.

Implementing an ISO 9000-compliant quality system will have both positive and negative effects upon individuals in your organization. On the positive side, the ISO 9000 registration project will call attention to unnecessary policies, processes, and procedures that frustrate people and contribute to unnecessary costs within the organization. For example, the responsibility and authority sections of the ISO 9000 standards ensure that individuals who change jobs will not have to conduct a massive search for someone to help them understand their new positions. They won't have to guess from the previous output of the function what to do, nor make it all up and hope for the best. ISO 9000 requires documented processes and procedures.

On the negative side, people do not like change that is done *to* them, and if improperly implemented, the ISO 9000 registration project will be perceived as forced change. For example, if standard operating procedure is minuteless meetings and an ISO 9000-inspired procedure requires written minutes and definitive action items, employees may perceive that the ISO 9000 registration project is simply adding administrative overhead that gets in the way of real productivity.

ISO 9000 registration activities are especially stressful for the individuals who are regarded as sole resident experts. These are the competent people who have been around "forever" and know how things really get done in the company. Unfortunately, everything is in their heads. As innocent and right as documenting processes may seem, to the sole resident expert documentation becomes a threat. What was once his or her exclusive knowledge now becomes part of the standard way of doing business. Is it any wonder, then, that some individuals in the company, however subtly, might resist ISO 9000 registration?

There are other reasons people in the company may be less than enthusiastic about ISO 9000 registration. The point is, be aware of people as individuals. Although you can generalize about the reaction and attitudes of departments with the company, don't expect those generalizations to hold true in every instance for every individual. Across an organization there are many attitudes that must be dealt with and many ways to classify people according to their attitudes.

Thus far we have divided an organization along functional lines—manufacturing, design/development, service, marketing/sales, and executive management. Using teams to bring people from these organizations together can reduce some of the differences in departmental mindsets toward ISO 9000. However, even within teams you will have to address a different set of dynamics—individual attitudes. In the following section, we'll take a look at one helpful way to classify individual attitudes toward ISO 9000 registration.

ISO 9000 AND INDIVIDUAL ATTITUDES

People's attitudes toward ISO 9000 registration, indeed toward the whole idea of quality system management, are bounded by two extremes. At one end of the spectrum are the quality purists, at the other end, the extreme pragmatists. The spectrum of attitudes in between is defined in Figure 1-1.

The Quality Purist

Quality purists are the radicals of the quality world. They are the early adopters of the quality world. Their view of quality is cutting edge theory. They read every new quality book as soon as it is published. They want to implement every new theory *now.*

In terms of ISO 9000, a quality purist will view ISO 9000 as a regressive step to inspection-oriented quality or to a bureaucratic implementation of quality. The quality purist's support for the ISO 9000 registration project will be only as a means to an end—total quality management (TQM).

The problem for you as a driver of ISO 9000 registration is not the motivation of quality purists, but their zeal. In their enthusiasm for total quality management, quality purists will fight interim

FIGURE 1–1
Extreme Attitudes toward the ISO 9000 Registration Project

Attitude	*View of ISO 9000 Project*	*Your Message*
Quality purist	It is a step backward in quality	Show how the project addresses improvement of processes and lays a foundation for shared quality values through the deployment of the company's quality policy.
Quality advocate	It advances the quality system	Encourage their quality enthusiasm. Arm them with the business rationale for ISO 9000 and make them your missionaries to the organization.
Pragmatist	It may benefit the business	Provide numerous examples of how the business will be helped by the project. Make them examples of success.
Extreme pragmatist	It is a necessary evil	Stress any immediate pressure to become registered and also the idea of competitive advantage and disadvantage.

steps necessary for timely ISO 9000 registration that are less than ideal from a TQM perspective. They will try to expand the scope of the ISO 9000 registration project well beyond what is required for registration. If a little quality is good for the organization, then a whole lot more is better. A praiseworthy attitude, perhaps, but one that will cause your project schedule to slip and the costs of ISO 9000 registration to rise.

Quality purists can be strong allies in your organization's drive for ISO 9000 registration, but only if you can convince them that the project is, indeed, a stepping stone, and not a stumbling block, to total quality management. There are many parts of the ISO 9000 standard that reinforce that concept. A quality system based on the ISO 9000 model will bring the company's processes under control. Once under control, continuous and innovative improvement can be made to the processes. Process improvement is a foundational element of total quality management. Also, ISO 9000 requires that the company quality policy be clearly articulated to all employees. This too is an element of total quality management.

The point to make to the quality purist is that although the ISO 9000 standard addresses quality system management in a more rudimentary manner than does total quality management, the ISO 9000 standard is not anti-TQM, but rather foundational to TQM. The ISO 9000 standard does not require a company to implement inspection-oriented quality systems. Rather, it allows each individual organization to address the control of quality in whatever way works for it. If teamwork, empowerment, and strategic quality planning are how you control quality, you must be able to demonstrate to the third-party registration agency that, as documented, your system is capable of producing products that consistently meet customer requirements and that people's behavior is consistent with the documented system.

The key to dealing with quality purists is building credibility. If you are going to position ISO 9000 registration as a stepping stone to total quality management, you must have a road map of how you are going to get there. You need to build hooks to total quality management into your ISO 9000 registration project plan. Chapters 3 and 4 address techniques for creating a credible ISO 9000 registration project plan that addresses the cultural changes necessary for future implementation of TQM.

From the people management perspective, the more you involve quality purists in the ISO 9000 planning process, the easier it is to channel their enthusiasm for quality in the right direction and set their expectations for the scope of the ISO 9000 registration project. Far better to be negotiating the scope of the project at the planning stage than sending a confusing message to the organization's people during the registration effort.

The Quality Advocate

The quality advocate holds that quality should be pursued for its own sake. Quality for quality's sake is the ethical high ground. The quality advocate needs no proof of business benefit beyond his or her simple faith that "Quality pays." It's not a case of rejecting a business rationale for ISO 9000 registration, but rather the belief that a business-based reason for pursuing ISO 9000 registration is irrelevant. The quality advocate believes that ISO 9000 registration should be accomplished because it is the right thing to do, and because it is the right thing to do, the business will benefit.

The difference between the quality purist and a quality advocate is that while a quality purist may actually resist ISO 9000 as a step backward in quality, the quality advocate will more likely seize the opportunity to advance the company along the quality continuum. Laying our cards on the table, the authors definitely fall into this category. What we personally learned in implementing our ISO 9000 registration project at NCR and how we personally changed our behaviors is a lesson that will prove helpful in dealing with quality advocates in your organization.

To make ISO 9000 viable in the eyes of the organization, we had to make registration a business necessity. We had to stop preaching "do quality" and start helping the organization use quality to achieve business objectives. When dealing with quality advocates, you don't want to change their motivation, only their methodology.

The most effective way to enlist the aid of quality advocates is to make them your confidants. When working with them, empathize with the position that you're pursuing ISO 9000 registration because it is right, but also emphasize that it is the business value of ISO 9000 registration that will drive it through the organization. Share with them your long-range quality strategy. Arm the quality advocates with a sound business rationale for ISO 9000 registration and let them be your missionaries throughout the company.

The Pragmatist

A pragmatist views quality as being valuable only when it advances the business of the company. Unlike the quality advocate, the pragmatist does not accept at face value that improved quality necessarily produces improved business results. Consequently, pragmatists will consider an ISO 9000 project valuable if and only if they feel that it is required in order to sell into specific markets or that it provides a competitive advantage for the company. In the absence of that need, a quality pragmatist may accept other benefits, such as the elimination or reduction of waste, as valid reasons for conducting the project, but will judge that value in terms of the return on the company's investment in registration.

In working with pragmatists, make as broad a case as possible for all of the business benefits that the company will realize from the project. Beyond immediate customer or regulatory pressure and arguments of competitive advantage or disadvantage, make a case for operational benefits like reduced waste, increased productivity, and the like. Convinced of the business value of ISO 9000 registration, pragmatists can be as staunch ISO 9000 registration project supporters as the quality advocates.

The Extreme Pragmatist

The extreme pragmatist is a person who perceives the notion of quality for quality's sake as dangerous and potentially damaging to the company because "too much" quality is distracting from real business concerns. The value of any special quality effort must be judged in terms of specific impact on profitability of the business.

An extreme pragmatist will support ISO 9000 registration only if it addresses a clear and immediate business need and only if the project can be rigidly controlled. In the absence of any immediate external pressure to be ISO 9000 registered, the extreme pragmatist will resist the initiation of a registration project.

Extreme pragmatists will try to limit the ISO 9000 project to no more than the minimum required for registration. Their goal is registration, not necessarily improvement of the quality system. It is this attitude, especially if the extreme pragmatist is a member of executive management, that can severely hamper your ISO 9000 registration project. Quality purists and quality advocates will view the minimalism of the extreme pragmatist as a signal that the organization doesn't really care about quality. Pragmatists will feel pressure to be more rigorous in their expectations of a business return on ISO 9000 registration.

Working with the extreme pragmatist is one of the most difficult challenges you will face during the ISO 9000 registration project. Extreme pragmatists may openly oppose you at every opportunity, or support you verbally in an open meeting, only to return to the workplace and chide employees for working on the ISO 9000 project instead of doing "real work."

How do you deal with extreme pragmatists? Very carefully. When you need their support, be sure you have a strong business case prepared that supports whatever request you are making. Stress immediate needs for the project like customer or regulatory requirements. Call attention to the increased ISO 9000 registration activity taking place throughout the world and point out the competitive advantage that your organization gains by leading your competition or the competitive disadvantage you will have if beaten by your competitors to ISO 9000 registration. As you make visible improvements to the quality system that result in improvements to the company's bottom line, emphasize these victories to the extreme pragmatist. Any time you have hard data that demonstrates a positive impact from the ISO 9000 registration project on the business, make sure the extreme pragmatists know about it.

It is also important to recognize that no matter how well you plan and prepare for ISO 9000 registration, you will never convince everyone that registration is the right thing to do. And you are foolish to try. You must be concerned with building a critical mass of support for the ISO 9000 project, not with converting the unsaved. Extreme pragmatists are not likely to be, and probably won't ever be, missionaries for ISO 9000 registration. Don't try to force them. Make a business case for whatever support you need, but, in general, isolate them from the project—until you have success and then make sure that they share in it. It's tough to knock a project when people are applauding.

And what of those who never come around? Let those who resist you to the end become an insignificant minority surrounded by the evidence of the project's success. The project will speak for itself.

Real People

The four attitudes of Figure 1–1 are stereotypes to be sure. Within each category, you will find gradations of attitude. You will encounter a few individuals at each of the extremes, but most people in your organization will fall somewhere in the middle. Whatever attitudes you encounter, work to establish a win-win relationship with all. As the quote that opens the chapter says, "Challenges can be stepping stones or stumbling blocks. It's just a matter of how you view them.'' Most people will support something that *they perceive* benefits them. Each person will see ISO 9000 registration through different eyes, and you must show them the picture they want to see.

Sure, it may be true that if you aren't ISO 9000 registered your company will be shut out of a key market. But a quality purist is not so much focused on key markets as he or she is on pursuing ISO 9000 registration as a stepping stone to total quality management and wanting to know how you are going to get there. Conversely, a pragmatist isn't all that interested in a flowery vision of quality as next to godliness. He or she wants to know the impact on the bottom line. Show it.

To motivate real people to buy into ISO 9000 registration, try to understand their expectations. Tailor your communications to meet those expectations. That's neither as easy nor as difficult as it sounds. Examples of effective communication are covered throughout the book.

HOW ARE WE GOING TO GET THIS DONE?

Armed with background about the International Organization for Standardization and the origins of the ISO 9000 quality system standards, a basic understanding of the rationale behind international adoption of the ISO 9000 standards, a sensibility for the potential impact of the ISO 9000 project on the departments that make up your organization, and an understanding of the potential impact of the ISO 9000 project on individuals within those departments, you are ready to begin introducing your organization to the ISO 9000 standards.

Successful ISO 9000 registration of your quality system is your ultimate goal. *ISO 9000: Motivating the People, Mastering the Process, Achieving Registration!* is a rational, step-by-step approach to planning, implementing, and maintaining ISO 9000 registration—the stepping stone response to the question ''How are we going to get this done.'' The first step is to overcome the change-resisting inertia of the organization. We'll address that issue in Chapter 2.

Chapter Two

Getting Started: Overcoming Organizational Inertia

Every body persists in its state of rest or of uniform motion in a straight line unless it is compelled to change that state by forces impressed on it.

Sir Isaac Newton
The Law of Inertia

Unlike many other projects undertaken by a company, ISO 9000 registration will dramatically affect a company's existing corporate culture. The effort to become registered to ISO 9000 will drive many changes in company processes and procedures, but it will also drive personal behavioral changes. People's status within the company will change. Old skills will be replaced with new skills, and although the potential gain from ISO 9000 registration is great, it is not without perceived risk to many individuals within the company.

As Harvard professor Rosabeth Moss-Kanter so aptly notes, change may be exhilarating when done *by* us, but it is disturbing when done *to* us.[1] To many people, the changes required by the ISO 9000 registration project will be perceived as change that is being forced upon them. These people may unconsciously or consciously put up road blocks in the way of the ISO 9000 registration project. This reluctance to change, reluctance to roll up the corporate sleeves and get started on ISO 9000 registration, is what we call "organizational inertia"—the tendency of a company to stick to traditional ways of doing things.

THE PURPOSE OF THIS CHAPTER

The information in this chapter will help you understand and overcome organizational inertia and get your ISO 9000 registration project rolling. You'll become familiar with the objections people most often raise about ISO 9000 registration, and you'll learn how to deal with them. You'll learn how to prepare for the necessary missionary work you must do to prepare the organization for ISO 9000 registration. In short, you'll learn how to position ISO 9000 registration as change that is being done *by* the people of the company, not change being done *to* them by some outside force.

From our experience and verified by our conversations with other companies that have gone through the ISO 9000 registration process, underestimating the impact of cultural change on the ISO 9000 registration effort is almost universal. Replace the word "body" in Newton's Law of Inertia with "company" and you have, in a nutshell, the situation you face when initiating your ISO 9000 registration project. Like a boulder poised at the top of a hill, a slowly accelerating locomotive, or a speeding bullet, every company persists in its state of rest or of uniform motion in a straight line unless it is compelled to change that state by forces impressed on it. ISO 9000 registration is a force that compels change. A successful ISO 9000 registration project hinges on your ability to get people making changes rather than viewing the results of the ISO 9000 registration effort as change forced upon them.

Perhaps the best way to emphasize this point is to step back for a moment—step out of the world of theory and personalize some of the objections to ISO 9000 registration you will encounter at the beginning of the project. Your company's ISO 9000 informational meeting may not go exactly like the one that follows, but the first time someone stands before management to explain the ISO 9000 standards, he or she will surely confront a full range of human dynamics.

WELCOME TO THE REALITIES OF CORPORATE CULTURE!

Eight-thirty and people begin filing into the conference room. Supervisors from around the organization arrive first. Tossing their notepads on chairs around the perimeter of the room, they gather in small groups waiting for the meeting to start. Middle managers arrive next, a few picking out seats around the big conference table in the middle of the room, a few venturing hesitantly to the coffee cart near the door. A couple of managers offer compliments to you, the company's newly appointed ISO 9000 champion, who called the meeting. A few ask you what this ISO 9000 stuff is all about. Their comments reinforce your hunch that most of the people at this meeting know very little about ISO 9000, a few know just enough to be dangerous.

Senior managers begin arriving about 8:35. They grab rolls and coffee. Most have stacks of papers under their arms—in-basket material they plan to browse during anticipated slow parts of the meeting. Not a good sign. They corner each other and some of the middle managers with casual questions about business issues as they take their seats at the table. None of the questions is about ISO 9000. The small groups of supervisors and middle managers break up. When the company president enters the room at 8:40, everyone is seated, ready for the meeting to start—the company's first informational meeting on ISO 9000.

As the ISO 9000 champion, you are well prepared. Since it was announced that you would lead the company's effort to become registered to the ISO 9000 standards, you have done a lot of homework. You've read everything about ISO 9000 you could get your hands on. You understand the intent of the standards and some of the specifics. Most importantly, you appreciate the need for the company to become registered and see a lot of ways to leverage the ISO 9000 registration effort into the company's long-term quality strategy.

The company president opens the meeting with a few remarks. Quite a cross-section of company management has been invited to this first ISO 9000 meeting. Seated around the table are the senior executives whose approval, support, and commitment will be crucial to the success of the project. Some are listening intently to the company president. Others are already flipping through the material from their in-baskets. Among the middle managers and supervisors in the room, some will become members of the ISO 9000 project team—the people who will do the lion's share of the work writing the quality manual, assessing the readiness of the company for registration, defining and implementing quality processes and procedures. Others around the room will probably drag their feet on the effort. Some will actively resist the project.

Suddenly, in one of those off-the-wall leaps the human mind sometimes takes, you find yourself thinking back to high school physics class and good old Sir Isaac Newton and his law of inertia—*Every body persists in its state of rest or of uniform motion in a straight line unless it is compelled to change that state by forces impressed on it.* The enormity of the ISO 9000 registration effort hits home. You and your team are the force that will have to compel the corporate body to change its course. The company president finishes his remarks, and the floor belongs to you.

You begin by giving some background about the ISO 9000 standards. Your first overhead lists reasons why the company should seek registration—market demand, international acceptance of the standards. . . . "Why do we have to be registered to these European standards?" The interruption comes from one of the supervisors at the edge of the room. "The whole single-European market isn't moving that fast." You are ready for this question. You explain that the set of ISO 9000 quality system standards are international standards, not European standards. The European Community has adopted the standards, but so have over 90 countries around the world with such diverse economies as Australia, China, Mexico, and Brazil. Major organizations like the British Defense Agency, Ameritech, and British Telecom require their suppliers to be registered if they want to achieve preferred supplier status, or even to do business at all. Others, like Pacific Bell Telephone, use their own checklists derived from the standards to survey or assess their suppliers.

The final "s" of "suppliers" has not yet escaped between your teeth when the vice president of marketing announces, "I have no knowledge of any customer who is requiring us to become ISO 9000 registered." Again, you are ready. You counter that if the company waits until sales people start getting questions from customers to begin an ISO 9000 registration effort, its customers will belong to competitors with the foresight to become registered ahead of the power curve. The company will be 12 to 24 months behind right out of the gate. At the mention of 24 months, eyebrows raise around the table. You quickly skip past some of your introductory material and move right into a discussion of the registration process.

"How much will all this cost?" asks the company controller, followed by, "It sounds like the third-party registration agencies really have a racket going." One long-time director of engineering chimes in immediately. "Speaking of rackets, once this project is completed, you can start a lucrative consulting business with the experience you'll have here. Think you'll need a partner?"

When the chuckles subside, you address the budget question by providing some typical third-party assessment costs, compiled through benchmarking other companies who have gone through the ISO 9000 registration process. However, because you realize that third-party assessment costs are only a portion of the total cost of ISO 9000 registration and that the true cost of ISO 9000 registration is the time and resources required to document and implement an ISO 9000-compliant quality system, you launch a discussion of the path to registration—the things the company must do and the amount of effort you think it will take to become registered.

Reacting to the extent of the ISO 9000 registration effort, one of the engineering managers clears his throat. "You know," he says, "we've committed to getting a lot of product out the door this year. We just don't have the time to devote to a project that's going to distract people from their jobs."

"Every body persists in its state of rest or of uniform motion . . .," you think, but before you can answer, another engineer echoes the sentiment of the first. "To save time, it's best not to mess up the system we have," she says. "Just add a few things that will convince the third-party agency to register us. Then we don't spend a lot of money *or* waste a lot of time."

One of the software project engineers chimes in. "I think it might be better to have two separate quality systems," he suggests. "The real way we do our work is just fine, but if it's not good enough for registration, we could document a new system, but follow the old way."

"Wouldn't it be better to just bring in a consultant to set up an ISO 9000-compliant system?" asks the vice president of manufacturing. "In the long run it would probably be faster and cheaper to have an expert create our quality system for us."

"I think I remember seeing something about a software package that will generate an ISO 9000 quality manual with very little work on our part," adds a supervisor from Information Services.

By this time, no one is paying much attention to the flow of the presentation. Another corner is heard from. ''You know,'' says a regional sales manager, a person noted for his propensity to create controversy. ''It would really be best to scrap our current quality system and start over.'' This suggestion generates a lively discussion, but no concrete decisions, except that you should distribute minutes and set up another meeting.

People start leaving the conference room. A manager whom you had hoped to make part of the registration project team pulls you aside. ''Do you think this project has any chance?'' she asks. ''Top management may have authorized the project, but when push comes to shove, will they support it?'' You shrug, thinking again of good old Sir Isaac.

ANTICIPATING RESISTANCE TO THE ISO 9000 REGISTRATION PROJECT

To paraphrase the old *Dragnet* television show, the meeting described above is true, only the names have been changed to protect the not-so-innocent. In one form or another, we heard all of the comments expressed in the scenario when we introduced the ISO 9000 standards to our organization. You will too. You will face the same range of human dynamics. Some people in your organization will obviously be against the project. Others will endorse ISO 9000 registration. Many, however, will make no commitment. You won't know where they stand, and possibly, they won't either. Others who are clearly supportive of the project will be concerned that management will not deliver adequate resources when it comes time to take action.

You'll be given a plethora of suggestions for how to proceed with the ISO 9000 registration effort. Most will be expressed as easy-cost-effective-I-only-want-to-help suggestions; however, you need to understand that many of those suggestions are likely subtle expressions of resistance to change, of organizational inertia. Understanding that will help you address the issues raised and convert ISO 9000 registration from a change being done to the organization to a change being done by the organization.

Remember the engineer's suggestion to ''simply'' add the ISO

9000 requirements to the requirements of the current quality system and the software project leader's suggestion to make the ISO 9000 requirements into a separate quality system that would coexist with the existing system? Both these suggestions are fraught with problems of conflict and redundancy. In the first case, conflict will occur whenever an organization adds procedures to address the ISO 9000 standards that give instructions different from current procedures. For example, a new procedure that directs test records to be logged and archived would conflict with a current procedure that calls for test records to be verified and disposed of. The organization's people wouldn't know which procedure to follow. The two-quality-system organization is just a larger version of the same problem. There are now two systems rather than two sets of procedures within the same system. Confused employees will not only wonder which system to follow, but question the basic integrity of a duplicitous quality system.

In dealing with suggestions like these, which essentially say "We don't want to change," you must be careful to deal with both the overt suggestion and the underlying psychological resistance to change. A good tactic is to focus on those areas of your quality system that are likely ISO 9000 compliant already. For example, rather than point out that your manufacturing organization does a poor job of measurement tool calibration, point to the organization's process for discarding obsolete material as an example of an ISO 9000-compliant procedure. Don't stress that your development organization doesn't conduct design reviews; focus on the efficient process for maintaining training records.

Let your audience suggest areas that are not ISO 9000 compliant. They know where the problem areas are; your job is not to point out the obvious (and embarrassing) areas of concern, but to guide people to discover them for themselves. Remember, change done by us is exhilarating; change done to us is disturbing.

UNCHAIN THE EXPERTS

Note that we are not recommending communicating an oversimplified picture of the ISO 9000 registration effort by focusing only on what's right with the organization's quality system. Clearly, it's the "what's wrong" that will require the greatest effort. What we are recommending is that to allay the fears of the organization and overcome initial resistance to the ISO 9000 registration project, the "what's wrong" be positioned as an *enhancement* of your organization's existing quality system, not as a radical departure from the current way of doing business.

In point of fact, radical approaches to the ISO 9000 standards, such as the regional sales manager's suggestion to "scrap the current quality system and start over," create resistance and confusion among the troops. Although it might be easy to resist the start-over-from-scratch approach, there are other, less dramatic but equally ill-advised approaches to ISO 9000 registration that will tempt your organization with the illusionary promise of being a fast-track to success.

Very early in the ISO 9000 registration effort, someone, like the vice president of manufacturing in our introductory scenario, will likely suggest that an outside expert, a consultant, be called in to create an ISO 9000-compliant system. In many ways, this approach makes sense. An outside expert brings to the table an understanding of the ISO 9000 standards and the registration process that is likely not available in-house. Consultants can provide interpretations of the ISO 9000 standards, suggested documentation systems and structure (not content), and auditing services and training. In this capacity, an ISO 9000 consultant is a valuable resource.

However, as any good consultant will tell you, he or she does not have an understanding of your organization's corporate culture, the individual personalities of the people in your organization or on your ISO 9000 registration team, nor an understanding of your company's current business situation, nor of any of a number of idiosyncratic elements that will affect your implementation of that consultant's suggestions. A consultant can create a format and structure for your ISO 9000 documentation, but if a consultant creates your actual quality documentation, it cannot possibly accurately reflect the culture. There will be no sense of ownership of the documentation by the people who work within the system.

In short, hiring a consultant does not do away with the organization's involvement in ISO 9000 registration. In many ways, such as bringing the consultant up to speed on the workings and culture of the organization, hiring a consultant will involve additional effort. The caveat is simple: before retaining a consultant, understand what the consultant can and cannot do for you. A good consultant will help your organization achieve ISO 9000 registration, but he or she cannot do it for you. Ultimately, ISO 9000 registration is your organization's responsibility.

Closely related to unchaining the experts is the benchmarking-as-panacea approach to ISO 9000 registration. The temptation is to find an organization that has been registered to ISO 9000 and transplant its quality system into your organization. Don't misunderstand: like working with a good consultant, benchmarking ISO 9000-registered companies is a valuable exercise. We did a great deal of benchmarking that proved invaluable in preparing system documentation. We picked up ideas not only about what to do but also about what to avoid, which most certainly helped us shorten our implementation schedule.

However, because a given company's quality system reflects its corporate culture, one company's quality system will not plug and play into another company's culture. Quality system documentation from one company—even if that company is ISO 9000 registered—will not necessarily produce an ISO 9000-compliant system in a company with its own unique corporate culture. A "borrowed" quality system does not engender ownership among the people who must function within the system. Ownership of the quality system is very important.

Consider the case of a multinational corporation marketing-organization that was seeking ISO 9000 registration. In this organization, management wrote *all* quality system documentation. To speed the registration process, they did so with no input or review from the individual contributors who did the actual production work. The documentation was wonderful. It described a system compliant with the ISO 9000 standards in every respect.

Unfortunately, as Shakespeare's Macbeth so aptly phrased, the documentation was "full of sound and fury, signifying nothing." The documentation did not accurately describe the way people did their jobs. When the third-party registration agency visited the company for the actual registration assessment, they stopped the assessment by noon of the first day. "We feel like you lied to us," they told the company's management. "Your documentation describes a quality system that is in compliance with the standard, but your company does not follow the documentation." They added, "Call us back when you are serious about registration."

In an effort to bypass the problem of organizational inertia by ignoring it, this organization overlooked a key ISO 9000 concept: an ISO 9000-compliant system has two dimensions: (1) the system as documented complies with the requirement of the ISO 9000 standards, and (2) people operate consistently within the system. By leaving people out of the documentation of the quality system, this company denied them any ownership in the quality system. Rather than overcoming people's reluctance to change, management only intensified it. Consequently people did not follow the new system but continued functioning as they always had. A documented quality system, which may well be ISO 9000-compliant, that is not followed will not pass the scrutiny of a third-party assessment. An ISO 9000-compliant system must not only be documented such that it is compliant with the standards (something management, a consultant, or a benchmark can provide); it must also be followed by the people who actually produce the product or service that is the output of the system.

ISO 9000 registration will gain credibility with your organization's people if you demonstrate that changes are not being made solely for the purpose of registration, but for system improvement, i.e., making it easier for people to do their jobs. Employee conformance to a documented system cannot be externally motivated. So that the subtlety of that point is not lost, let us be specific: *The only approach to ISO 9000 registration that works is to improve the company's quality system for the benefit of those who function within it; ISO 9000 registration is a by-product of quality system improvement.* Changes thus become changes initiated by the organization for the benefit of the organization, not changes forced upon it from the outside.

MANAGEMENT COMMITMENT

One concern we heard a number of times during the early stages of our ISO 9000 registration project, and which surfaced when we became involved with other companies seeking ISO 9000 registration, was that senior management would not be fully committed to the effort. Management may bless the program at its inception, but that may be before they realize the full scope of the ISO 9000 registration effort.

One story related to us concerned a company that had set aside a room in their facility as a ''war room'' for their registration effort. A sign was put on the door that simply read ''ISO 9000.'' A few weeks later, the sign on the door read ''I$O 9000.'' A few more weeks of planning, and the sign was altered once again. It now read ''I$O 9,000,000!'' Although the cost of ISO 9000 registration need not be astronomical, the changes to the sign indicated that this company was finding the project to be much larger in scope than anticipated. The obvious question is: will management remain committed when the ''$'' is added and the zeros keep mounting?

No one wants to devote time to a project that he or she suspects will come to naught. No one wants an unsuccessful project as part of his or her employment history. People are willing to put in the hours of work necessary to assess the quality system only if they have faith that management will respond with the resources required to make changes. Until employees are convinced management is serious about ISO 9000 registration and serious about improving the organization's quality system, they will be less than fully committed to the registration process. However, contrary to common belief, management commitment is not a factor that is beyond your influence. Gaining management commitment is a factor that can be planned for, just like the project budget, scheduled target date, or any other critical element that is part of your ISO 9000 registration project plan. Gaining management commitment and communicating that commitment credibly to employees is one of the critical success factors for achieving ISO 9000 registration. We'll look more closely at this issue and other critical success factors in Chapter 4.

PERSONAL PREPAREDNESS

Thus far in this chapter we have focused on overcoming organizational inertia and getting your ISO 9000 project moving. However, before addressing your organization's reluctance to move forward, you must first overcome any tendency *you* might have to resist change. You must overcome the initial sense that ISO 9000 registration is an overwhelming effort. Ancient wisdom says that the longest journey begins with a single step. In the case of ISO 9000 registration, that first step is preparing yourself for the task ahead. To be fully prepared to move the organization forward toward ISO 9000 registration, you must have a basic understanding of both the overt requirements of the standards and the intent of those requirements and a basic understanding of how implementing those requirements will affect the culture of your organization.

The first step in gaining such understanding is to read ISO 9000 documentation and commentaries. Today there is a great deal of helpful literature commenting on various aspects of the ISO 9000 standards. This information, much of which was not available when we began our ISO 9000 registration effort, is extremely valuable. However, diving into this commentary without having basic knowledge of the actual text of the ISO 9000 standards is more than a little like leaving *Moby Dick* unopened and writing your term paper based on the movie or *Cliff's Notes*. It's important that you wrestle with what the ISO 9000 standards mean to your organization before you read outside interpretations of the standards. Figure 2–1 lists available ISO 9000 publications and their purposes. Sources from which to obtain these publications are listed in Appendix A.

When you have a working knowledge of the ISO 9000 contractual standards (ISO 9001, 9002, and 9003) and how they might apply to your organization, you're ready to expand your reading to include books that provide interpretations of the standard by industry experts. Comparing your interpretations to the experts helps focus your own thinking—remember, disagreeing with the "experts" does not mean you are wrong. You must interpret the ISO 9000 standards within the context of your organization. The generic interpretation you glean from your reading can provide additional insight, but in the end, you must necessarily go with your judgment as to what the standards mean for your organization.

You will find that ISO 9000 books on the market can be classified into three categories. The first category provides a generalist's viewpoint. These books provide you with a little bit of everything

FIGURE 2–1
ISO 9000 Publications

ISO 9000 Publications	Purpose
ISO 9000:1987 *Quality Management and Quality Assurance Standards—Guidelines for Selection and Use* (will become ISO 9000–1)	A guideline to help in the selection of the appropriate contractual standard for an organization.
ISO 9001: 1987 *Quality Systems—Model for Quality Assurance in Design/Development, Production, Installation, and Servicing*	Contractual standard applicable to companies that both design and manufacture products or that produce computer software or design and offer services.
ISO 9002: 1987 *Quality Systems—Model for Quality Assurance in Production and Installation*	Contractual standard applicable to companies that manufacture products designed elsewhere.
ISO 9003: 1987 *Quality Systems—Model for Quality Assurance in Final Inspection and Test*	Contractual standard applicable to companies that assemble and sell components manufactured elsewhere.
ISO 9004: 1987 *Quality Management and Quality System Elements—Guidelines* (will become ISO 9004-1)	Describes a quality system more comprehensive than required by the contractual standards.
ISO/DIS 9000–2 *Quality Management and Quality Assurance Standards—Part 2: Generic Guidelines for the Application of ISO 9001, ISO 9002 and ISO 9003*	Describes the intent and application of each paragraph of ISO 9000 contractual standards.
ISO 9000–3: 1991 *Quality Management and Quality Assurance Standards—Part 3: Guidelines for the Application of ISO 9001 to the Development, Supply and Maintenance of Software*	Describes application of ISO 9001 to the development, supply, and maintenance of software.
ISO 9004–2: 1991 *Quality Management and Quality Systems Elements—Part 2: Guidelines for Services*	Guidelines for implementing a quality system in a service organization.
ISO/DIS 9004–3: *Quality Management and Quality Systems Element—Part 3: Guidelines for Processed Materials*	Guidelines for implementing a quality system in a processed material organization.
ISO 9000 Compendium—International Standards for Quality Management	Contains all of the documents listed above, plus additional material on auditing quality systems, developing a quality manual and the *Vision 2000* document, which describes the ISO strategy for the future of the standards. *Highly recommended.*

about ISO 9000—ISO 9000 history, interpreting the standard, quality system documentation structure, a primer on registration bodies, sample quality manuals, and the like. Depending on the author's area of expertise, any one of these topics may be given more in-depth treatment than the others. Examples of this type of material are James L. Lamprecht's *ISO 9000: Preparing for Registration,*[2] and *The ISO 9000 Handbook,* edited by Robert W. Peach.[3]

The second category of literature you will encounter is strict interpretation of the ISO 9000 standards. An example of this category is *The Handley-Walker Guide to ISO 9000,* published by the Handley Walker Consulting Group.[4] Generally, most available ISO 9000 seminars offered through consulting firms and educational institutions also take the strict standard interpretation tack.

The third category of ISO 9000-relevant information addresses individual parts of the standard and the registration process. To date, this literature primarily pertains to general auditing principles and applies examples of those principles to cases based upon the ISO 9000 standards. *The Quality Audit—A Management Evaluation Tool,* by Charles A. Mills,[5] is an excellent example of a book in this classification.

The most common source of reference literature about ISO 9000 are book lists put out by a number of publishers. Although many offerings are very good, you need to exercise some discrimination in selecting ISO 9000 material sight unseen. Some books will provide new information, but many books in the field merely rehash what is currently available regarding ISO 9000 documentation. And, you should always understand that the interpretations of ISO 9000 given in these books are formulated generically, that is, *outside the corporate culture of your organization*. The common characteristic of generic ISO 9000 literature is that it will offer advice on what to do but leave the *how* questions of implementation to your imagination and initiative. You will find little advice regarding the organizational dynamics that an ISO 9000 registration effort arouses. You won't find an answer to the basic ISO 9000 registration question, "How are we going to get this done?"

Implementation techniques for achieving ISO 9000 registration is what this book is all about. It takes you from awareness through registration to maintaining a registered quality system, addressing organizational dynamics along the way. The next step is preparing a sound ISO 9000 registration project plan. This topic is addressed in Chapter 3.

THE NCR EXPERIENCE[6]

The first step in overcoming organizational inertia is overcoming your personal tendencies to resist change. The previous section described several sources for familiarizing yourself with the ISO 9000 standards. When we first embarked on our ISO 9000 registration project, many of these sources were not readily available, which in some ways was a disadvantage. However, it did force us to do our homework on the ISO 9000 standards themselves. The only documents we had to work with were the standards of ISO 9001–9004 and a draft copy of what has become ISO 9000–3, the guideline for application of the standards to software. There was no *ISO 9000 Compendium,* nor was there the ISO/DIS 9000–2 guideline to help us understand the intent and application of the standards. We found no books that embellished upon the standards. Seminars were few, distant, and costly.

In the absence of other documents, we used the ISO 9004 guideline to help us understand the intent of the ISO 9001 standard to which we planned to be registered. We visited an NCR sister plant in Dundee, Scotland, to gain some first-hand experience with the ISO 9000 effort in progress there. We attended AT&T/NCR-sponsored seminars on ISO 9000 and consultant-sponsored seminars on ISO 9000 basics. We reviewed available literature on quality systems auditing.

Armed with this information, we felt confident that *we* were ready for ISO 9000 registration. Quite frankly, though, we had doubts about the organization. We knew that ISO 9000 registration was a big project, that there would be some resistance, so we set about raising the level of awareness of the ISO 9000 standards with others in the organization. Because we believed that the standards offered a springboard for leveraging our long-term quality strategy, we began building a case for ISO 9000 registration. We enlisted the company president as an ally and several key members of the executive staff. We made our initial pitches for ISO 9000 registration based on business rationale, rather than from a quality advocate point of view. We made sure that influential people within the organization were aware of the standards and how they might contribute to the success of the organization. We tried to anticipate who might resist the ISO 9000 registration effort and why.

It was during our premeeting sales calls on management that many of the issues discussed in this chapter surfaced. Some we were able to address immediately, others we could not, but we made sure we were prepared by the time of the first informational meeting.

To involve management right from the start, we divided the ISO 9001 standard into sections and determined which executive staff member owned each task described. We formally sent each member of the staff a memo describing the ISO 9001 standard, its intent, and its relevance to the company. We attached the appropriate sections of the standard to the memos and requested that they review them prior to a scheduled informational meeting. This process will be discussed in greater detail in Chapter 5.

Because we had prepared for both an understanding of the ISO 9001 standard and for the psychological impact it might have on the organization, we were able to keep our meeting under control. To be sure, we did not get 100 percent buy-in from everyone in the room, but we did present a strong enough case so that we could move ahead to actual planning of our ISO 9000 project.

Planning for ISO 9000 registration—for many organizations, therein lies the rub. Our informational meeting got people excited about ISO 9000 registration. Now they wanted to know what to do. All this ISO 9000 stuff was still new to the organization. If we were going to capitalize on the enthusiasm the informational meeting generated, we had to provide a plan—not just a list of milestones, but a plan that defined behaviors we expected from both employees and management, defined the resources required to achieve registration, and included a realistic target date for registration. Developing that plan is the subject of the following chapter.

Chapter Three

Creating Your ISO 9000 Registration Project Plan

A good deal of the corporate planning I have observed is like a ritual rain dance; it has no effect on the weather that follows, but those who engage in it think it does. Moreover, it seems to me that much of the advice and instruction related to corporate planning is directed at improving the dancing, not the weather.

Russell L. Ackoff
Creating the Corporate Future

Planning isn't sexy. Swashbuckling, shooting from the hip, snatching victory from the jaws of defeat—that's sexy. Never mind that swashbuckling spills some blood, shooting from the hip you miss more often than you hit, and more often than not, one who reaches into the jaws of defeat gets chomped before snatching victory. There's a certain glamour in reacting to a crisis that isn't found in the perceived banality of planning.

"Planning leads to paralysis," says the swashbuckling, hip-shooting, victory-snatchers. "Lace up the corporate Nikes, and just do it."

Although we will be the last to defend procrastination behind the barricades of planning, we will be the first to stress that ISO 9000 registration requires far too much integration to "just do it." A working plan is a must. Indeed, developing a comprehensive, ISO 9000 registration project plan that is accepted by and credible to management and employees is a critical success factor for an ISO 9000 registration effort.

THE PURPOSE OF THIS CHAPTER

This chapter looks at some of the basic principles of good planning applied to the ISO 9000 registration project and to the NCR Network Products Division experience. It discusses three key activities involved in creating a working and credible ISO 9000 registration project plan: (1) determining an appropriate ISO 9000 registration schedule; (2) analyzing ISO 9000 registration project activity; and (3) determining resources required to achieve ISO 9000 registration. The chapter examines the thinking behind each activity, pulls them together into a systematic approach to ISO 9000 registration project planning, and explores the influence of the corporate culture on the registration project plan.

To borrow Russell Ackoff's metaphor, the intent of this chapter is not so much to improve your dancing as it is to provide you a means of changing the weather. More than helping you create a project plan, the chapter provides you a means of gaining control of your ISO 9000 registration project.

However, before we discuss the ISO 9000 project planning process, or before you begin preparing your ISO 9000 registration project plan, let us be clear on the reason for planning. Without understanding why it is that you need a written plan in the first place, it is easy to fall into one of two traps—preparing a plan specifically to please upper management, and/or preparing only a list of milestones that is not a plan at all but merely a tracking mechanism that ultimately does no more than remind you how far behind your ISO 9000 registration project is. So, before we look at the three key activities in preparing an ISO 9000 registration plan, we will first discuss these two planning traps, and then the only valid reason for preparing a written ISO 9000 registration project plan. We'll introduce the planning traps by addressing a question you will very likely be asked in the course of planning your ISO 9000 registration project: "Why are we going through all this work? Why prepare a documented plan?"

WHY PREPARE A DOCUMENTED PLAN?

First planning trap: We need a documented plan because upper management wants one. From a personal survival perspective, that's certainly a compelling reason to prepare a plan. However, a management requirement should not be the priary reason for preparing an ISO 9000-registration project plan.

Granted, documented plans are excellent communication tools that help management allocate appropriate resources to the ISO 9000 registration project. But an effective plan is not written for management; that is, the plan should not be confused with the presentation of the plan, which will be discussed in Chapter 5.

The ISO 9000 registration project plan is owned by the individual or team developing it. The plan must be *their* tool, reflect *their* thinking, and be *their* conclusion as to the appropriate registration target and milestone dates, the actions required to meet those dates, and the resources required to support those actions.

Unfortunately, much planning in the corporate world begins from the premise "What can we sell to management?" Often the "goodness" of the plan is measured by the degree of acceptance it receives from upper management, not on the adequacy of the plan elements to achieve the desired goal. Planners who start from the premise of "the possible," as they perceive it, rather than from the ideal state to which they aspire, may achieve their plans but often at the expense of their objectives. They may be good dancers, but they have little impact on the weather. This is an especially important distinction in the case of ISO 9000 registration project planning. Plan versus presentation is not a trivial or mere semantic distinction.

ISO 9000 registration is a complex exercise in that it demands the coordinated involvement of virtually every department within the company. It is a labor-intensive effort. And let's face facts: In today's corporate world there just aren't a lot of people sitting on their hands with nothing to do. The "lean and mean" trend of late dictates that everyone in the company has a full plate of responsibilities. If ISO 9000 registration goes on the menu, something must come off. A project plan that lightly glosses over the resource issues relating to ISO 9000 registration in order to sell the concept of ISO 9000 registration to senior management sets a false set of expectations for both management and employees. It is neither workable nor credible.

In their book *Cynical Americans*, authors Kanter and Mirvis found that, by and large, American workers are a cynical lot.[1] An underlying cause of this cynicism is the failure of society in general, the corporation specifically, to meet the expectations set in the minds of people. The cynical cycle is set up because of reinforced, but unrealistic expectations coupled with the consequential failures.

The implications of this research for your ISO 9000 registration project is that a failed effort is fuel on the fire of organizational cynicism.[2] It is extremely difficult to rejuvenate the failed project, which is all the more reason to ensure that the premise of your ISO 9000 registration project plan is declarative, "This is what it will take to get registered," and not interrogative, "What can we sell to management?" The project plan is the place to set proper expectations and establish workability and credibility for the ISO 9000 registration project.

Second planning trap: We need a documented plan so we have a way to track progress on the project. Sure you do, but the ISO 9000 registration project plan needs to be more than a milestone list or Gantt chart. The plan must not only define where you are going; it must also address how you are going to get there. A list of milestones is to your ISO 9000 registration project plan what the table of contents is to a book: a milestone list is an organizational structure; it is a means of breaking the larger project into understandable and manageable segments. A milestone list is not definitive of the project itself.

Resource issues (which we'll discuss in some detail later in this chapter) that you must consider in formulating your ISO 9000 registration project plan include the number of people who will be involved in the project, how these people will be selected, what training they will receive, the process you will use to manage the registration project, the tools available to facilitate the registration project, the communication structure that will keep both management and employees informed about the project, and reward and recognition issues. Resolution of these resource issues is the real work of the registration project; milestones on the Gantt chart merely reflect that resolution. They are not a plan for actually accomplishing the objective.

How does this distinction play out during your ISO 9000 registration project? When the milestone chart is viewed as "the plan," the maxim "work expands or contracts to fill the time allotted" becomes operational. Effort increases as the deadline approaches. It's tempting to declare victory on the deadline date even if there are a few loose ends that must be cleaned up during the next phase of the project. See the danger there?

On the other hand, if milestones are based on specific accomplishments completed with specific expenditure of resources, then project management and project tracking are meaningful and effective. Let's look at an example.

A key milestone in any ISO 9000 registration project is the writing of a quality manual. But how does one begin to judge if the quality manual is adequate? More importantly, does making that judgment take place within the existing schedule, or is it now an additional task beyond the milestone? What impact does that have on the downstream schedule?

A milestone-driven plan provides no real methodology for answering those or similar questions other than a subjective evaluation of the "goodness" of, in this case, the quality manual. But let's take a look at a resource-driven quality manual milestone.

Assume that a team is chartered to put together the quality manual and estimates are that each team member will spend 30 hours per week for six weeks to prepare the quality manual. Each week, reporting on time spent, reviewing what was accomplished, and evaluating if 30 hours is still a correct estimate, provides a constant check on the progress of the quality manual. Certainly the hourly estimate required to complete milestone activities can change, but it does so after review and for rational reasons.

The point not to be lost is that once an actions/resources-based plan has been accepted as valid, progress tracking and evaluation becomes a logical, not a subjective, exercise. The logic is: Here are the resources we said were required to prepare a quality manual with these characteristics. Here are the resources we've expended. Here are the characteristics of what we've accomplished. Are we on schedule (expending resources at the rate we expected and accomplishing what we thought we would), behind schedule (more resources, less accomplished), or ahead of schedule (fewer resources, more accomplished)? Given any of these scenarios, what must we do to stay on schedule?

Continuously monitoring the project in the above terms provides a better assessment of the adequacy of the quality manual than an arbitrary evaluation of "goodness" at the milestone date. It takes the ISO 9000 registration project plan beyond merely tracking the project to facilitating a method for managing the project. The weather becomes more important than the dancing.

The only valid reason for planning: We need to establish the right combination of actions and resources to achieve timely registration. Now we're on the right track and approaching the significant rationale for developing an ISO 9000 registration project plan. The sentiment expressed in the above subhead is absolutely true. However, bear in mind that no such plan exists.

Writing your ISO 9000 registration project plan is not a search for the right mix of schedule, actions, and resources. Planning is not a *search* exercise; it is a *creation* exercise. It is not a case of finding some pre-existing balance of schedule, actions, and resources that result in registration. It is an exercise in defining actions and determining resources that will achieve registration on the schedule required by your organization.

In other words, there is no one right ISO 9000 registration project plan. The activities, required resources, personnel requirements, and cultural parameters of your organization are unique. Ultimately, your plan depends on and reflects that uniqueness.

Obvious? One would think so. Yet we have received requests from organizations seeking ISO 9000 registration to help them audit their quality systems *against our quality manual*. Their ISO 9000 registration project plan was to find an already registered quality system, benchmark the system, and then overlay the registered system on their own *modus operandi*.

Benchmarking others' ISO 9000 registration projects can be helpful to your ISO 9000 registration project. Indeed, we spent a great deal of time benchmarking the projects of others before writing our ISO 9000 registration project plan. However, it is a major mistake to take someone else's plan and overlay it on your project and expect the resulting quality system to work. Benchmarking will not show you what to do, but rather how to approach doing it, whatever "it" may be.

Understand before you begin the planning process that planning is a learning experience. It is the exercise of putting the plan together, not the plan itself, wherein lies the real value of planning. Planning your ISO 9000 registration project must be approached from that perspective. If it is not, at best you'll wind up with a list of milestones that will help you track how far behind schedule you are. You will dance; you will not change the weather.

A WORKING AND CREDIBLE PLAN

The operative words in creating an ISO 9000 registration project plan are "working" and "credible." An effective plan is not one where every detail and every possible contingency is examined and debated before being committed to paper. An effective plan is a working document. It is both flexible enough to accommodate unforeseen developments and rigid enough to keep the project on track. It is credible in the eyes of your organization. People believe in it. They perceive the milestone dates are realistic. They understand the rationale for the dates, and they believe the dates can be achieved. An effective, working plan for ISO 9000 registration achieves three key objectives:

- It establishes a registration target date and the interim milestones that must be accomplished to meet that date.
- It defines the actions the organization must take to achieve the interim objectives at each milestone.
- It determines what resources are required to meet the schedule (i.e., support the defined actions necessary to achieve the interim milestones).

Bearing in mind that documenting an ISO 9000 registration project plan is not done merely to please upper management or to provide a tracking mechanism for the project but is done to create a combination of actions and resources that allows your organization to achieve timely ISO 9000 registration, let's look at each of the three key objectives of an ISO 9000 registration project plan in more detail.

DETERMINING AN APPROPRIATE ISO 9000 REGISTRATION SCHEDULE

"How long did it take you to get registered?" That's probably the most common question we're asked and also the most irrelevant. As discussed earlier, there is no right plan for ISO 9000 registration.

Each organization's ISO 9000 registration project plan is a unique blend of activities, resources and personnel requirements, and corporate culture, and therefore, each organization's quest for ISO 9000 registration has its own optimal duration. Defining optimal requires a broader business view than is usually taken when scheduling quality projects.

For example, consider the following scenario of ISO 9000 registration schedule setting. Management catches the ISO 9000 bug and suddenly registration to ISO 9000 becomes a company priority. A team is chartered to "get us ISO 9000-registered as soon as possible," which usually means the end of the next quarter or some other Herculean time frame. The ISO 9000 project team, whose merit review hinges on accomplishing ISO 9000 registration, counters management's "as soon as possible" deadline with a "realistic schedule" that "allows for contingencies" and achieves ISO 9000 registration "in a reasonable time frame." Management responds to this proposal with a "stretch objective" and the admonition that ISO 9000 registration is "critical to the organization."

At this point, discretion becomes the better part of valor for the members of the ISO 9000 project team. They don the mantle of good corporate citizens and pledge to "do everything possible to meet the aggressive schedule." Schedule negotiation comes to an end, milestones are cast in concrete, management considers the project as good as done, and ISO 9000 project team members advise their spouses not to count on a year-end bonus.

What's wrong with this picture?

A schedule is not a negotiated compromise between those who want to be registered "as soon as possible" (usually upper management) and those who argue for an "achievable schedule" (usually those assigned responsibility for registration). *From the enterprise viewpoint, there is a point in time at which the organization should become registered to achieve maximum return on its investment in the registration process.* Between now and that point is the optimal duration of the ISO 9000 registration project.

During the planning phase, there may be many discussions within the organization about where the point of maximum return is, but these are far different from discussions focused on the ISO 9000 registration target date. These discussions are not about how long the registration effort should take, but about when registration should be achieved. They are not about dancing, but about the weather. They are analogous to discussions that take place about market windows for proposed product development projects. For every organization seeking ISO 9000 registration, there is an optimal market window for registration. A schedule should never be set independent of market influences. That is, the schedule should never be separated from the business reason for seeking ISO 9000 registration in the first place. That reason is market pressure.

Yes, for the quality advocate there are abundant reasons why improving the quality system, independent of ISO 9000 registration, is the right thing to do and will make the company and the world a better place, ad infinitum. (This, by the way, is the position we wholeheartedly endorse.) However, the reality of the business world is "the business of business is business." Initially, you will be far more successful in most organizations developing a business reason for ISO 9000 registration than taking a semi-moralistic, "it's the right thing to do" approach.

As discussed briefly in Chapter 2, setting the schedule for ISO 9000 registration is a market-driven process with the degree of market pressure (or market opportunity) setting the pace. Are customers asking about your organization's ISO 9000 registration plans? Is an ISO 9000 registration requirement cropping up in bid requests that your organization responds to? Are customers regularly auditing your operation as part of their bidding process? Is your company looking at new markets in countries with ISO 9000 registration requirements? Where is the rest of your industry in regard to ISO 9000 registration? Are you at a competitive disadvantage by not being ISO 9000 registered or could you gain competitive advantage by being registered?

The above questions are representative of the questions you need to ask to determine the true urgency of ISO 9000 registration for your organization. Obviously, if your company is losing bids because it is not ISO 9000 registered, achieving registration as soon as possible is not an unrealistic desire. If ISO 9000 registration is being considered as part of a move into a new market, then registration timing should coincide with that move.

The point is, and it bears repeating, that ISO 9000 registration should be a market-driven event. There is a market window for ISO 9000 registration with the same implications as the market window for a new product program. Timing actual ISO 9000 registration to a window of opportunity for your company provides the best return on your ISO 9000 registration investment and will engender the organizationwide commitment to ISO 9000 registration required for a successful effort.

A second observation about the scenario depicted earlier: As commonly conceived, there is no such thing as a *stretch objective*. Stretch objective has too often become a euphemism for any objective that is achievable only through superhuman effort and perchance, divine intervention. If a set of actions necessary to achieve the objective are defined and sufficient resources to support those actions are available, the schedule is not a stretch. If actions have not been defined and/or sufficient resources to support defined actions are not available, the schedule is impossible. A schedule cannot be set independently of actions and resources. No schedule is valid until the actions required to achieve it are defined. No registration deadline is realistic if sufficient resources are not provided to support the actions defined as necessary and sufficient to achieve it.

An additional point touched on previously should also be made again here: Planning an ISO 9000 registration project should always start with the "ideal" schedule, not a schedule perceived as "possible." Although it may turn out that the ideal schedule cannot be achieved given the organization's available resources applied to traditional activities, beginning with the ideal may well drive thinking towards nontraditional ways of accomplishing the objectives.

An example from our ISO 9000 registration experience makes this point clear. To be prepared for a third-party assessment, we needed assurance that all employees were aware of and understood our division's quality policies. Working from a traditional premise, which dictated that the quality assurance organization prepare a training class and conduct it for all employees, we quickly realized that given quality assurance resources and the number of division employees, there was no way we could educate *all* employees in the given time frame. Our alternatives appeared to be to push out the schedule or risk having a third-party assessor encounter an employee who was not familiar with NCR Network Products Division quality policies.

However, because we were working from a market-driven schedule (our division could gain competitive advantage by being ISO 9000 registered prior to 1992), we focused on the ideal—was there some non-traditional training method that would allow us to train all employees and still meet the optimal registration date?

Our real problem was a lack of quality assurance people to conduct training within the time frame required. We obviously needed to recruit more trainers. The question was who, and how, would they be adequately trained to present the material? Here we borrowed an idea from our benchmarking and opted for the Xerox LUTI method (learn, use, teach, inspect). Our quality steering team (senior executives) was reviewing and editing the company's quality policies. We trained this group to present the quality policies to their direct reports, who in turn presented the policies to their direct reports and so forth.

In this manner, our trainers increased geometrically, and all employees were exposed to the quality policies within our scheduled time frame. In addition, follow-up on the training by quality assurance found that the training had significant impact and credibility with employees *because it was conducted by their management*. Management-conducted training gave the quality policies credibility and specificity to individual work areas. Was the training as complete and pure as we would have liked it? Probably not. But the credibility and specificity achieved far exceeded anything a quality assurance-presented class could have provided. And from the ISO 9000 registration perspective, we were confident that a third-party assessor would find our people versed in the company's quality policy.

In summary, then, there are several points to keep in mind in determining your ISO 9000 registration target date. First, there is an optimal point in time at which your organization should be registered to achieve maximum return on its investment in the registration process. Second, that point in time is market-driven; that is, it is based on external forces acting on the organization, and not driven by arbitrary internal mandates. Third, in setting a target registration date, start with the ideal date and determine activities and resources required to meet that date. And fourth, don't fall into the trap of an unsupported stretch objective. If resources are not available, look for alternative activities and/or adjust the target registration date accordingly.

To do the latter, you must view your organization's ISO 9000 registration project as a system and analyze ISO 9000 activities in terms of that system. This is the second key activity in creating an ISO 9000 registration project plan.

ANALYZING ISO 9000 REGISTRATION PROJECT ACTIVITY[3]

ISO 9000 registration project planning is most effectively conducted when viewed as a system. In process management terms, a system consists of various inputs that go into a process or work activity that produces a measurable output. Based on measurement of the output, one adjusts either the inputs or the work activity to achieve the optimal results. There are six steps in system analysis:

- **Defining the system to be investigated**. In other words, putting a boundary around the process. In the case of an ISO 9000 registration project, your documented project plan defines the system. It defines the output (ISO 9000 registration), it defines the process (the actions the organization must take to achieve registration), and it defines the input (the resources required to support the necessary and sufficient actions).
- **Defining what the system should accomplish**. If the output of the system is ISO 9000 registration, what the system needs to accomplish is creation of an ISO 9000-compliant quality system. This seemingly obvious statement, however, is often ignored in an organization's concern for registration. Actions focused on ISO 9000 registration rather than on quality system improvement produce a disjointed effort. The fundamental approach to ISO 9000 registration taken in this book is that *improvement of the quality system drives registration, not the reverse.*
- **Defining the elements of the system and their relationships to each other**. System here refers to the project plan-

ning system for ISO 9000 registration, not the quality system itself. In that sense, the registration plan must address three variables: (1) How fast do we want to be ISO 9000 registered? (2) What are the characteristics required for an ISO 9000-compliant quality system? and (3) What will it cost to achieve time/requirements objectives? Relationships and interactions between these three elements must be considered in preparing the ISO 9000 registration project plan.

- **Defining the measurable performance desired**. Your ISO 9000 registration project plan must clearly define the three project variables from the bullet item above in declarative terms: (1) This is the optimal registration date. (2) These will be the characteristics of our ISO 9000-compliant quality system. (3) This is what it will cost.
- **Consider the effectiveness of various actions**. Remember, there is no one right ISO 9000 registration project plan. Planning is not a search exercise; it is a creation exercise. Once you have defined the measurable performance of the ISO 9000 registration project (target date, quality system characteristics, registration project cost), you need to look at alternatives for achieving the results in terms of their impact on the variables "how fast," "what characteristics," and "what cost." For example, can time leading to registration be more effectively reduced by adding more people to the project (commitment of resources) or by providing more training and better tools to fewer people (quality of effort) or by focusing registration activities in a different direction (allocation of effort)?
- **Implement the most effective methods**. Obvious? Yes. However, from our previous discussions, understand that "most effective" must consider the cultural impact on the organization. Changing a culture takes time and will have an impact on your schedule. Our ISO 9000 registration schedule allowed for assessment training and preparing companywide communication about the assessment in order to counter some negative cultural elements. The key point is that to evaluate effectiveness, you must look beyond short-term cost. You must consider the issues raised by organizational behaviors.

Figure 3–1 puts the above discussion into a graphical format. The ultimate objective of the planning system depicted in Figure

3–1 is ISO 9000 registration (at the far right of the figure). In order to achieve this objective, your organization must have an ISO 9000-compliant quality system. In order to achieve an ISO 9000-compliant quality system, the project manager moves to the left through the figure to determine what actions and resources need adjustment in order to achieve the desired results. *The ISO 9000 registration project plan is a summation of the resources required to support desired actions to achieve the defined results.*

As Figure 3–1 implies, resources provided to the organization and actions initiated affect the relationship between how fast the quality system becomes ISO 9000 compliant, what characteristics that system exhibits, and how much the ISO 9000 registration project costs. Decisions about resources and actions must be clear about which of the variables they are attempting to affect, and what impact that change will have on other variables.

For example, adding more people to the project (resource) to cut time to registration (variable) will increase the cost (variable) of the ISO 9000 registration project. However, adding more people (resource) can also be done with the intent of modifying the characteristics of the quality system (variable), which will affect the project cost (variable), and may or may not affect the time to registration (variable).

Take another example: Internal assessment of the existing quality system finds that the organization's documented processes would be ISO 9000-compliant with minor modifications; however, the people are not following them. The ad hoc activities of the people are getting the job done, and although they are different than sanctioned processes and procedures, they could be documented and modified to be ISO 9000-compliant. Allocating effort to document the existing system (action), and by implication change the behavior of the people working within the system, will drive one set of relationships among quality system characteristics, time to registration, and cost (variables). Scrapping the existing procedures and documenting what the people are doing (action) drives another set of time to registration, quality system characteristics, cost relationships (variables).

Almost any combination of resource allocation and actions put into your ISO 9000 registration plan affects all three results variables. The point of our discussion is that in planning the ISO 9000 registra-

FIGURE 3–1 *ISO 9000 Project Planning Viewed as a System*

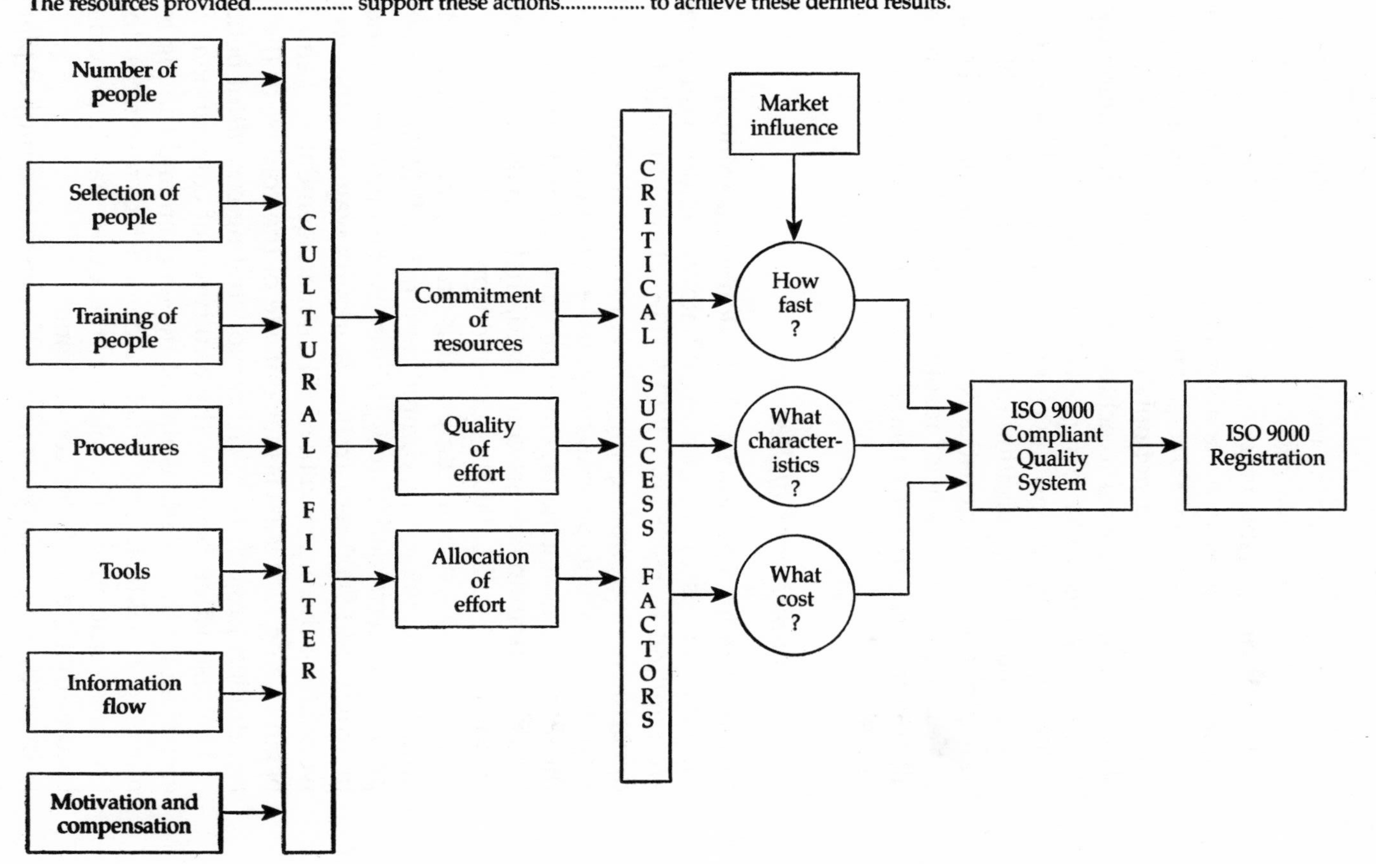

tion project, when putting resources into or defining actions as part of your plan, you must clearly understand two things. First, what is the primary variable you are trying to affect. Second, what is the impact on the other two variables and is the result acceptable. This approach makes ISO 9000 registration project planning a fact-based activity that is focused not only on the target registration date, but also on actions required to achieve the target registration date and the resources required to support those actions.

Moving to the left on the chart, we come to three categories of actions that the organization can take to alter the variables of time to registration, characteristics of the quality system, and cost of the project: (1) commitment of resources, (2) quality of effort, and (3) allocation of effort. Let's take a closer look at each of these action categories.

Commitment of Resources

"Commitment of resources" has a double meaning. In one sense, the emphasis is on resources. Whatever actions you determine are required to meet your ISO 9000 registration schedule, some department or group is going to have to commit resources, be those resources funding, people, or capital equipment. Commitment of those resources is a management behavior, a highly visible behavior as far as employees are concerned, that signals the organization is sincere in its ISO 9000 registration project.

In a second sense, the emphasis is on commitment as in dedication. The organization's commitment to the ISO 9000 registration project is determined (through the eyes of employees) by the ways in which ISO 9000 registration works its way into the everyday work life of the organization. When management and employees begin raising ISO 9000 issues outside of the context of the actual registration project, they are demonstrating *committed* behavior.

The distinction between the two types of commitment are exemplified by the relationships of the chicken and the pig to your morning breakfast. The chicken committed resources to your breakfast—the eggs. The pig, on the other hand, provided the bacon—that's a *dedicated* commitment.

In putting together your ISO 9000 registration project plan, you need to give consideration to both types of commitment. Obviously, increasing available resources can affect the time to registration, but so can increasing the dedicated commitment of a smaller number of people. Total resources can affect project cost in both a positive and negative direction. More resources obviously means more short-term project costs, but if adding resources early can prevent later consequences, such as a second third-party assessment or driving a marketing advantage that results in an increase in sales revenue, then adding resources has a positive effect on costs. Increased resources can also permit a broadening of the scope of a quality system or a more in-depth review of the system. Fewer resources, and the opposite is true.

Quality of Effort

A continuum of effort for ISO 9000 registration ranges from actions motivated by a "let's do as little as we need to in order to get by" attitude on one end, to a "let's use this process to move our organization toward total quality management" attitude at the other extreme.

Unequivocally, behavior at the "as little as needed" end of the scale is going to create problems for your ISO 9000 registration project. A group that takes a declared extreme pragmatic approach will sooner or later find themselves scrambling to patch the quality system. They'll find themselves with processes and procedures that don't work together. Patching the quality system saps resources that should be expended on the business of the business.

Ironically, the same result, misspent resources, occurs if behavior runs to the quality purist end of the spectrum. As important as the quality system is, people should not lose track of the fact that the quality system is a means to an end, and that end is the business of the business. Yes, a quality system must be continuously improved, but when dedication to process starts to choke the flexibility needed to operate the business, it's time to reevaluate one's perspective.

Your ISO 9000 registration project must strike a balance between the extremes of these two behaviors, sometimes swinging in one direction, sometimes in the other. Extreme pragmatists will put the emphasis on schedule and cost, quality purists on the characteristics of the quality system. You must keep the focus of ISO

9000 registration on the market-driven reasons for seeking registration in the first place and never let the registration process become an end in itself.

As a driver of your company's ISO 9000 registration project, you must decide where on the scale you want the people of your organization to perform. Moving to the left in Figure 3–1, you select and tailor resources to match the actions you want to support. The relationship between resources and actions is discussed in the following section.

Allocation of Effort

The third category of action that you must concern yourself with is where people in the organization apply their effort. Again, the problem is one of balance. Some of the issues you will have to consider are:

- Do you allocate resources to modify your quality system or modify behavior within the existing system?
- Do you allocate resources for in-depth improvement in limited areas of the quality system, or do you expend your resources on a more broad-based approach to quality system improvement?
- Do you allocate effort to "registration now," or do you take time to plant seeds for future quality system initiatives?

During your ISO 9000 registration project, allocation of effort questions will arise with regularity. We spoke earlier about an ISO 9000 registration plan requiring flexibility. The ability of your organization to react to resource allocation issues quickly and correctly has a major impact on meeting your registration target date. The obvious question, of course, is how do you plan for unforeseen circumstances? How do you plan for flexibility?

For every question of resource allocation that arises during your ISO 9000 registration project, there is some optimum balance of effort that will allow the organization to achieve the results it has defined for target registration date, characteristics of the quality system, and the cost of the project. If the organization over-focuses on any one of the variables, the others will suffer accordingly and the registration project will be in jeopardy.

Left to their own devices, people play to their preferences. Organizational pragmatists make decisions from the perspective of cost and schedule. Quality advocates first and foremost consider the "goodness" of the quality system that is being created. If you knew every possible allocation of effort contingency that would arise during your ISO 9000 registration project, you could define specific actions people should take. Unfortunately, you don't know every contingency, and you never will. Nonetheless, the most common method of allocating effort, and one which leads to the paralysis of planning so often cited by the just-do-it crowd, is trying to identify every last contingency.

Certainly you can and should plan for likely contingencies, but knowing every possible "gotcha" is an impossible task. Far better to use your plan to define decision criteria that can be applied when resource allocation questions arise.

Take an example from our experience. Two fundamental principles of our ISO 9000 registration project were: (1) improvement of the quality system drives registration, not the reverse, and (2) our target registration date was market-driven and not subject to compromise. When allocation of effort issues arose, discussion on how to proceed always began from the same premise—take the course of action that will produce necessary improvement in the quality system *and* maintain the target registration date.

This admittedly ideal set of decision criteria took any question of resource allocation out of an either/or context and put it in a context of looking for a way to accomplish both objectives. It focused us to look at the impact of the allocation of effort on all three result variables. We made fact-based allocation of effort decisions. The point is, in order to keep a level of consistency in your registration program, you must define fundamental decision principles, up front, in your ISO 9000 registration project plan.

DETERMINING RESOURCES REQUIRED TO ACHIEVE ISO 9000 REGISTRATION

At this point in the planning process you have defined a specific, market-driven target registration date. You have a defined set of characteristics for your organization's quality system. You have a cost figure based on what the organization is willing to spend to achieve the defined quality system by the specific registration target date. You have completed the first key activity in creating an ISO 9000 registration project plan.

You have also defined actions that will achieve your defined results. You have defined both the commitment of resources required and the level of personal commitment you require. You have addressed issues of the breadth and depth of the quality system, and you know where you need to allocate your effort. You have completed the second key activity in creating an ISO 9000 registration project plan. In essence, you *have* a plan—with one important exception—the allocation of resources required to support the actions you have defined.

Earlier we stressed the importance of beginning the ISO 9000 registration planning process from the ideal. The plan you have at this point is an ideal. The key activity that remains is matching the organization's available resources to the actions you have defined. We are now at the far left side of Figure 3–1. At this point in the planning process you may well find, as we did, that available resources don't line up with your ideal plan. In that case you must trade off resources to achieve desired results.

Recall our example of quality policy training for our people. We did not have the number of people required to accomplish the training in the required time frame. We could not supply the resource. However, we could provide train-the-trainer education for a limited number of people. We could change the procedure we used for organizationwide education. We could provide people with tools to help educate others in the quality policies. And that's what we did. By changing the input to our registration process (resources) and the activity (allocation of effort) we were able to maintain the desired target registration date (results).

Returning to Figure 3–1, "number of people," "selection of people," and "training of people" are all listed in the far left column as organizational resources as are "procedures," "tools," "information flow," and "motivation and compensation." These general categories cover resources that the organization can provide to support the actions you have defined as being necessary and sufficient to achieve ISO 9000 registration. There are any number of ways these resources can be used to support actions. Major effects of these resources are summarized in Figure 3–2.

FIGURE 3–2
Effect of Resources on ISO 9000 Registration Activities

Allocated Resources	*Affected Actions*
Number of people	Impacts the breadth and depth of quality system improvement and the time to registration.
Selection of people	Impacts the quality of effort by the orientation (pragmatist/purist/advocate) of the people.
Training of people	Impacts personal commitment of people by providing understanding of and rationale for ISO 9000 registration.
	Impacts quality of effort by providing a clear and comprehensive understanding of the goals and objectives of the ISO 9000 registration effort.
	Impacts allocation of effort by clearly defining the decision criteria for determining expenditure of resources.
Procedures	Impacts commitment of resources by defining what activities need to take place.
	Impacts the quality of effort by defining the methodologies used to pursue registration.
Tools	Impacts commitment of resources by enhancing productivity of people involved in the registration project.
	Impacts the quality of effort by providing people with better methods of evaluating the quality system.
Information flow	Impacts all three categories by providing people with the objectives and rationale for ISO 9000 registration and progress toward registration and current issues.
Motivation and compensation	Impacts all three categories of actions by providing incentives consistent with the desired results.

Providing resources is a primary function of management in the ISO 9000 registration project. Resources are the control knobs, if you will, of your ISO 9000 registration project. As you track the progress of your ISO 9000 project and find yourself ahead or behind schedule (as determined by the relationship between resources expended versus quality system characteristics achieved), you will necessarily alter your activities. Once you choose to alter activities, you must adjust the resource knobs and match resources to the activities that must be supported. Activities cannot be changed independently of resources. It all fits together—resources provided must support the actions necessary and sufficient to achieve the desired results.

MANAGING THE CORPORATE CULTURE

One of the elements of the ISO 9000 registration project planning system illustrated in Figure 3–1 that we have yet to address is the *cultural filter*. The cultural filter, the basic behavioral elements of your company's corporate culture, has the ability to either amplify or weaken the impact of the resources devoted to ISO 9000 registration.

Any resource provided to improve actions associated with the commitment of resources, the quality of the ISO 9000 registration project, or the allocation of organizationwide effort, will not be fully effective unless it is in harmony with the existing corporate culture. Despite the fact that "corporate culture" has become a business buzzword, it is still conceptually valid. The complex web of organizational interactions and values that make up the corporate culture can sink the best of project plans.

For example: you have developed an internal audit procedure that calls for members of one group of your organization to audit the activities of another in preparation for the third-party ISO 9000 assessment (our approach, by the way). How will the people of your organization react to such a plan? Will they view cross-department assessments as an opportunity to improve their operations, or as having the potential to show them up in front of their peers? Will organizations cooperate with the audit teams, or will they try to cover deficiencies in order to make themselves look better than they are? Will the audit teams do a thorough job, or will the temptation be to be lenient in hopes of receiving leniency in return?

In our ISO 9000 registration project, those specific questions represented just some of the cultural considerations we needed to incorporate into our planning process. How are cultural issues addressed?

When confronted with cultural barriers to your plan, you basically have two options—change the plan or change the culture. Sometimes changing the plan may be the best choice. Other times, education or even brute force can be used to change the culture, but it will take time. In our project, we used a number of communications vehicles to explain, demystify, and deterrorize the concept of an assessment. In the training we provided to assessors, through companywide communications, and by individually meeting with managers around the company, we communicated the basic idea that an assessment was a fact-finding, not fault-finding activity. The message was that the assessment process would provide us with opportunities to improve, not an excuse to pinpoint blame. We made it clear that managers did have accountability (otherwise we would have had no credibility with employees), but that management accountability lay not in the number of quality system nonconformities that were found but *in what management did to correct those nonconformities*.[4] In addition, we subjected our quality assurance organization and the division vice president's office to the internal assessment with the same rigor (if not more) as the rest of the organization.

Did we change everybody's behavior? No. But we did create a critical mass of individuals who were willing to give the process a chance and who conducted and cooperated with the assessment process. We uncovered deficiencies in our quality system and initiated corrective actions in a timely manner. We held to our promise not to place blame for nonconformities; we strictly monitored follow-up corrective action. Today, internal and external assessments are considered part of the way we do business by the majority of our people.

The point to take home is that when putting together your ISO 9000 registration project plan, you must consider the impact of ingrained organizational behaviors on your plan. If planned activities and corporate culture are in conflict, your options are to change the plan, or change the culture. Each of these options will have an impact on the results of your project. How you make the decision to change behavior or change the culture will depend on the decision criteria you have set up in the plan itself.

CRITICAL SUCCESS FACTORS

The remaining element of Figure 3–1 not yet addressed is that labeled "critical success factors." Critical success factors are elements of the corporate culture that must be in place in order for ISO 9000 registration to take place. Understanding critical success factors can help you get more benefit out of your ISO 9000-driven activities. This important element is the topic of Chapter 4.

THE NCR EXPERIENCE

We first became aware of the ISO 9000 standards in late 1989 through quality and trade press publications. This initial awareness became more acute when we learned that another NCR plant, Dundee, Scotland, was actively pursuing registration. We obtained copies of the standard, reviewed them, and recognized the value of both the standards and the effort of obtaining registration to our pursuit to improve our division's quality environment.

Coming from an admittedly quality advocate persuasion, we also saw that ISO 9000 registration could be leveraged into future Baldrige Award application. As we quickly learned, however, by working with upper management, a far more persuasive argument for pursuing ISO 9000 registration was the potential for competitive advantage of early registration.

During the first half of 1990, we laid the foundation for our ISO 9000 registration project plan. We benchmarked the ISO 9000 plan and activities of NCR's Dundee plant (not their quality system). We also benchmarked with and obtained quality manuals from other companies on the cutting edge of ISO 9000 registration. We attended seminars put on by consultants and also by third-party registration agencies. We read the existing literature on ISO 9000 and pursued formal quality system auditing training and ASQC auditor certification. Given the functions performed by our division, it was determined that we should focus our efforts on ISO 9001 registration.

After much discussion about what was possible, we came to a consensus that ISO 9000 registration was indeed a market-driven event. As a substantial number of our products are sold overseas, we felt we would be at a competitive advantage if we could be registered prior to 1992. We also anticipated increased interest in

ISO 9000 with consequent pressure on third-party registrars. If we could beat the rush, we would not be put at competitive disadvantage by having to wait for a spot on the registrar's schedule. With our target date established, we identified the milestones in Figure 3–3. The activities necessary to achieve these milestones and the resources provided to support those actions will be discussed in subsequent chapters.

FIGURE 3–3
NCR Network Products Division ISO 9000 Registration Project Schedule

Event	*Plan*	*Actual*
Appoint ISO 9000 registration project champion	6/90	6/90
Identify executive owners of ISO 9001 sections	6/90	6/90
Present ISO 9000 registration project plan to division vice president and staff	7/90	7/90
Individual meetings with executive owners of ISO 9000 sections	7/90	7/90
Train ISO 9000 department champions	8/90	8/90
Conduct internal self-assessment of the quality system to ISO 9001 standard	8–9/90	8–9/90
Compile and analyze results of internal self-assessment of the quality system to ISO 9001 standard	9/90	9/90
Present the results of the internal self-assessment to the division vice president and staff	9/90	9/90
Develop plans to improve quality system in accordance with ISO 9001 standard	10/90	10/90
Implement plans/write division quality manual	10–12/90	12/90
Conduct internal "independent" assessment to ISO 9001 standard	1/91	1/91
Correct deficiencies found during "independent" assessment to ISO 9001 standard	2–3/91	3/91
Conduct third-party pre-registration assessment	3/91	4/91
Correct deficiencies found during third-party pre-registration assessment	3–6/91	7/91
Conduct first third-party registration assessment	6/91	8/91
Correct deficiencies found during first third-party registration assessment	6–10/91	10/91
Conduct (possible) second third-party registration assessment	11/91	N/A

Chapter Four

Understanding Critical Success Factors

If wishes were horses, then beggars would ride.

Mother Goose

In working with other organizations on ISO 9000 registration, we have often seen what we call the "if wishes were horses syndrome." I wish management were more committed to the project. I wish employees would internalize the quality system concept. If wishes were horses, then beggars would ride, and ISO 9000 registration would be easy.

But wishes aren't horses and wishing doesn't address cultural issues that may be barriers to your company's ISO 9000 registration. Because doing so allows you to define cultural issues in terms that can be addressed in your ISO 9000 registration project plan, expressing the hopes and fears of your organization as *critical success factors* prevents cultural issues from derailing your ISO 9000 registration effort. Rather than just wishing you had management commitment, you can plan to achieve it. Rather than just wishing employees internalized the quality system concept, you can plan to make it happen.

THE PURPOSE OF THIS CHAPTER

In the previous chapter we made the bold, but well-reasoned, conclusion that there is no one right ISO 9000 registration project plan. The activities, required resources, personnel requirements, and cultural parameters of your organization are unique. Ultimately, your ISO 9000 registration project plan will depend on and reflect that uniqueness. Each organization's ISO 9000 plan will necessarily be different from that of any other organization. Having said this, we hasten to add that certain critical success factors are common to all ISO 9000 registration projects.

In this chapter, we'll identify seven critical success factors for ISO 9000 registration. We'll look at each one in some detail in order to understand how each factor affects the ISO 9000 registration project. Having gained this understanding, we'll provide a methodology that allows you to use critical success factors to effect cultural change in your organization.

THE NATURE OF CRITICAL SUCCESS FACTORS

The best way to understand the nature of critical success factors is to take an example from the physical world. Although it is the capital city of Bolivia, the city of La Paz has no fire department and does not need one. La Paz sits at 12,000 feet above sea level. At that altitude, oxygen in the air is so thin that it's difficult to light a cigarette, much less support major combustion. Oxygen is a critical factor for combustion. It is necessary. Without oxygen, combustion cannot occur. But oxygen is not sufficient for combustion. Fuel to burn and a heat source to cause ignition are also required. Fuel and a heat source are also necessary to start a fire. Together, oxygen, fuel, and a heat source are necessary and sufficient to produce and sustain combustion. Oxygen, fuel, and heat are critical success factors for combustion.

By the same token, critical success factors for ISO 9000 registration are those activities both necessary and sufficient for registration to occur. By "necessary" is it understood that if a factor is absent, the ISO 9000 registration project will be unsuccessful. The necessary factors are also "sufficient" if when taken together, they define a complete set of activities that must be completed before ISO 9000 registration can occur.

Necessary and *sufficient* are stringent requirements for critical success factors. By applying both requirements, you define specific issues you must address (with defined ISO 9000 registration activities) to achieve ISO 9000 registration. You both ignite and sustain the ISO 9000 registration process.

Although they may find unique expression in any given organization, the following seven critical success factors are common to *all* ISO 9000 registration projects:

1. Management commitment to ISO 9000 registration.
2. Employee commitment to ISO 9000 registration.
3. A clear and comprehensive organizational understanding of the ISO 9000 standard.
4. A clear and comprehensive understanding of the organization's quality system.
5. A communication structure for effectively communicating within the organization.
6. Institutionalization of the ISO 9000 quality system concept.
7. A comprehensive certification plan accepted by both management and employees.

When you look closely at that list, you will recognize many attitudes in your organization that are often vaguely expressed as statements of hope or fear. For example, "I *hope* that when it comes time to commit some real resources to this project, management will support us," or "I'm *afraid* that people are just going to look at ISO 9000 registration as more bureaucracy that gets in the way of doing their jobs."

Defining fear is the first step in confronting it; casting vague hopes as concrete objectives is the first step in fulfilling them. As an antidote to negative attitudes, critical success factors are best expressed as positive statements beginning with the words "We need . . ." or "We must have. . . ." The "we" expression indicates buy-in by all those involved in the project. "Need" or "must have" expresses the criticality of each factor.[1] Let's take a closer look at the "Critical Seven" as they relate to cultural change and ISO 9000 registration.

THE CRITICAL SEVEN

1. Management Commitment to ISO 9000 Registration

Somewhat rotund comedienne Rosanne Arnold notes that she would do anything to be thin . . . short of diet and exercise. Management commitment to ISO 9000 must go beyond doing anything to be certified short of personal involvement in the process. Management commitment must go beyond just allocating resources to the ISO 9000 registration project. Management must have a personal stake supported by a personal belief in the rightness of the ISO 9000 registration effort.

Despite the wave of quality consciousness flowing through the business world, concern about management's real commitment to quality efforts is practically universal among companies seeking ISO 9000 registration. "How do we get management commitment to ISO 9000 registration?" is one of the most frequently asked questions we encounter. We cannot pretend that acquiring such commitment is simple. It is not. However, the approach to management commitment *is* straightforward. As a driver of the ISO 9000 registration project, you cannot just wish for management commitment. You must plan for it. You must design activities into your ISO 9000 project plan that require active management involvement.

Plan for management involvement in making presentations, in conducting training, in the communication effort, in the progress review process, wherever and whenever you determine it is appropriate. The key is making management involvement part of your plan and not a series of ad hoc requests. You must define management commitment in terms of specific behaviors; for example, set up specific committees with very specific charters and require that a member of management be a part of that team. Set up criteria for measuring the effectiveness of that team.

If management knows specifically what you want them to do and the impact that their involvement will have on the ISO 9000 registration project, you have a better chance of involving them in the project than if you simply say, "We need your commitment," and expect them to figure out what to do.

2. Employee Commitment to ISO 9000 Registration

As you might expect, management commitment to ISO 9000 is only half the equation. Although management commitment is a major concern of many ISO 9000 registration projects, employee commitment is no less important and often equally as difficult to achieve. Again, the reason for the difficulty can be attributed to lack of planning and definition of desired behaviors.

The common *modus operandi* for kicking off major initiatives (including ISO 9000 registration) in most corporations is starting with an awareness campaign. Motivation becomes the word *de jour,* and employees are inundated with communication about the importance of, the rationale for, the urgent need to, and so forth and so on about the "new" initiative. What's missing is a specific call to action that links the new initiative with new behavior and relevant results.

As was the case when building management commitment to ISO 9000 registration, the presence of a comprehensive ISO 9000 registration project plan that clearly defines specific employee activities and management activities is the catalyst for commitment. For example, one way to fulfill the ISO 9000 requirement that employees understand their job responsibilities and authority is to ensure that all employees have a current job description that defines their role in the quality system. Ensuring that his or her job has such a description is something each and every employee can do immediately that impacts ISO 9000 registration.

The second step in securing employee commitment is creating a vision of how these activities will improve the employee's lot. In other words, there must be a connection between ISO 9000 registration, what employees must do to achieve registration, and how the achievement of registration will improve the work life of employees.

Recognizing that employee commitment to ISO 9000 registration is indeed a critical success factor for your project enables you to plan activities directed at building employee commitment as part of your ISO 9000 registration project plan.

3. A Clear and Comprehensive Organizational Understanding of the ISO 9000 Standard

The operative word is "organizational." To effectively achieve ISO 9000 registration, there must be a common organizational understanding of the ISO 9000 standard to which your company seeks registration, not myriad individual interpretations. This is not to say that there ought to be an official interpretation handed down from on high. Quite the contrary. An organizational perspective can only be arrived at through the involvement of many individuals of differing perspectives. The organizational interpretation is a blending of viewpoints; facilitating the blending process is a critical success factor for ISO 9000 registration.

However, organizational understanding of ISO 9000 standards, albeit necessary for success, is not in and of itself sufficient to guarantee success. Unfortunately, understanding of ISO 9000 standards is virtually the exclusive focus of many ISO 9000 registration efforts. In essence, that focus equates the ISO 9000 standards with the organization's quality system; it assumes them to be one and the same, which is, in fact, dangerously untrue.

ISO 9000 is a set of standards used to evaluate specific segments of an organization's quality system. It is not the definition of that organization's or any other organization's quality system. The danger lies in assuming that if all of the parts of a quality system are ISO 9000 compliant then the quality system as a whole is functioning smoothly. Because a quality system encompasses more than is stated in the ISO 9000 standards, this assumption is simply not accurate. A quality system can be judged in the context of the ISO 9000 standards, but ISO 9000 compliance is not sufficient for a smoothly functioning quality system, which brings us to the next of our critical success factors for ISO 9000 registration.

4. A Clear and Comprehensive Understanding of the Organization's Quality System

"Quality system" is a rather abstract concept for most organizations. Product developers think in terms of a development process. Industrial engineers think in terms of manufacturing processes. Marketing people understand a product introduction process. Salespeople respond to quotas. Defining and rendering understandable the system that relates the activities for which departments are accountable to each other and to the abstract concept of "quality" is not as easy as sketching a flow chart. Nonetheless, unless such understanding is achieved, it is unlikely that a quality system will withstand the scrutiny of a third-party assessment.

From the practical perspective of having an efficient and effective quality system, the situation is worse. A quality system that lacks interdepartmental accountability will be fraught with problems as the interfaces between processes inevitably and repeatedly break down and reform and break down and reform. The reason is simple: The ISO 9000 standards concern themselves with processes and procedures; the functioning of the quality system also depends, however, on the interfaces between those processes and procedures. The ISO 9000 standards very clearly define the types of processes expected to be in place, but they say almost nothing about the interfaces between those processes.

A vivid example is the leap of faith between Section 4.4.3 *Design Input* and 4.4.4 *Design Output* in ISO 9001, the most stringent of the ISO 9000 series. Section 4.4.3 lists specific requirements for handling design inputs. Section 4.4.4 defines specific characteristics of design output. On the subject of the design process itself, the standard is silent, yet it is inarguable that the design process is a key element of a quality system. It is the interface between design input and output.

Management of a quality system takes place at the interfaces between processes. Management of a quality system focuses on the behaviors of the people within that system. It is on those behaviors that a third-party assessor will ultimately judge the functioning of a quality system (see discussion of Figure 7–1). Attacking quality system improvement from processes up does not provide the systematic view required for an effective and efficient quality system. Yes, process management and sectional ISO 9000 compliance is important, but bottom-up compliance must be done in the larger context of an effectively and efficiently functioning systematic approach—a top-down approach. You need both.

5. A Communication Structure for Effectively Communicating within the Organization

Critical to the success of the ISO 9000 registration effort is a communication structure that consists of ways and means of communicating with your organization. A communications structure includes a communications plan that defines specific key messages that will be included in individual communications and the media through which those messages will be repeated. Whether evaluating an existing communication structure or establishing new communications vehicles to promote the ISO 9000 registration project, necessary and sufficient criteria should be applied. Are sufficient means available to communicate your messages to your organization, or are other communication vehicles necessary?

Communication is critical to the ISO 9000 registration project, but in planning your program you must be careful not to substitute communication for substance. Writing in *Quality on Trial,* authors Roger and Maynard Howe and Dee Gaeddert note that having recognized the need to improve quality, companies tend to shift the corporate communications department into high gear, pumping out slogans, designing logos, and ordering buttons and mugs printed with the quality message. When challenged, these companies respond that these methods "build quality awareness." Although quality awareness is certainly a necessary element of success, equally certain is that quality awareness is not sufficient in and of itself to ensure the successful integration of quality, in this case ISO 9000 requirements, into ongoing business practices. A communications plan must include communication of concise, easily understood actions that employees can immediately take to move the organization in the desired direction.[2]

6. Institutionalizing the ISO 9000 Quality System Concept

Institutionalization is visible behavior that signals that ISO 9000 is part and parcel of the way the organization does business. For example, ISO 9000 conformance is routinely considered when processes and procedures are changed and when reorganizations take place. ISO 9000 conformance is also considered when employees are transferred to new positions that may require a new skill set.

Some necessary elements of institutionalization are defined by the ISO 9000 standards (e.g., an audit program or naming of an ISO 9000 management representative). Your task is determining whether or not the stated requirements of the standard are sufficient to firmly establish the quality system concept in the culture of the organization. If not, additional activities may have to be initiated.

7. A Comprehensive Certification Plan Accepted by Both Management and Employees

As discussed in Chapter 3, a plan that integrates milestones, activities, and resources and is credible in the eyes of management and employees is absolutely necessary to achievement of ISO 9000 registration. Mapping activities defined within that plan to the critical success factors described in this chapter allows you to address ISO 9000 within the context of cultural change. While others fail because they only wish they could change the culture, you can be actively changing your organization's culture.

CRITICAL SUCCESS FACTORS AND CULTURAL CHANGE

Critical success factors are the cultural and structural foundation upon which an ISO 9000-certifiable quality system is built. And while people may preach a lot about cultural change in connection with ISO 9000, because it revolves around soft, difficult to manage issues, practicing cultural change is often overlooked and usually goes unaddressed in most ISO 9000 registration project planning. People spend more time wishing management and their peers behaved differently and less time actively trying to change the culture. As a result, organizations expend more resources than necessary on ISO 9000 registration, run into more obstacles than are necessary, and, in general, increase the overall time required to achieve ISO 9000 registration (or fail at it altogether).

Factors that are both necessary to ignite and sufficient to sustain an ISO 9000 registration project are those that make corporate cultures "notoriously slow to build and hard to change."[3] But, you say (and rightly so) time is a luxury that most organizations confronted with ISO 9000 registration do not have. Given the urgency of ISO 9000 registration, cultual change has to happen now! Faced with the challenge of changing an organization's culture, designated change agents set about with missionary zeal to convert the masses on the need for change. In doing so, they focus on changing people's attitudes. Little or no attention is given to changing behaviors. Although people can be motivated to change their attitudes, a change in attitude in and of itself is a poor predictor of behavior—and unless behavior changes, there is no cultural change. Direct experience is a key factor in determining how people will behave. The more narrowly focused the definition of a behavior is, the more likely it is to be internalized.

The implication for your ISO 9000 registration project is that you should not put all your cultural change eggs in the basket of attitudinal change. If you are going to change the corporate culture, you need to provide specific actions for people to take. You can't just tell people what to believe; *you must show them what to do and provide them the opportunity to do it.* Preaching attitude change must be accompanied by practicing cultural change through specific activities and defined behaviors. Don't just tell management they need to be committed to ISO 9000 registration; set up a requirement for them to review the progress that their departments are making toward registration at monthly staff meetings. Nothing will derail your ISO 9000 registration effort faster than revving up the work force with enthusiasm only to leave them with their motors running and no place to go.

USING CRITICAL SUCCESS FACTORS

In Chapter 3 we stated that an ISO 9000 project plan is more than a list of milestones. It is an exercise in balancing schedules, resources, and activities. The question we raised and deferred in Chapter 3 was how you can get more bang for the buck from the activities that are part of your ISO 9000 registration project. The answer is to direct planned ISO 9000 registration activities at cultural change driven by the "Critical Seven." Using a matrix like that found in Figure 4–1, you can evaluate and plan for the relationships between planned ISO 9000 activities and critical success factors.

Figure 4–1 is a portion of the matrix used to evaluate the NCR Network Products Division registration project (the full matrix is shown in Appendix B). Readers familiar with Quality Function Deployment (QFD) will recognize a variation of QFD matrix analysis.[4] The left side of the matrix lists the seven critical success factors for ISO 9000 registration. In QFD terms, these are the "whats"—those requirements that must be met in order to achieve success.

FIGURE 4–1 ***Critical Success Factors Related to Elements of the ISO 9000 Project Plan***

WHATs versus HOWs

Strong relationship:	●	9
Medium relationship:	○	3
Weak relationship:	△	1

Critical Success Factors ("Whats")	Elements of the ISO 9000 Registration Project Plan ("Hows")	1 Ownership of the ISO 9000 sections	2 Ownership of the system at the elementary level	3 Empowered department champions	4 Assessment training	5 Quality policies	6 Quality manual	7 Review meetings with department champions	8 Internal assessments/audits	9 Bonuses	Critical success factor coverage	
Management active commitment to registration	1	●	○	○		●	○				27	1
Employee active commitment to registration	2	○	●	●	○		○	○	○	○	36	2
Clear and comprehensive understanding of the ISO 9000 standard	3	○	○	○	●	△	●	●	●		46	3
Clear and comprehensive understanding of the quality system	4	○	○		●	●	●	○	○		39	4
Communication structure	5				○	△	△	●	△		15	5
Institutionalization of the ISO 9000 quality system concept	6	●	●	△	○	●	●	○	●		52	6
Comprehensive registration plan accepted by management/employees	7	●	●	●	○			○			33	7
Importance of activities to success		36	36	25	30	29	34	30	25	3		
		1	2	3	4	5	6	7	8	9		

Across the top of the matrix is a sample of the activities we implemented to achieve ISO 9001 registration. These are the "hows"—the activities that describe how you will meet the requirements listed at the left.

The symbols at the intersection of the rows and columns define the relationship between critical success factors and activities that are a part of the ISO 9000 registration effort. These relationships can be defined as strong, medium, weak, or nonexistent. The stronger the relationship, the more impact a planned activity has on a critical success factor. Using a matrix like Figure 4–1, you can evaluate the relationships between planned activities and critical success factors. For example, the planned activity "Internal assessments/audits" has a strong relationship with the critical success factor "Clear and comprehensive understanding of the ISO 9000 standard," a medium relationship with "Employee active commitment to registration," a weak relationship with "Communication structure," no relationship with "Comprehensive registration plan accepted by management/employees," and other levels of relationship with the other critical success factors.

There is no inherent relationship between any ISO 9000 registration activity and a given critical success factor. Activities are what you make them. By examining the relationship between activities and critical success factors, you can have activities that create impact beyond their stated objectives. You can stop wishing for cultural change and start planning for it.

A completed Critical Success Factor matrix provides you with a powerful evaluation and planning tool. If any row of the matrix is empty, nearly empty, or consists of only a few weak relationships, you have identified a critical success factor that is not being adequately addressed. In your planning process, you must then decide if another activity must be added to your ISO 9000 registration project or if you can get more mileage from existing activities by modifying them so that they address neglected Critical Success Factors. If any column is empty, nearly empty, or consists of only a few weak relationships, you have identified a planned activity that may be of little value to the overall ISO 9000 registration project.

Be aware that in Figure 4–1 (and the full matrix in Appendix B) the symbols at the intersections of rows and columns are based on our experience with the NCR organization. To a greater or lesser degree, the seven critical success factors are already present in all organizations. The degree to which they are present will determine how much emphasis must be accorded each factor in an ISO 9000 registration project plan. Completing the critical success factor matrix should not be regarded as a discovery of the universally correct mapping of activities to critical success factors. Because every organization is unique, no such universal one-size-fits-all matrix exists. Completion of the matrix is part of the creation process inherent in good planning. For your organization, planned activities and the relationships of those activities to the Critical Seven will necessarily be different from ours.

For example, if ISO 9000 registration is driven by senior management, you will not need to spend as much effort gaining their commitment as if the impetus for ISO 9000 registration comes from the Quality or Marketing organization. Nonetheless, because it is a critical success factor, active management commitment to registration must be present to achieve ISO 9000 registration. The point is, if management commitment is clearly high in your organization, you need not expend as much effort in selling ISO 9000 registration to management (or the rest of the organization) or involving management as visibly in the ISO 9000 registration process as you would if that commitment were not present.

You can also weigh the relationships and determine a couple of other helpful facts. Assign each relationship the following value: 9 for strong, 3 for medium, 1 for weak, and 0 for no relationship. You can then total the values down each column. In Figure 4–1, these totals are found in the row labeled "Importance of activities to success." The higher the number, the more completely a planned activity addresses the critical success factors. Comparison of the column totals will give you a relative ranking of the importance of each proposed activity to the success of your project. In the example, "Bonuses," with a total of 3, are not very helpful in fulfilling the critical success factors.

You can use these column totals to prioritize resources and/or look for ways to beef up activities, making them applicable to more critical success factors. For example, there is wide latitude within the ISO 9000 standards for the criteria of an acceptable quality policy. At one extreme, a quality policy is simply a statement of the importance and role of quality in the organization. If you map that statement against the critical success factors, you find that it has very little overall impact on the organization. However, if you expand the concept of quality policy to encompass the idea of a collection of quality policies that address major functions of the business and incorporate dissemination of those quality policies into the training structure of the organization, the impact of the quality policy is considerably increased. More critical success factors are affected and to a greater degree.

You can also total the values across each row. In Figure 4–1, these totals are found in the column labeled "Critical success factor coverage." The higher the number, the more activities you are initiating that address a given critical success factor. Comparison of the row totals will give you a relative ranking of how well the total planned activities cover each critical success factor. In the example, "Institutionalization of the ISO 9000 quality system concept" is very well covered with a total of 52. This analysis will tell you if you have planned too few, too many, or enough activities and whether they are the right ones.

You can perform a sanity check on these row totals. For example, the ranking for your organization might show that your ISO 9000 registration project plan involves putting in place a sophisticated communication structure to keep people informed about the project. However, when you do a sanity check, you may realize that your organization already has a communications structure in place that can be used to keep people abreast of project progress. It doesn't make sense to set up a separate system for ISO 9000 communication. Or your ranking may tell you that despite the obvious fact that employees and management are not committed to ISO 9000 registration, you have too few activities specifically designed to build that commitment.

A word of caution here. The numerical values you calculate for the rows and columns on your matrix should not be taken as precise measures. They provide a sanity check—does it make sense to expend more effort on a communications structure than on gaining management commitment to the project? Critical success factor analysis is important, but don't get hung up on the process to the detriment of doing real work. The intent of the exercise is to help you make the right decisions about the way you expend your resources, not to create an impressive chart.

A second key point—critical success factor analysis should continue throughout your ISO 9000 registration project. Organizational dynamics change. At different stages of the registration effort, you will need to concentrate more on some critical success factors than others. For example, early in the project, management commitment and employee commitment are extremely important. The communication structure becomes important when key events, like a third-party assessment, are taking place. If your emphasis on critical success factors is out of sync with the stage of the project, you'll find yourself doing a lot of retrenching and replowing of old ground. In Chapter 5, we'll look at how analysis of critical success factors helps you at a key stage in your ISO 9000 registration project—presenting your ISO 9000 registration project plan to your management.

THE NCR EXPERIENCE

It would be nice to say that the critical success factor charts you find in this chapter and in Appendix B served as the guiding model of our ISO 9000 registration effort. Nice, but untrue. If the truth be told, the actual charts were put together after the project was completed in an attempt to understand why it was successful and to locate any general principles we could apply to other projects. However, without giving it a formal name, we did continually analyze critical success factors throughout our ISO 9000 registration project.

For example, we recognized very early in the project that the existing communications structure in our organization was not robust enough to support the ISO 9000 registration effort. Consequently, we created "Quality Briefs," a publication of our division quality assurance organization, through which we communicated project rationale and progress to all employees. We also set up a number of teams and formal review meetings specifically targeted at ISO 9000 project activities, again with the intent of keeping the rationale for the project in front of people and documenting that real progress toward registration was being made. Most activities we planned were not viewed only as a means to their desired end, but also as an opportunity to communicate.

In addition to the criticality of a communication structure, we recognized very early in the project the critical impact of management commitment to the project. We also recognized that our market-driven target date for registration did not afford us the luxury of first changing management attitudes and then initiating new behaviors. Consequently, in light of the criticality of management commitment, we looked at every ISO 9000 registration activity with an eye to involving key management personnel.

For example, we could have defined a simple quality policy and disseminated it throughout the organization via the communications structure we had established. This process would have met the requirements of the ISO 9000 standards. However, it would have had little impact on management commitment. Noting this, we elected to create what might be considered a lengthy quality policy document that at first glance might seem like overkill. As a stand-alone document, it probably is. However, our quality policy was never positioned as a stand-alone document. Each member of the executive staff was required to present the complete set of quality policies to his or her direct reports, providing interpretation relevant to his or her specific organization. In turn, members of the next level of reports then presented the quality policies to their direct reports and so on.

This training methodology was a clear departure from our organization's usual one. As a result, there was a clear perception on the part of employees that management was committed to the intent of the quality policies because they took the time to discuss them. The ripple effect was an increase in employee commitment to the ISO 9000 registration project. Survey forms were given to employees at each management training session; overwhelmingly, there was a positive response to management's involvement in the training. This message was relayed to management, reinforcing their commitment behavior.[5]

The point of this discussion of critical success factors is that by understanding the critical nature of both management and employee commitment, we were able to expand an activity—the writing and dissemination of quality policies—to impact a broader segment of the ISO 9000 registration effort. Through critical success factor analysis, we moved beyond wishing the corporate culture was different to taking concrete action to change the existing culture.

Chapter Five

Presenting the ISO 9000 Registration Project Plan to Management

Our problem in making a talk to convince or impress others is just this: to plant the idea in their minds and to keep contradicting and opposing ideas from arising.

Dale Carnegie
The Quick and Easy Way to Effective Speaking

You have just spent several weeks wrestling with the ISO 9000 standards. You have gained understanding of both the standards and how ISO 9000 requirements pertain to your organization. You've been on the stump throughout your organization, sharing your understanding with others. In some cases, you've gained enthusiastic support. In others, the support is more tentative. But despite some pockets of resistance to an ISO 9000 registration effort, all in all, you've overcome initial organizational inertia and created an atmosphere ready for ISO 9000 registration.

Most importantly, you've put together a plan to register your organization to ISO 9001, 9002, or 9003—a plan that takes advantage of the environment for change that you've created. Your plan is well conceived. It establishes a market-driven registration target date and milestones that must be accomplished to meet the date. It defines the actions the organization must take to achieve the interim objectives at each milestone. It determines what resources are required to meet the schedule. Further, you have mapped your planned activities to your organization's culture. You are confident that your plan will not be derailed by cultural issues.

Now the moment of truth is at hand. It is time to present the ISO 9000 registration project plan to management. A carefully prepared

ISO 9000 plan certainly smoothes the way for acceptance, but acceptance of the plan is not automatic. Consider that you are about to ask executive management to commit a significant amount of human and financial resources to the ISO 9000 registration project. Your task is to convince them that ISO 9000 registration is necessary to your organization's business success and is worth the investment. And although there is no silver bullet approach that can guarantee acceptance of your plan, as Dale Carnegie advises, your strategy for management acceptance of your project plan should be to "plant the idea [of ISO 9000 registration] in their minds and keep contradicting and opposing ideas from arising."

THE PURPOSE OF THIS CHAPTER

Winning acceptance of your ISO 9000 registration project plan involves more than a pulsating presentation. Presenting the ISO 9000 registration project plan is not a singular activity; it is a three-phase activity consisting of prepresentation activities, the presentation itself, and postpresentation activities. This chapter breaks down each of these phases into specific actions you should take to smooth the way for gaining acceptance and building commitment for your ISO 9000 registration project plan.

A basic premise of this book is that managing the ISO 9000 registration project requires that you consider cultural issues and their impact on the project. In keeping with that premise, this chapter also introduces you to the notion of having two agendas for your ISO 9000 management presentation. Overtly, the management presentation is intended to gain management approval of your ISO 9000 project plan. However, a subtle agenda you should carry into the presentation goes beyond the basic requirement of approval and addresses the cultural issues of gaining commitment to the ISO 9000 process, creating an environment favorable to ISO 9000 registration, and promoting a quality-focused culture.

Using the management presentation of the ISO 9000 registration project to address both the requirement to gain approval of your project plan *and* to address cultural issues is an extension of the critical success factor analysis discussed in the previous chapter. Using this methodology, you gain a level of control over cultural issues that otherwise might derail even the best of plans. Let's take a closer look at the concept of two agendas and then move into the activities of each of the three phases of the presentation process.

TWO AGENDAS

Overtly, the purpose of presenting the ISO 9000 registration project plan to executive management is to gain approval of the plan. However, as we saw in Chapter 4, there is substantial benefit in using ISO 9000 activities to build and nurture a quality-oriented culture. The executive presentation is no exception. You can use it to pursue more than one agenda, to accomplish more than one objective.

The overt agenda, as described above, is securing approval of the ISO 9000 registration project plan. In order to accomplish this objective, you must inform executive management about what ISO 9000 is and convince them that ISO 9000 registration is necessary to your organization's business success. The second agenda is more subtle.[1] Think of the second, subtle agenda as the mirror image of the main, overt agenda. Rather than being a completely separate agenda, which has been hidden from view to disguise its intent, the subtle agenda is a supporting structure that enhances and facilitates the accomplishment of your overt objectives. The notion of two agendas and their relationship is shown in Figure 5–1.

Understanding the interrelationship of the two agendas in Figure 5–1 helps you put ISO 9000 into a context of total quality improvement that will have long-term benefits for your organization. While you are informing the executive staff about ISO 9000 as a quality system concept, you can also be promoting the quality agenda of enhancing the quality system. While you are convincing the executive staff that ISO 9000 registration is necessary for business success, you can be creating a win-win environment ripe for quality improvement. While seeking management approval for your ISO 9000 registration project plan, you can be building management commitment to the plan. Let's look at these interrelationships a little closer and determine how they can be used to structure information that is important to the presentation of ISO 9000 to executive management.

FIGURE 5–1
Two Agendas for the Management Presentation Meeting

Overt Agenda	*Subtle Agenda*
Inform the executive staff about what ISO 9000 is	Promote a quality-focused culture
Convince the executive staff that the project is necessary	Create a win-win environment
Gain approval of the plan	Gain commitment to the plan

Informing/Promoting

Because your management may never have considered the concept of a quality system before, or thought about the quality of your organization's day-to-day activities apart from its impact on specific products, your presentation message should inform or remind executive management of the quality system concept and its relationship to the ISO 9000 standards. Your organization's management must clearly understand that each ISO 9000 standard is a quality *system* standard, not a quality *product* standard. If your organization's executive staff thinks the ISO 9000 project is about product certification, they will not understand your later request for resources. In their experience, no product certification will ever consume the quantity of resources required by an organization-wide ISO 9000 registration effort.

At the same time, you need not avoid talking about product quality. In fact, a product quality discussion is a natural opportunity for you to enter the promotion mode of the presentation process. After all, the purpose of having a good quality system is to produce good quality products. However, an ISO 9000 registered system does not make any guarantees about product quality. ISO 9000 registration simply means that your organization's quality system is capable of producing consistent quality products. Based on your organization's customers' requirements, your organization determines the level of product quality and implements a quality system that consistently delivers that level of quality. Herein lies your opportunity.

Today, nearly every organization has heard the continuous im-

FIGURE 5–2
Improvement to a Controlled Quality System

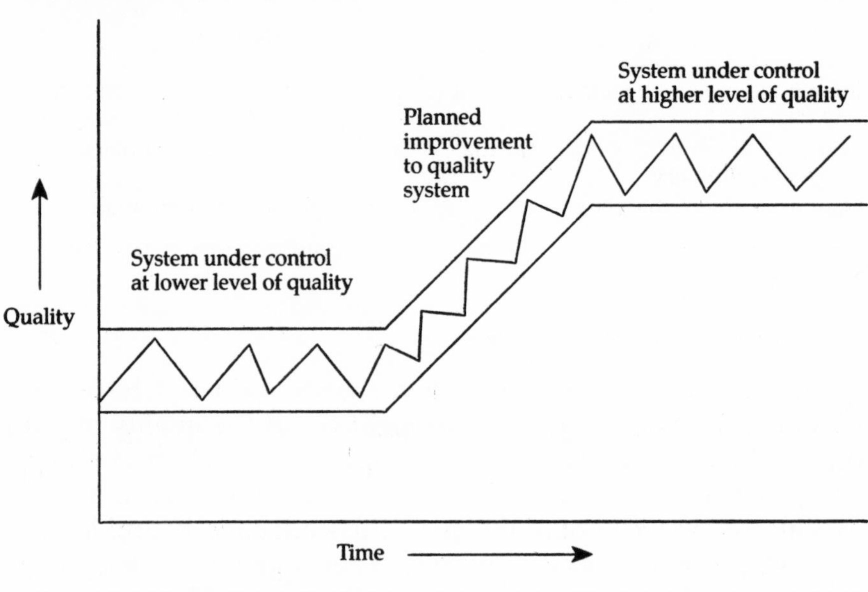

provement story. And in theory, it is a pretty hard argument to ignore. Continued success in business requires continuous product and process improvement. Many organizations accept that notion but fall short on implementation. Many never seriously start a continuous improvement effort because, quite frankly, they don't know how to start. They never attack basic systemic issues.

ISO 9000 provides a systematic starting point for an organization. If your management desires your organization to produce products of higher quality than it currently does, ISO 9000 will help it do that. If your system is compliant with ISO 9000, it is under control. You can improve it while using ISO 9000 to maintain control. This improvement/control relationship is shown in Figure 5–2.

The point made in Figure 5–2 is that once the ISO 9000 project has brought your quality system under control, you can then improve it for the purpose of producing higher quality products. You will be able to hold the gains in improvement by using ISO 9000 requirements to keep your system under control. You can improve a system that is not in control, but without control the system can and often does backslide easily. The ISO 9000 standards provide the control mechanism that allows for planned process improvement and prevents backsliding when improvements are made.

Although increased awareness of ISO 9000 is making people more knowledgeable about the standards, you may still have to convince some individual executives that ISO 9000 is *not just a European standard.* A comment made to one of us recently was "Why don't we [Americans] come up with our own set of quality standards, like ISO 8000, or something, instead of trying to follow a European standard." This was not said in an anti-European frame of mind, but it expresses a common misconception—that ISO 9000 is a European standard. Actually, ISO 9000 is an *international* standard. ISO 9000 has been adopted by countries around the world as well as by the European Economic Community. Americans, Canadians, Japanese, Europeans, and others from many nations had a part in the creation of the ISO 9000 standards.

The value of an international standard is that it facilitates international activities. International air traffic standards facilitate international air travel. Likewise, international quality system standards facilitate international commerce. If you have a supplier halfway around the world that has been registered to an ISO 9000 standard, you know some things about that supplier's quality system without ever having seen it. You have a higher level of confidence in the supplier's capability to deliver products of consistent quality as a result of the supplier's adherence to an internationally accepted standard, than the confidence you would have if the supplier complied only with some unknown local standard.

It is also important that your executive staff know the origins of the ISO 9000 standards, who the International Organization for Standardization is, who represents your country in that organization, and how the ISO conducts its business. This material is covered in Chapter 1. If you do a lot of business in Europe, you may need to make the relationship of the ISO 9000 standards to the European Economic Community a part of your presentation process. Certainly, if your company does or is planning to do significant business in Europe, ISO 9000 registration should play a significant role in your marketing strategy. However, to maintain credibility with your audience, you should make clear to your executive management that even the European Economic Community has passed no blanket legislation requiring non-European companies to be registered to an ISO 9000 standard as a prerequisite to doing business there.

The EEC has, however, determined to regulate certain products for reasons of safety or strategic importance. To one degree or another ISO 9000 quality system registration is a part of the regulation of those particular products. More information about the current status of these particular EEC product regulations is available from your national government. In the United States, the Department of Commerce provides information on this subject. To date, however, ISO 9000 registration requirements are primarily driven by individual customer requirements, not legislation.

That ISO 9000 is a worldwide standard is information that your organization needs to make decisions about its registration effort. But the worldwide nature of ISO 9000 also provides you with the opportunity to move beyond ISO 9000 registration and promote a quality-focused culture.

Because of the widespread acceptance of the ISO 9000 standards for quality systems, as more and more companies become registered, ISO 9000 registration will become a de facto ante to play in the global marketplace. From a marketing perspective, ISO 9000 registration will not provide your organization with any competitive advantage. If your goal is to sustain a quality leadership position in your industry, your organization will have to enhance its quality system beyond the requirements of ISO 9000.

An important part of the presentation process for the ISO 9000 registration project plan is conveying to the executive staff that the requirements of ISO 9000 are not the pinnacle of quality systems. Once you reach ISO 9000 registration, you may have come a long way from where you were, particularly if you had no documented quality system in place before you started, but you are still a long way from total quality management. As seen in Figure 5–3, an ISO 9000-compliant quality system is on the minimum requirement end of the spectrum of world-class quality systems.

In terms of the quality journey as depicted in Figure 5–3, achievement of ISO 9000 is a significant milestone because it is the dividing

FIGURE 5–3
The Quality Journey

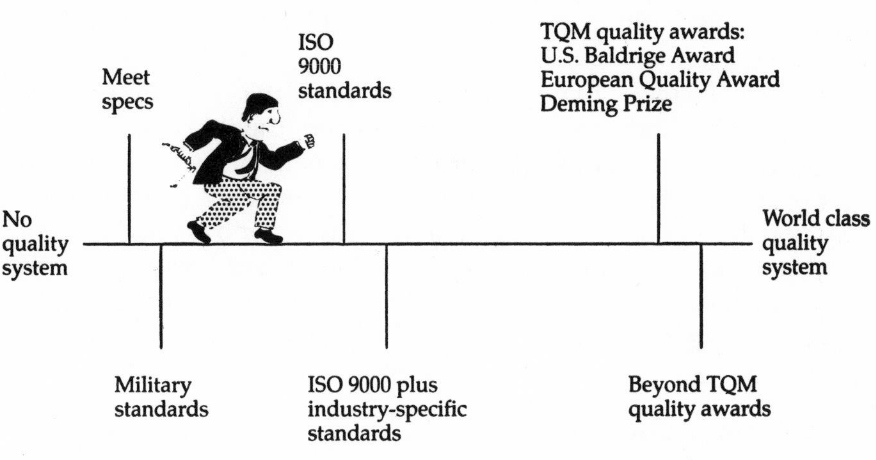

line between an ad hoc approach to quality and truly looking at quality as a system. To the left of ISO 9000, quality efforts focus on specific product-focused criteria like meeting specifications or conforming to specific standards. ISO 9000 moves away from product-specific criteria to system criteria. ISO 9000 gets away from looking at every single product to looking at the system that creates every single product. If the system is sound, then the products produced by that system will be of consistent quality.

The key word is consistent. An ISO 9000-compliant quality system will produce products of consistent quality, which is not necessarily to say superior quality. For a company to use quality as a competitive advantage, it is necessary to move beyond the basic requirements of ISO 9000 by enhancing the quality system. Criteria in the Deming Prize, the European Quality Award, and the U.S. Malcolm Baldrige National Quality Award—to the right of ISO 9000 standards in Figure 5–3—are expansions of the basic requirements of ISO 9000. For example, ISO 9000 requires a systematic approach defining customer requirements. Baldrige and other quality award criteria put much more emphasis on the specific methods used to understand and translate customer requirements into product requirements. The criteria for these awards also address strategic quality planning, information and analysis, fact-based decision making, effective use of human resources, and a company's responsibility to the community and environment—issues that are only marginally addressed by the ISO 9000 standards.

The point to make to your management team is that as comprehensive as the quality award criteria may be, those criteria cannot be addressed until a basic quality system is in place. ISO 9000 is a set of criteria that defines a basic quality system. Achieving ISO 9000 registration sets the stage for moving beyond ad hoc quality efforts to systematic improvements. It also provides the people of the organization with a clear, short-term goal and the opportunity to celebrate success.

Convincing/Creating

Convincing executive management of the value of the ISO 9000 registration project to your organization is best done by relating the ISO 9000 registration project to management concerns—first and foremost among them, money. Although quality advocates may cringe, the fact of the matter is that outside of the glossy magazine success stories of companies that focus on quality, there is an underlying skepticism among business leaders that quality really does pay. Writing in *Quality on Trial,* authors Roger and Maynard Howe and Dee Gaeddert note:

> much has been written about attempts to change the priorities of the corporation in modern society. However, as the hundreds of line executives we have interviewed are quick to point out, none of these changes, including the emphasis on quality, is possible if the corporation is not profitable and does not provide a reasonable return to its shareholders. When the dust settles and the sun sets in the west, bottom-line results keep the lights on and turn the crank of the corporate world.[2]

By the nature of their responsibilities and the criteria by which they are judged and by which they are rewarded, executive management is interested in knowing what return they will get for investing company resources in ISO 9000 registration. Therefore, to convince executive management of the value of ISO 9000 registration, you must relate the cost of registration to its benefits in return-on-investment-like terms. Potential contributions of ISO 9000 registration to hard and fast financial measures must be forcefully addressed in the presentation of your ISO 9000 registration project plan.

Of course, as quality advocates in your organization will be quick to tell you, not all quality benefits are tangible, nor will all benefits from improved quality bring about a short-term return on investment. Unfortunately, the quality community has not always been successful in making that point with executive management. And while the quality advocates may balk at your return-on-investment (ROI) approach to convincing executive management of the value of ISO 9000, that approach helps create a win-win environment for both management and the quality community. If ISO 9000 registration does indeed lead to quantifiable business benefits, then the precedence is set and credibility established for future quality initiatives. It is a win-win situation.

We recommend that you explain the benefits of the ISO 9000 registration project using the following three major headings in the following order:

1. ISO 9000 registration impact on sales and revenue,
2. ISO 9000 registration impact on specific company problems, and
3. ISO 9000 registration impact on the company's internal operations.

Let's look at each of these headings in some detail.

ISO 9000 registration impact on sales and revenue. The impact of ISO 9000 on an organization's sales and revenue can be expressed both negatively (failure to become ISO 9000 registered will result in lost sales and revenue) and positively (ISO 9000 registration has the potential to increase sales and revenue). Both approaches provide valid arguments for ISO 9000 registration in the abstract. Depending upon your organization's circumstances, you may choose to emphasize one tack over the other.

For example, one line of argument holds that today, market requirements are driving ISO 9000 registration. A growing number of companies are requiring ISO 9000 registration of their suppliers as part of supplier management programs. British Telecom is a major example. Within many large and multinational companies, internal divisions are requiring their internal suppliers to be ISO 9000 certified. And strangely enough, we have even heard of cases where companies who are not themselves registered to ISO 9000 are requiring their suppliers to become registered.

If your organization's customers are already making ISO 9000 a requirement of doing business, then you have an obvious tie-in between sales and revenue and ISO 9000 registration. It becomes fairly straightforward to compare the value of a specific customer or customers to the cost of ISO 9000 registration. It is also credible to postulate other customers making ISO 9000 a requirement of doing business and extrapolate their value into the equation.

However, even if you don't have specific customers demanding ISO 9000 registration, the prevalence of companies using the standards as part of their supplier management programs provides evidence enough that the trend has started. It becomes only a matter of time until such a requirement from *your* customers will be forthcoming. If you wait to pursue ISO 9000 registration until there is customer demand, you may find your customers unwilling to wait for your organization to achieve registration. They may very well take their business to competitors who had the foresight to pursue and achieve ISO 9000 registration before your company is out of the starting blocks. The ISO 9000 plans of your competitors is a good piece of information to have when you present your ISO 9000 registration project plan to executive management.

The above examples fall into the negative category. If your organization doesn't seek ISO 9000 registration, it may lose sales and revenue. In some organizations, the negative approach carries a lot of weight. In others, a positive approach to the benefits of ISO 9000 registration will fare better. ISO 9000 registration can provide your organization with a competitive advantage that expands sales and revenue opportunities. Making ISO 9000 registration a part of your organization's sales story creates expectations with your customers that your organization can live up to, but that your unregistered competitors cannot. Your organization not only produces a superior product or service, it produces that product in a quality system that is registered to an internationally accepted quality standard.

In short, to convince executive management that ISO 9000 registration has an impact on sales and revenue, you must relate ISO 9000 registration to your organization's specific *marketing* environment. Note that we did not say *quality* environment. If we may be allowed a bit of digression here, we have seen too many quality initiatives, ISO 9000 registration among them, fall flat because the organization failed to integrate quality into ongoing day-to-day business activities. To gain management commitment to ISO 9000, to institutionalize ISO 9000 within your organization, and to implement a quality system approach in your organization, you must integrate ISO 9000 with other key business initiatives. Quality benefits are difficult for executives to grasp. Marketing benefits are considerably easier for them to evaluate. Selling ISO 9000 necessarily involves talking in the language of executive management.

In addition to scenarios such as those described above, you should be aware of two specific ISO 9000 implementations that may affect the business fortunes of your company. First, if your organization currently does or plans to do a significant amount of business in Europe, you should make yourself familiar with any EEC directives that affect your product. To find out whether your company's products are regulated by the EEC under one of these directives, contact the government agency in your country that is responsible for international trade. Products regulated by the EEC are those that have safety requirements, like children's toys and implantable medical devices, or are of strategic importance to the EEC, like telecommunications products. Some of these directives promote registration to the ISO 9000 quality system standards.

You should also be aware that certain contracts like those with military or other government organizations may require ISO 9000 registration. Some allow ISO 9000 to be a substitute for other requirements. In 1993, the US Department of Defense began allowing the Army, Air Force, and Marines the latitude to accept ISO 9000 registration in place of certain other military quality standard requirements. At some future time the ISO 9000 standards, with some supplementary requirements, may actually replace the US military quality system standards as a contractual requirement.

If your company is affected by either of these cases, ISO 9000 registration, or lack thereof, can have a significant impact on sales and revenue.

ISO 9000 registration impact on specific company problems. Every company has problems that refuse to die. Like creatures in some B-movie horror story, they arise from the grave at nearly every meeting. Stakes through the heart and silver bullet solutions may seem to do the job, but sooner or later, the problems arise once more and stalk the organization.

As discussed earlier, recurring problems are often the result of the lack of a systemic approach to quality management. ISO 9000 requirements provide an excellent framework for a systemic approach to solving persistent problems of an organization. Addressing the potential of ISO 9000 to solve specific problems is a convincing argument for pursuing registration, and it also creates a win-win environment for the quality community. Let's look at just a few examples.

Operating costs are a continuing concern of executive management. Quality professionals know that inadequate supplier management is a major contributor to those costs. Beyond supplier management, partnering with suppliers is the mark of a world class organization. Although the idea of partnering with suppliers is today a generally accepted paradigm, an organization can't start down the road to partnership without first understanding the basics of building a supplier relationship. ISO 9000 provides a basic framework for such relationships. Convincing executive management that the purchasing requirements of ISO 9000 provide a framework that will reduce operating costs creates a win-win environment that opens the door for the quality community. How purchasing is implemented is up to the organization. The solution may be a just-in-time (JIT) system, or it may be implementation of tighter inspection controls. The point is, once management accepts that ISO 9000 can reduce operating costs by establishing requirements for purchasing, the environment is created to implement a broad range of supplier management activities even leading up to the establishment of supplier partnerships.

Corrective action is another area of ISO 9000 where the same principles of convincing/creating can be applied. The ISO 9000 standards require that a system of problem correction be in place but do not define the nature of this system. Definition of the corrective action system is up to the organization. The point is, once management has accepted the business value of ISO 9000, they have by default accepted the need for a corrective action system. The internal debate switches from whether or not the company needs a corrective action system to how elaborate a corrective action system should be installed, which essentially changes the way quality planning is viewed and implemented.

In making your ISO 9000 presentation, you should keep in mind that all general company problems are sooner or later manifested as someone's personal problem. Sooner or later someone inherits de facto ownership of the problem. The tighter you can tie ISO 9000 to solving such personal problems, the more commitment you will gain from individuals who have inherited the woes of the company. Robert Block, in *The Politics of Projects,* states it like this: "A good politician is able to read the players in his arena, and to understand what they want and need. This insight allows him to devise solutions that work, since workable solutions inevitably involve changing the opinions or actions of the players."[3]

For example, if you know that your vice president of engineering is perceived as having ownership of a development cycle time that is too long, you might show him or her how the ISO 9000 project can be used to improve the design process by placing more emphasis on front-end product planning for the purpose of eliminating defects that later must be found and corrected. Although development cycle time is not mentioned by any ISO 9000 standard, opening the eyes of the vice president of engineering to how application of the standard will help him or her solve cycle time problems gains you an ally for ISO 9000 registration project plan approval.

Another good convincing/creating technique is relating ISO 9000 to topics currently in vogue in the business press—for example, flattening the management structure of the organization. If your management has been talking about flattening the organization, you can point out the ISO 9000 requirements for documented responsibility and authority. You might suggest that as part of the ISO 9000 registration project, your organization give more responsibility and authority (along with appropriate training and qualification) to people closer to the actual design or manufacture of your product, creating the potential for eliminating layers of management. This might be a difficult concept to sell in your organization as a discrete proposal, but when incorporated within the ISO 9000 framework, it borrows credibility from the ISO 9000 standards themselves. Acceptance of the standards creates an environment more receptive to new concepts and ideas.

ISO 9000 registration impact on the company's internal operations. Many functional managers intuitively buy into the importance of quality, but they have a hard time relating the "quality is a good thing" concept to specific activities they can implement. The ISO 9000 registration project gives these managers specific things to do. Processes and procedures must be documented and brought under control. People's behaviors must be brought into line with documented processes and procedures. Employees in their charge must be properly trained and qualified to perform assigned tasks. The company embarks on ISO 9000 registration, and suddenly, managers have specific responsibilities and accountabilities for quality that are associated with a deadline—your organization's ISO 9000 registration target date.

In convincing management that ISO 9000 registration will have a positive impact on your organization's internal operation, the logical flow of the argument is that behaviors, not just attitudes, must change before there will be any noticeable improvement. Unfocused quality initiatives that aren't related to business needs may change attitudes, but they seldom change behaviors. Because you have tied the ISO 9000 registration project to business issues such as sales and revenue preservation and enhancement, and you have established a deadline for registration, you are driving changes in the behaviors of the organization's people. If those behaviors produce positive results, you will have created an environment ripe for further quality improvement.

Individual contributors will come to a similar understanding as their behaviors change to meet the requirements of ISO 9000. As they participate in design reviews, keep Statistical Process Control (SPC) charts, or perform other tasks that relate to procedures that are put in place during the ISO 9000 registration project, individual contributors will become more comfortable with the idea of quality as a part of the way your organization does business. Quality becomes real to them because they are doing it. Again, positive experiences lead to behavior changes.

Another benefit, albeit less tangible, of the ISO 9000 registration effort is employee motivation. Quality has been called a journey with no destination, or a race with no finish line. This race appears to be one you could lose, but never definitely win. Under such circumstances, it can be difficult to motivate people to run the race. Vague quality initiatives are difficult to sustain precisely because they have no end objective. In this regard, the ISO 9000 registration project is different. It has a definite endpoint—achieving registration. What has come to an end is the *project* for achieving registration, not your quality efforts. Once you achieve registration, your organization still needs to apply effort to maintaining registration and improving its quality system.

In the early 1960s, US President John F. Kennedy set a goal of putting a man on the moon before the decade was out. In 1969, American astronaut Neil Armstrong took a "giant leap for mankind." Logistics problems that were not even known at the time of President Kennedy's declaration had to be solved before his vision became a reality. Would human beings have landed on the moon prior to the 1970s if a goal had not been set? Doubtful. However, because a goal had been set, a call to action issued, resources (both human and material) were applied to reach that goal. Seriously setting a goal for ISO 9000 registration can provide a rallying point when unanticipated problems arise. Achieving or maintaining ISO 9000 registration provides a sense of urgency to solve system breakdowns when they are discovered, rather than letting problems fester and infect the morale of the entire organization.

Additionally, when the goal of ISO 9000 registration is reached, you have an opportunity to celebrate. Hard work that results in success is good for morale, and celebration of success feeds that good morale. People can be proud that they have worked together to accomplish something worthwhile. That success can be the breeding ground for future success. People who have learned to work together now have a forum to work together in the future.

Approval/Commitment

After introducing executive management to the ISO 9000 standards and convincing them that the project will definitely benefit the company, the next step in the presentation process is gaining management approval of the ISO 9000 registration project plan. Approval of the plan means that both the schedule and the required resources are agreed to. It means that executive management agrees to endorse the project as defined by the schedule and agrees to provide the resources you require to gain registration by the time called for in the schedule.

However, ISO 9000 registration project plan approval and commitment to the ISO 9000 registration project plan are not one and the same. If executive management approves *your* plan, that is only half the battle. That is the overt objective. The subtle objective, your ultimate goal, is having executive management commit to *their* plan. This is not merely a semantic distinction. Unless your executive team takes ownership of and responsibility for the success of the ISO 9000 registration effort, you will be continually fighting an uphill battle for resources and the executive mind-share required to adequately address ISO 9000 registration.

How do you get executive commitment? There is only one way, and that is through credibility. Building credibility is not done by trying to change executive management's opinions and beliefs. It is done by understanding their concerns, thinking the way they think, and putting the ISO 9000 registration project into their context. The presentation process provided in this chapter is designed to build credibility. It begins by positioning ISO 9000 in terms of sales and revenue benefits to the organization. It moves to tying ISO 9000 to the resolution of specific organizational problems—problems for the organization in general and problems of significance to people key to the success of the effort.

The final step in the credibility chain is convincing executive management that you have a valid plan for achieving ISO 9000 registration, that is, a plan that management is comfortable supporting as its own. The planning process described in Chapter 3 becomes critical at this point. If your ISO 9000 registration project plan consists of little more than a list of milestone dates and a huge "trust me," you may get approval of a plan, but you will certainly not have commitment to ISO 9000 registration. On the other hand, if you are able to walk executive management through the systematic approach to ISO 9000 registration introduced in Chapter 3 (see Figure 5-4) applied specifically to your organization, you will build a credible case for your plan.

Your presentation of the ISO 9000 registration project plan should follow a logical sequence from the right of the diagram.

FIGURE 5–4 *ISO 9000 Project Planning Viewed as a System*

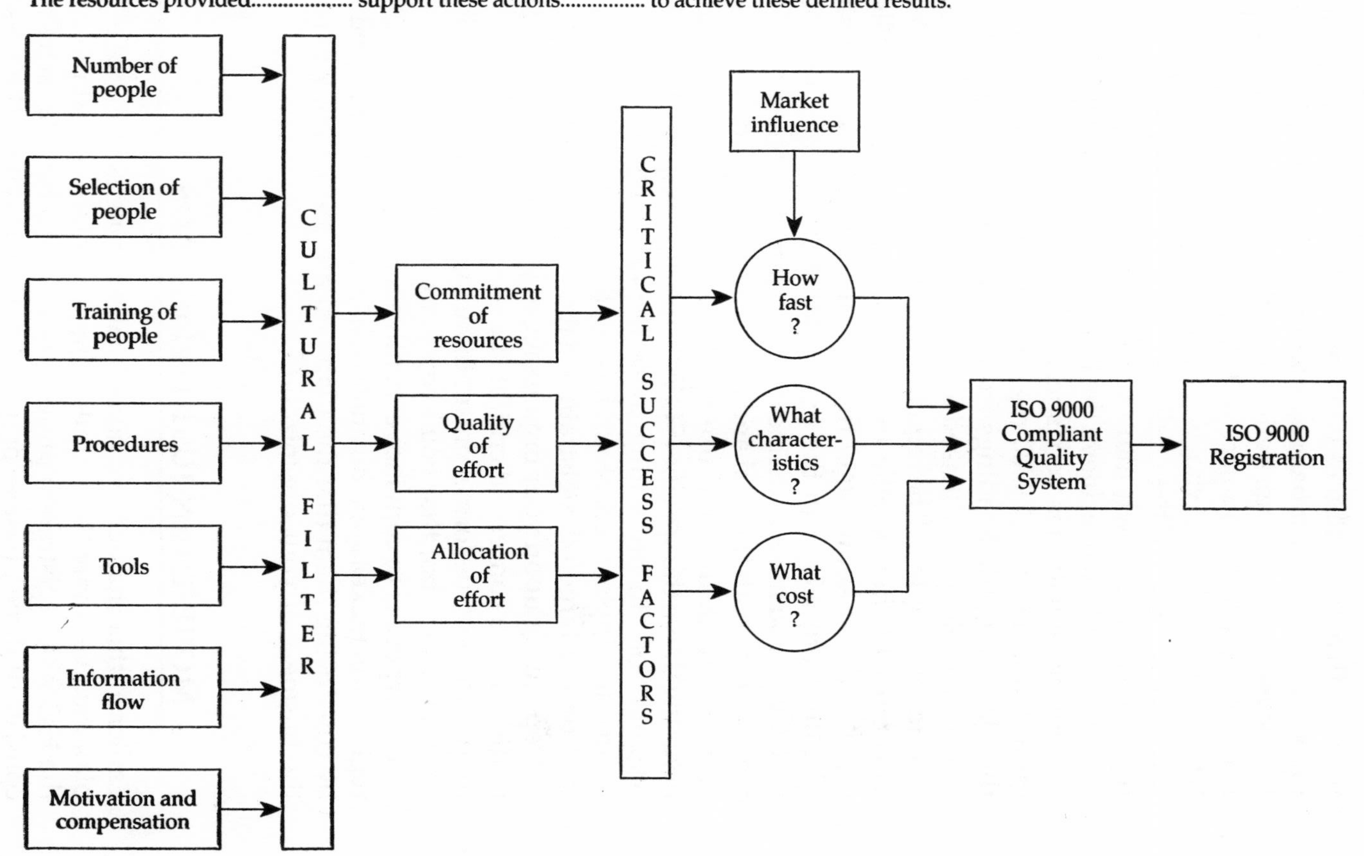

Begin with a discussion of your target registration date—why it is market driven, why it has sales and revenue impact. Be prepared to discuss the target registration date in business terms—if the date is pushed out, what impact will that have on sales and revenue? If the date is pulled in, what will that do to the cost of the project and the characteristics of the quality system? Next, break the targeted registration date down into interim milestones and describe the activities required to achieve the interim milestones. The final step in your presentation is very specifically defining the resources required to achieve ISO 9000 registration within the parameters of the plan using the headings from the diagram in Figure 5-4.

For example, you will need to lay out for executive management how many people will be required to achieve ISO 9000 registration. You must further be able to define what capabilities (skills and organizational knowledge) these people must have. You should identify from where in the organization you think these people will come. You need to define the procedures involved in ISO 9000 registration, both internal and external to your company, and the costs involved. In short, use Figure 5-4 as a high-level guide for breaking down the specific ISO 9000 resource requirements of your organization. In presenting these requirements, be prepared to define the ripple effect of not having those resources and the impact on the targeted registration date.

Depending upon your organization, you may or may not want to discuss the concept of critical success factors. We suggest that for purposes of the formal presentation, you be prepared to discuss cultural issues, but that you keep your focus on business issues. Your purpose is to convince executive management that ISO 9000 registration makes good business sense. You must build credibility by convincing them that the plan you are presenting will benefit the business of your organization.

MORE THAN JUST OVERHEADS

Earlier in this chapter, we noted that winning acceptance of your plan involves more than a pulsating presentation, that presenting the ISO 9000 registration project plan is not a singular activity but consists of three phases—prepresentation activities, the presentation itself, and postpresentation activities. All of the information presented in the previous section might, indeed, be formally presented as part of your executive management presentation of the ISO 9000 registration project plan. However, your chances of having your ISO 9000 registration project plan approved increase dramatically if you spend time before the formal presentation "planting the idea [of ISO 9000 registration] in the minds of your audience" and finding out from where "contradicting and opposing ideas" will arise. The success of your ISO 9000 registration project will be greatly enhanced if you spend time after the presentation following up on key points.

Prepresentation Activities

Prepresentation is the seed-planting and objection-finding phase of the presentation process. It is a time for building allies among those who will be in attendance at your executive management presentation, for identifying possible objections to your ISO 9000 registration project plan, and for identifying individuals who will be significant roadblocks to the project. The more thorough a job you do up front greasing the skids for the ISO 9000 project, the better able you will be to use actual presentation time to focus on the elements of your registration project plan.

Unfortunately, all too often, important prepresentation activities are skipped in the rush to put together and deliver an executive management overview of ISO 9000. When prepresentation activities are skipped, much of the valuable formal presentation time must be spent addressing issues that detract from the focus of the presentation. The meeting degenerates into a debate, and little is decided. Plan approval is delayed, and even if the plan is approved, chances are there is inadequate commitment to make the plan work.

Prepresentation activities can be divided into two primary tasks—identifying potential objections and preselling ISO 9000 and your registration project plan. A closer look at these two areas is required.

Identifying objections. The Dale Carnegie strategy admonishes us to "keep contradicting and opposing ideas from arising." The best way to do that is to answer arguments before they arise. To do this, you must know your audience. Who are the members of the executive staff? What motivates each of them? Where will they likely stand on your plan?

To address this issue, list each member of the executive staff, what you think his or her position will be on your ISO 9000 proposal, and what strategy you might apply in dealing with that person. Anticipated objections can be addressed in your formal presentation before they arise in the form of a question. Addressing objections as part of the presentation rather than waiting to address them when they arise (or ignoring them and hoping that they don't arise) has several advantages. First, it allows you to position the objection and address it offensively rather than defensively. Second, when you address an objection as part of the presentation it has no champion. If one of the people in your audience brings up the objection, that person has de facto ownership of the objection. The objection carries whatever credibility that person has in the organization and depending upon the personalities involved, the discussion of the objection may degenerate into a personal issue.

For example, if the manufacturing area is operating at 100 percent capacity with constant pressure from sales to deliver more, it is likely that the vice president of manufacturing will make the argument that his or her people have no time to devote to this project. However, if you are aware of this objection before your formal presentation, you can address the resource issue generically by positioning the manufacturing vice president's problem as a general, organizationwide issue. Knowing the issue beforehand also gives you an opportunity to explore potential solutions—for example, you may research how other manufacturing organizations in the same situation have addressed this issue.

If you do not know the members of the executive staff well enough to know what their motivations are, talk to those who do know them. The better you can relate your ISO 9000 registration project plan to the specific needs of individual members of the executive staff, the more acceptable your plan will be to them.

Although addressing objections as part of the formal presentation rather than waiting for them to arise will minimize conflict, it will not necessarily eliminate it. Even when you intend to address a controversial point in the presentation, to the extent that you can, have backup documentation that goes beyond what you present. This backup documentation should be expert-based, that is, it should be in the form of books, magazine articles, government papers, presentations at conferences, press releases, surveys from your customers that ask for ISO 9000 registration, and the like. Remember, a key to your success is establishing credibility. If contrary arguments arise from the executive staff, such arguments should be with the experts rather than with you. In that case, your credibility will remain intact.

For this reason, it is helpful to index any points that you run across in your personal preparation for the ISO 9000 project. As you come across useful pieces of information, note the material so that you can find it later when you need it. There are various personal computer programs that allow you to do this easily, but you can accomplish the same thing with an index card file.

Preselling your plan. Dealing with objections is a necessary, but negative aspect of formal plan presentation. The positive side of the equation is building alliances by preselling your ISO 9000 registration project plan as part of your prepresentation activity. Meet with selected members of the staff prior to the meeting to presell your plan. This presales meeting is a short discussion of your presentation with a given member of the staff for the purpose of appraising both the presentation and the likely response of the staff member.

For those staff members who will favorably support your plan, a presales meeting enables you to provide them with information prior to the presentation meeting that will help them formulate supporting arguments for the meeting. It helps build a sense of ownership in the plan on their behalf. Here, you may have to bury your own ego a little. If a member of the staff makes comments that you have already thought of, give the staff member credit and "add" his or her suggestions to your plan. You'd be surprised at how quickly buy-in is achieved.

Meeting with those staff members who are not favorably disposed to ISO 9000 or your registration project plan also gives you the opportunity to hear their objections in advance of the meeting. Knowing the problems they have with your plan, you will have time prior to the presentation to research win-win solutions. This meeting will help you relate your presentation to their perspective. Also, it often happens that if someone has once presented their objections to you in person, they may not be as vocal in a public meeting as they would if they were responding for the first time.

In general, the point of preselling your plan is twofold. First, making your audience as familiar as possible with the ISO 9000 standards and your registration project plan prior to the formal presentation of that plan, and second, making you as familiar as possible with the various positions of the executive staff regarding the ISO 9000 standards and your registration proposals. "If you know your enemy and know yourself, you need not fear the result of a hundred battles."[4] That wisdom is as relevant today in your "battle" to gain approval and commitment to your ISO 9000 registration project plan as it was when Chinese general Sun Tzu penned it in 500 BC. The time you spend in prepresentation activities will benefit your formal ISO 9000 presentation.

The Formal ISO 9000 Presentation

Earlier sections of this chapter have discussed much of the key information that needs to be presented to executive management. The body of your presentation must rely heavily on logic and reasoning, using the systematic model of ISO 9000 registration as a guide. In your presentation, you are building the case that the project is necessary and that your ISO 9000 registration project plan is the right plan for your unique organization. You are showing your executive management how the project has something of value for them. This part of the presentation consumes the most time and must be very sound and well thought out. However, the first three and the last two minutes of the presentation are perhaps the most important to your success.

In the first three minutes, you introduce your subject. More than likely, you are one of a number of topics on the agenda at the executive staff meeting. You must grab your audience's attention. You must divert their attention from what they were previously discussing and focus it intently on the presentation of your plan. You must make them want to hear what you are going to tell them.

When you get up to make your presentation, walk with purpose. Face your audience. Let a couple of moments of silence pass as you look at them and then make a bold statement of fact. This statement could be one of several relating to elements of the body of your presentation. For example:

> About two months ago, our largest competitor began working on a project that will put us at a great competitive disadvantage unless we respond. That project is not related to a new product feature, or even a new product line. It is something far more revolutionary than that. They are overhauling their entire system of design, manufacturing, and servicing, and unless we respond in kind, they could reduce overhead and cycle times and gain market share at our expense. It is their intention to become registered by the end of next year to the internationally accepted standards for quality systems known as ISO 9000. I stand before you today with a proposal that will not only neutralize their efforts, but will solve some of the very problems that frustrate many of you in this room today.

We do not suggest that you state any falsehoods, or even exaggerate any truths in the opening statement. However, you must make your case for ISO 9000 registration boldly. Remember, the key to success is credibility. End your introduction with clear statement of the action you expect executive management to take as a result of your presentation—for example:

> At the end of my presentation, I am going to ask you to commit to a plan of action that will address the issues I have just raised. The purpose of my presentation is to convince you that my plan is worthy of your commitment.

In the final two minutes, you must move your audience to do exactly what you have come to ask them to do—approve and commit to your ISO 9000 registration plan. Summarize the main points of your presentation and stir your audience to act on your recommendation. The introduction of your presentation is a bold statement of fact. The body relies heavily on logic. In it you build the case that the project is necessary and will deliver several benefits to the company. The conclusion will be a call to action and as such will contain an element of emotion. You convince people with logic; you move them with emotion.

We are not talking about false emotion, but a genuine, from-the-heart, appeal for action:

> I have shown you the reasons why we must gain this registration and have laid out a plan that addresses all of the critical factors that will make the registration effort successful and of great benefit to us all. We must not sit idly by while our competitor plots to gain advantage of us through the registration of their quality system. We must take the lead to retain the lead. Please join me in endorsing and committing to this plan that will not only provide the benefits we have discussed here today, but will assure us a prominent position in the world marketplace.

If your company has a slogan or dogma that has credibility with the organization, use it in your presentation. For example, a concluding sentence might take the form:

> This plan will help us maintain our competitive edge—please join me in committing to it so that together we can continue to **Do Our Best to Be the Best.**

The example opening and concluding statements are not meant to be used verbatim. Your words will fit your culture and particular circumstances. These examples are given to convey the style, intensity, boldness, and emotion that we advocate be used in your own opening and concluding statements.

Postpresentation Activities

There is a lot of work that goes into preparing the ISO 9000 registration project plan. As you have seen, there is additional work that goes into preparing the presentation of the plan. When the plan is approved, there is still work to be done. Even though you have gained approval of and commitment to the plan, do not assume that automatically means action. You must take the approval as empowering you to begin to carry out the plan. Quoting again from *The Politics of Projects:* "If you overstep your boundaries, the difference will be apparent, but if you underestimate your authority, you may never realize what you could have done."[5]

If the plan calls for individuals from each functional organization to participate in a cross-functional implementation team for the project, then as soon as the plan is approved, set up meetings with the executive staff members to determine who will represent each area. When those people are appointed, contact them and inform them of their appointment and their initial responsibilities as team members. The key is act fast. If you do not generate the sense of urgency, any residual enthusiasm created by your presentation will quickly die.

Just because the staff has approved your plan does not mean that they will attempt to determine what their personal responsibilities are. If the plan calls for them to do something, like convene a steering team, then you set it up. You are responsible for the logistics of the plan. No one else will begin to assume responsibilities on his or her own. It is our belief that top management involvement occurs because you define behaviors that they should exhibit, not because they do so inherently. In our experience, it is not that they don't want to participate. They just don't know what you want them to do. It's your plan. Tell them. Be specific.

Another postpresentation activity is to get the employees to commit to the plan. Recall from the previous chapter that employee commitment is a critical success factor for ISO 9000 registration. Just because top management approved the ISO 9000 registration project plan does not mean that employees buy into it. You have to sell them as well. Ask executive staff members to talk with their employees about the plan. Another method of building employee commitment is through department champions serving on your cross-functional implementation team. You might also use a communication vehicle like a company newspaper or magazine or an ISO 9000-specific publication to inform employees about the ISO 9000 registration project and the rationale for deploying it. These items should be included in the communications part of your plan.

The postpresentation activities are really just the execution of your plan. The point we are emphasizing is that approval does not mean that anyone will do anything differently than they did before, unless you get the ball rolling. It's your vision. It's your plan. It's your responsibility to make it happen. Look on plan approval as empowerment. Plan approval says you have the authority to act. Use it, or you most certainly will lose it.

The first thing to do after plan approval is to create a cross-functional team of department champions to lead the registration effort in the company's functional areas. The creation and use of this team is the topic of Chapter 6.

THE NCR EXPERIENCE

The presentation to the NCR Network Products Division executive staff was both to convince them of the necessity of ISO 9000 registration and to gain approval of and commitment to the ISO 9000 registration project plan. We decided from the beginning that ownership of the quality system belonged at the executive staff level, so prior to the meeting we divided up the sections of the ISO 9001 standard and distributed each section with a memo to the executive staff member who we felt owned each section. The memo asked them to read the attached section(s) of the standard and to be prepared for discussion at the presentation.

We then constructed a matrix of members of the staff and what we thought their position would be on the project: supportive, not supportive, or ambivalent. We established strategies for the three groups as follows: we intended to make early successes in the departments of those who supported the project as evidence to the ambivalent and nonsupporters that the project was viable and beneficial; we decided to find elements of the project that would solve problems that nonsupporters were wrestling with as a means of showing them the benefit of the project; we decided to display the early successes of the supporters to the ambivalent as a means of winning them over.

We constructed our presentation as described in this chapter: a strong opening; a logical body which listed general benefits to the company and specific benefits to individual departments; and a conclusion that appealed for approval and commitment. We had several articles and papers as backup material to support the claims we made in the presentation. We quoted four different authors who said that the standard would become a customer-driven condition of doing business, and that companies could use early registration to their competitive advantage, which enabled us to make a business case for ISO 9000 registration.

We did a certain amount of preselling of ideas to key members of the executive staff for the purpose of having support in the presentation meeting. We did not approach those whom we felt would be nonsupportive, which created some problems during discussions of the plan. We had to spend time in the presentation meeting addressing objections we could have handled before the meeting. We had to be quick on our feet, rather than having time to prepare a response after hearing the objections. Having the supporting material with us at the meeting helped in that regard.

The project was approved with the complete support of the vice president of our division, as well as several staff members. No one was openly opposed by the end of the meeting, although there were some members of the executive staff who were less than fully committed to the effort.

We began immediately after the meeting to implement the plan. We met with members of the staff during the week following the presentation to determine who would be department champions on the cross-functional implementation teams (see Chapter 6). We very carefully specified the type of individual we wanted on the team—someone with organizational experience, respect, and authority in the department. In some cases we were asked to recommend people, in other cases we were not, but in all cases the department champions met our criteria.

We went on from there holding meetings, performing training, conducting assessments, and defining behaviors where necessary. For example, we told the members of the executive staff that we needed them to form a quality steering team, headed by the vice president, whose responsibility was to define the high level quality policies and set strategic direction. This they did willingly.

The principles of this chapter made our presentation a success and set the tone for getting the project off to a good start. We were on our way.

SECTION

II

ENSURING ISO 9000 COMPLIANCE OF THE QUALITY SYSTEM

Chapter Six

Creating ISO 9000 Department Champions

It is unfortunate when final decisions are made by chieftains headquartered miles from the front where they can only guess at conditions and potentialities known only to the captain on the battlefield.

Wess Roberts
Leadership Secrets of Attila the Hun

The power sweep of the great Green Bay Packer teams of the 1960's was a thing of beauty. Fuzzy Thursten and Jerry Kramer pulling from their guard positions, creating a wall of blocking for running backs Paul Hornung and Jim Taylor; the Pack moved steadily down the field in "three yards and a cloud of dust" bursts. True, those great Packer teams had some outstanding talent, but what made them consistent winners year in and year out was their ability to function as a team, to execute coach Vince Lombardi's game plan. The Green Bay Packers were a *team* in more ways than just wearing the same color uniform.

Just as no one individual, no matter how talented, can carry a professional football team to victory alone, no one individual can assume responsibility for achieving ISO 9000 registration for your organization. No matter the size of your company, the scope of ISO 9000 registration is far too broad to be adequately addressed by one person. ISO 9000 registration is a team effort.

THE PURPOSE OF THIS CHAPTER

Putting in place the team that will lead your organization to ISO 9000 registration is an important part of your ISO 9000 registration project. In this chapter, we'll take a look at what it takes to build a strong team of ISO 9000 department champions—how you can identify and recruit individuals who can make your ISO 9000 game plan work. That last sentence is extremely important in its implications. As this chapter discusses, there are specific skills and character traits you should look for in selecting ISO 9000 champions. The implication of the sentence and the fact when implementing your ISO 9000 registration project plan is that people you want on your team might not always be "people of title."

Certainly, ISO 9000 registration requires management support, but the people at the department level—managers, supervisors, and individual contributors—are the people who really understand how ISO 9000 standards impact their organizations. They know the conditions and potentialities of the battlefield, so to speak. They understand how their departments function. They are in the best position to suggest resolution for process problems at the interfaces between organizations. In short, they are the best people to make ISO 9000 registration happen.

How you find such people within your organization, the education you provide to them, and how you continuously motivate them throughout the ISO 9000 registration project makes up the majority of this chapter. However, before moving on to the details of selecting your ISO 9000 team, a few words of caution are in order. As important as the team concept is to achieving ISO 9000 registration, as a primary driver of the ISO 9000 registration project, you must also be careful not to fall into the "team trap."

AVOIDING THE "TEAM TRAP"

Just as misery is said to love company, accountability loves a team. You are caught up in the "team trap" when you consciously or unconsciously invest success of the ISO 9000 project in the team, and consciously or unconsciously abdicate responsibility for success to the team. Teams must be guided, mentored, and disciplined toward a common goal. That is your job, and how well you perform will have a major impact on how well your team of ISO 9000 department champions functions. When putting together your team of ISO 9000 department champions, you should clearly understand two key points about teams.

First, understand that in a corporate situation, teams do not make decisions. Individuals make decisions. Teams make recommendations. As a driver of ISO 9000 registration, you will encounter situations where it proves impossible to achieve consensus or even compromise on issues. In such cases, you certainly should seek out and listen to all points of view, but eventually you will reach a point where a decision must be made.

For example, should your organization centralize or decentralize responsibility for distribution of quality documentation? (This issue is discussed fully in Chapter 8.) If, because of differing departmental views, your ISO 9000 team cannot arrive at consensus on this point, you should take responsibility to make a decision. Explain the rationale for your decision and immediately get on with implementation. You will no doubt still face resistance to your decision from those who perceive that they "lost," but you are better off in the long run making a decision and moving on to implementation than you would be trying to reach consensus while nothing is getting done. Either way, you will have to convince resistors, but in the latter situation, having made a decision and sticking by it, you leave no doubt as to what is the acceptable course of action.

The second key point to keep in mind about teams is that a collection of individuals is not necessarily a team. The primary characteristic that distinguishes a team from a mere collection of individuals is that everyone on the team is committed to a common goal. In the case of the ISO 9000 project, the common goal is achieving ISO 9000 registration. However, don't naively assume that everyone involved in the ISO 9000 project is committed to that goal. Many people involved in the project won't see the big picture. Their initial interest will be focused on *their* involvement and *their* responsibilities. As the driver of the ISO 9000 registration project, you must keep bringing people back to the enterprise view—the common objective of ISO 9000 registration.

In this chapter, we'll look at issues you need to consider in putting together a team to spearhead ISO 9000 registration. In our ISO 9000 registration project, we referred to this team as our "ISO 9000 department champions." People joined and left the team at various stages of the ISO 9000 registration project, but a core group was involved in the project from start to finish. They performed initial assessments of our organization's quality system, helped write key quality documents, and served as escorts for the third-party assessors who conducted our ISO 9000 registration assessment. This group provided continuity to the project from one phase to the next and ultimately was the reason for achieving ISO 9000 registration. And while we salute the effort of the people of our organization, we also realize that there are outstanding people in every organization. As a driver of the ISO 9000 registration project in your organization, your job is to channel the abilities and skills of these people in the most effective manner. People are only part of the equation. How you select, train, and motivate your ISO 9000 department champions will have a major impact on the success of your ISO 9000 project.

SELECTION OF ISO 9000 DEPARTMENT CHAMPIONS

The operative word in the subheading for this section is "selection." ISO 9000 registration is too important an issue to be left to a randomly designated group of people. It is too important a project to arbitrarily assign to people because they have the "right" titles or because they are "between projects" and "have the time." The ISO 9000 project leader must have at least input and at best final decision on who will be an ISO 9000 department champion.

Team selection involves both selecting the right people and selecting the right number of people. As mentioned before, people will join and leave the team at different points in the registration project. However, there will be a central core of people who will be with the ISO 9000 registration project from beginning to end. How many of these people you will have on the team depends on two factors.

The first factor in determining how many ISO 9000 department champions your project requires is the size of your organization. A larger organization requires more people dedicated to the ISO 9000 project. However, other factors mitigate the number of people required. As described in Chapter 3, the end result of an ISO 9000 registration project plan is threefold, consisting of a target registration date, a quality system with defined characteristics, and a budget for the registration project. In determining the number of people needed to serve as ISO 9000 department champions, you must consider all three elements—for example, more people on the team might allow you to meet the target date and enhance the characteristics of your organization's quality system, but it will do so at a greater cost to the organization. Explore the consequences of trade-offs.

A second factor to consider is the current state of your organization's quality system. If to date your organization has given little thought to documentation of its quality system, you will need more people on the team than if your company has already addressed quality system issues. Conversely, if your organization has already "discovered" many of the good practices defined by the ISO 9000 standards, fewer dedicated ISO 9000 department champions may be required.

Once you have determined the ideal size of your core team of ISO 9000 department champions, the next step is to determine whom you want on the team. Again, size of your organization plays a role in your decision making. In a small organization, you may know, if not personally then by reputation, most of the people in the organization. You will know the current projects that have priority for the organization, and you can plan the ISO 9000 project in the context of the organization's overall demand for resources. In a large organization, you will have to spend some time collecting this information. Your ISO 9000 registration project plan should reflect that you understand the resource requirements of the organization. Justifying ISO 9000 project resources in terms of the organization's overall direction provides additional credibility for you and for the ISO 9000 registration project.

When we discussed preparation of the ISO 9000 registration project plan, we noted that planning should always be done from the perspective of the ideal; that is, start the planning process with the assumption that the resources you need will be available. From that starting point, you can make adjustments to the plan with a better understanding of how those adjustments will affect the end result. This concept applies to the selection of ISO 9000 department champions as well.

In your initial ISO 9000 project plan, identify people you want on your team by name, if possible. If you cannot identify individuals, then you should establish specific characteristics of the people you are looking for. Characteristics are not the same as job titles. In fact, you want to specifically avoid job titles as a criteria for your ISO 9000 department champions. In selecting ISO 9000 department champions you must be focused on individual traits, abilities, and knowledge, not hierarchical status in the organization. Let's take a closer look at those characteristics.

Understanding of the Organization

Those individuals you identify as ISO 9000 department champions should have a working knowledge of the organization. Their understanding of the organization needs to go beyond just the documented functions. The people you want on your ISO 9000 registration project team need to understand the behaviors of people in the organization. They need to understand not just *what* gets done, but *how* it gets done.

ISO 9000 department champions should also be sensitive to the attitudes prevalent in the organization. They should have a sense of the corporate culture. They should understand what motivates the people in their organizations.

Credibility

Chapter 5 described a process for selling your ISO 9000 registration project plan to executive management. ISO 9000 registration needs to be sold to employees in the same manner—with an important difference. Obviously, one person cannot effectively sell one-on-one to every person in the organization. Therefore, the selling of ISO 9000 inside the organization must be accomplished by several people—your ISO 9000 department champions. *For these people to effectively sell the benefits of ISO 9000 registration, they must have credibility with the organization and the respect of the people they are working with.*

Credibility is a key criterion that you should look for in an ISO 9000 department champion. Credibility is often associated with honesty, but it really goes beyond whether or not a person is telling the truth. When a person is perceived as "credible," he or she is perceived as not just telling the truth, but as having a degree of understanding about the subject. Some people may be perceived as being honest, but if they are not also perceived as knowing what they are talking about (not just thinking that they do), they will have no credibility with the organization.

The basis of credibility is success. You want ISO 9000 department champions who have achieved success in their primary job functions—an engineer who is recognized for his or her contributions to successful products; a manufacturing supervisor whose area consistently meets product schedule and quality targets; a human resources representative with a people orientation. You want people who are viewed as the "heroes" of your corporate culture. Because of the role they will play in the ISO 9000 registration project, they must be team players as well.

Ability to Implement

In addition to being perceived as credible, an ISO 9000 department champion must have the ability to lead others where he or she chooses to go. An ISO 9000 department champion must not just communicate a credible message, he or she must inspire action.

Within any organization there are people who are sound strategic thinkers and others who are implementers or doers. ISO 9000 department champions can come from either group, but you must make sure that you have a good balance of both on a department basis. The strategists will help keep your ISO 9000 registration project on track and headed in the right direction. The implementers will ensure that actions are taken and completed that move you along the path toward registration. In choosing your ISO 9000 department champions, look for people who have a track record of successfully completing projects that they start.

Quality Attitude

Although the people you select as ISO 9000 department champions may not know all the buzzwords, they should be people who demonstrate a quality attitude in their primary job. This attitude should go beyond simply doing a good job. The people you want as ISO 9000 department champions should intuitively recognize the value of a systematic approach to quality. They should be customer-focused individuals who are not afraid to buck the system in support of customers.

The flip side of the coin is that although the people you choose as ISO 9000 department champions have a quality attitude, they should not be fanatics. As mentioned in Chapter 1, in any given organization, many people, especially in management positions, will be pragmatists when it comes to quality. They want to see a *business* return on the investment in quality. Your ISO 9000 department champions must be able to promote a vision of quality by talking the language of business.

Personal Characteristics

In addition to the specific characteristics described above, the people you choose as ISO 9000 department champions should be people who can function together as a team. They will no doubt be people with healthy egos, but at the same time, they should be willing to listen to others, be given to consensus building, and seek win-win solutions to cross-organizational differences of opinion.

ISO 9000 department champions should be people who can present ideas clearly, both verbally and in writing. They should be able to think on their feet, as they will be on the receiving end of many questions from people in their organizations.

The people you want are people who take personal responsibility for the projects to which they are assigned. An ISO 9000 registration project is a demanding effort, and even in the best planned projects, there will come a time when someone must step forth and make an extraordinary effort—training materials will have to be prepared to a next-day deadline; data will be required ASAP in order to make a process decision; someone will have to go to the hotel to drop off procedure manuals for the assessors at 8 AM on a Sunday morning.

ISO 9000 department champions you select will display the personality traits, indeed all of the characteristics described above, in varying degrees. Along with instilling in the ISO 9000 department champions a common objective of ISO 9000 registration, you will need to blend the personal characteristics of the ISO 9000 department champions into somewhat of a consistent perspective. This is accomplished through training.

TRAINING THE ISO 9000 DEPARTMENT CHAMPIONS

Although many of the characteristics described above are inherent in the individuals you select to be your ISO 9000 department champions, you will enhance the effectiveness of your ISO 9000 team through the training you provide. Providing proper training allows your ISO 9000 department champions to speak knowledgeably about the standards, about the importance of the standards to your company, and about the impact on the people of your organization. It helps build their credibility. Training also provides your ISO 9000 department champions with the skills and the tools they need to implement your ISO 9000 project plan. The manner in which you conduct the training and the attitude you project during the training creates a quality attitude in your ISO 9000 department champions. Although each organization is unique, there are some general principles that you should observe in putting together a training program for your ISO 9000 department champions.

Accept up front that while your training must be comprehensive, you cannot teach your ISO 9000 department champions everything. The primary objective of training ISO 9000 department champions is to provide them with enough information so they can function on their own, i.e., make decisions on the "battlefield" without having to rely on the "chieftain." Your training is sufficient when, combined with their individual initiative, it makes them credible with their fellow employees and comfortable with the ISO 9000 registration process.

The key elements of training you will need to provide are training in the ISO 9000 standards themselves and training in quality auditing techniques. These topics are covered in detail in Chapters 7 and 9 as part of the discussion of assessing your organization's quality system. Your ISO 9000 department champions will play a key role in the initial assessment and subsequent independent audits of your organization's quality system.

You will also need to provide your ISO 9000 department champions with background on the ISO 9000 standards from a *contextual* standpoint. Because these people will be your point people in the effort to sell the benefits of ISO 9000 registration into your organization, they need to understand more than just the "letter" of the standard. They must also understand the "spirit" of your ISO 9000 registration project.

As is the case with other types of ISO 9000 project training, you have options in how the training is delivered to your people. There are a number of outside consulting firms that provide excellent training on interpretation of the ISO 9000 standards. There are also excellent courses in basic auditing techniques. Your organization may have a training department that could prepare and deliver training for your ISO 9000 department champions. Or, you can develop your own training program. Once again, the point should be made that ultimately, the content and results of training the ISO 9000 department champions are your responsibility. Training should follow the needs identified in your ISO 9000 project plan.

The inside information on the ISO 9000 standards that the department champions receive in training, combined with the inside information they already possess on how their departments operate, make them local ISO 9000 experts within their departments. Creating experts of the ISO 9000 department champions is the inside track to motivating them.

MOTIVATING ISO 9000 DEPARTMENT CHAMPIONS

As "teaming" has become an accepted way of doing business, more and more books are being written on the topic, with various suggestions for motivating teams and individual team members. In their book *Empowered Teams*, authors Richard S. Wellins, William C. Byham, and Jeanne M. Wilson state that "there are three major forms of compensation for team members: base pay, skill-based pay, and some sort of bonus plan such as gain sharing."[1] We are not opposed to these methods, but we do feel that bonuses of one form or another should be considered rewards, a way of saying "thank you," more than as motivators.

It is our experience that the real *esprit de corps* of an ISO 9000 project team is not unlike the spirit that Vince Lombardi and other great coaches are able to build in their teams. Great coaches create a mystique, a special feeling of being part of a team. Even today, decades after the last great Lombardi-coached Green Bay Packer team took the field, there is still something special about the Packers. Whenever the Packers have even a mediocre season, the signs come out—"The Pack is Back"—a rallying cry around a still strong tradition of winning.

It is not melodramatic or hokey to believe you can create the same kind of dedication, loyalty, and will to win among your ISO 9000 department champions. This is not accomplished, however, with the corporate equivalent of cheerleaders and pep talks. You do not motivate ISO 9000 department champions per se; rather, you create an atmosphere in which their motivation is internally generated.

How do you do this? First, make sure that the ISO 9000 department champions understand the significance of their role in ISO 9000 registration. Let them know why they were selected. Emphasize the fact that they are people who are respected by their peers. As ISO 9000 department champions they are putting that credibility on the line. Therefore, you understand and expect that they will want to contribute to the planning of the ISO 9000 registration project. The motivation of ISO 9000 department champions comes from the fact that they take registration personally.

Second, establish a uniqueness for the ISO 9000 department champions. While not losing sight of the fact that achieving ISO 9000 takes a companywide effort, never miss a chance to establish the ISO 9000 department champions as a special entity in the registration effort. You do this in part just by holding ISO 9000 department champion meetings throughout the project. However, you can reinforce this message in other ways. For example, at one of your meetings have a member of the executive staff present to thank the team for achieving a specific milestone, or perhaps arrange an off-site celebration at a predetermined milestone.

Third, avoid demotivation, that is, anything that threatens the unity of the team. For example, earlier we mentioned bonuses. If one organization decides to offer a bonus to the ISO 9000 department champions from their department, you must not let that demotivate ISO 9000 department champions from other organizations. In your ISO 9000 registration project plan presentation to management (Chapter 5), outline the function you see for ISO 9000 department champions and stress the need to establish a companywide policy to reward these people.

Certainly, one of the key tasks that the department champions will have initially is to work within their individual departments to move them toward ISO 9000 compliance. This effort begins with an internal assessment of each department's current methods of doing things. The reasons for and logistics of this internal assessment is the topic of Chapter 7.

THE NCR EXPERIENCE

The ISO 9000 registration project plan presented to NCR Network Products Division executive management detailed specific time requirements for a core group of people required to facilitate ISO 9000 registration. Once the plan was approved, as part of the follow-up we did on the plan presentation meeting, we met with members of the executive staff and discussed the kind of people we were looking for to be part of the ISO 9000 registration project. In some cases we had specific people in mind; in others we stated the kind of people we were looking for.

Initially, there were 12 ISO 9000 department champions representing the seven different departments of the company plus the ISO 9000 project champion. The departments represented included quality assurance, customer services, development, finance, manufacturing operations, human resources, and product management. In addition to the seven ISO 9000 department champions designated as department leads, there were four additional people from development, and one additional person from manufacturing operations. These 12 people made up the core team who went through initial ISO 9000 training and participated in the first assessment of our quality system (Chapter 7).

We conducted training for these people over two days at our facility. The training was prepared and delivered by the ISO 9000 project champion. Internal training was selected for two reasons. First, we were concerned that training reflect the specific issues raised by our culture. Second, we were pursuing ISO 9000 registration at a time when affordable training was not easily available outside the company. The formal syllabus covered the background of the ISO 9000 standards and why they were important for our organization, interpretation and relationship of the ISO 9000 standards, assessing techniques and tools, and an overview of the ISO 9000 registration project plan as presented to management. However, much of the training time was a free-flowing discussion of how the requirements of ISO 9000 should be implemented in our organization.

Initially, the selected ISO 9000 department champions had some reservations that the project could be successful in our corporate culture. This is not a unique reaction. Because our training was internally delivered by the ISO 9000 project champion, he was sensitive to these issues and took the time to allow people to express their concerns. The discussion that took place helped create a common bond among members of the team. It took time, but as the project progressed, what appeared to be cultural barriers to ISO 9000 registration became challenges for the team and finally opportunities. We suggest that if outside training is selected (and there are good reasons to consider it) that you also work into your schedule a follow-up session that allows your ISO 9000 department champions to discuss the training from the perspective of your organization's culture.

Chapter Seven

Evaluating the Quality System: Conducting an Internal Assessment to the ISO 9000 Standards

Cast out first the beam out of thine own eye, and then shalt thou see clearly to pull out the mote that is in thy brother's eye.

Luke 6:42

Thus far, we have spent a great deal of time stressing the importance of laying a solid foundation for your ISO 9000 registration project. We've discussed overcoming the organization's initial reluctance to pursuing ISO 9000 registration, documenting your ISO 9000 registration project plan, addressing cultural barriers to ISO 9000 registration, presenting your plan to executive management and gaining both their approval and commitment, and building a critical mass of support by developing department champions for ISO 9000. All important stuff that we can't emphasize enough. However, sooner or later (and the sooner the better) you are going to have to evaluate your current quality system in terms of the ISO 9000 standard to which you are seeking registration.

Recall from Chapter 1 that there are three types of quality system assessments associated with ISO 9000: a first-party assessment, which is done internally by a company's own people; a second-party assessment, which is done by a customer team; and a third-party assessment performed by an independent agency with the intent of registering the quality system in a registry of compliant companies. It is the premise of this book that your organization is ultimately seeking third-party ISO 9000 registration. However, it is our recommendation that *before* you have your quality system assessed by a third party, you plan and implement a series of fairly formal internal assessments and audits.

By an "internal assessment" we mean that each department within an organization *examines itself* in the context of compliance to an ISO 9000 standard. This method is contrasted with the notion of an independent audit that is conducted by the organization's quality assurance organization or by people from another department in the company (See Chapter 9). Results of internal assessments are not intended to certify that an organization is or is not compliant with an ISO 9000 standard. They are not intended to be used as evidence for ISO 9000 compliance. Rather, the purpose of internal assessments is to better understand the status of your organization's quality system and lay the groundwork for the quality system improvements necessary to become registered to an ISO 9000 standard by an independent third party.

THE PURPOSE OF THIS CHAPTER

We should make it clear that an internal assessment is *not* a requirement for ISO 9000 registration; however, in keeping with the premise that one must address both formal ISO 9000 requirements and the cultural issues that can derail an ISO 9000 registration project, we endorse the concept of an internal assessment because it not only helps you identify strengths and weaknesses of your organization's quality system, but also provides another opportunity to build commitment to the ISO 9000 process.

This chapter puts forth the basics of evaluating your organization's quality system through an internal assessment performed by people in your company. It discusses the rationale of self-assessment—why we believe it is valuable and how we have seen an internal assessment create a positive environment for ISO 9000 registration. The chapter also discusses using the internal assessment as a markable milestone in the ISO 9000 registration project—an identifiable event that helps your organization overcome the reluctance to roll up its collective sleeves and get the ISO 9000 project rolling.

In order to conduct an internal assessment, your ISO 9000 department champions must have a clear understanding of what they are assessing. In Chapter 2, we talked about the two dimensions of a quality system: quality system documentation and behavior compliance with that documentation. In this chapter we introduce an assessment guide matrix that is a valuable visual tool for helping people understand the essence of quality system assessments and audits. The matrix is an excellent guide for defining and categorizing the specific areas your organization must change or modify to achieve ISO 9000 registration. Finally, the chapter provides you with a guideline for creating an Internal Assessment Report that is a working tool in moving forward toward a third-party audit and ultimately ISO 9000 registration.

WHY AN INTERNAL ASSESSMENT?

Those readers with even passing familiarity of formal auditing procedures will immediately note that the notion of an internal assessment conflicts with a core value of auditing—independence. Independence means that an auditor is not affiliated with the organization or function being audited. The reason for independence is obvious. Aside from potential conflicts of interest, well-intentioned people can get so close to a situation that they are unable to look at daily activities objectively. People become comfortable with specific practices to the point where it takes an outsider with an independent and fresh perspective to see that things are amiss.

If independence is so important to quality system auditing, why then do we recommend that the initial quality system assessment be performed by people within their own departments—a direct violation of the independence principle? The answer lies in a premise stated earlier: the only approach to ISO 9000 registration that works is to improve the company's quality system for the benefit of those who function within it; *ISO 9000 registration is a by-product of quality system improvement*. As detailed in the following sections and from the perspective of improving an organization's quality system, an internal assessment has several advantages over an independent audit.

Familiarity with the Area Being Assessed

In an independent audit, the auditor evaluates the quality system documentation to determine if the quality system as documented complies with an ISO 9000 standard. An independent auditor performs this activity without working knowledge of the activities represented by the documentation. He or she may find holes in the documentation, but there may also be processes in place in the organization that have not been documented. These processes may or may not be in compliance with the ISO 9000 standard, and an auditor will need to conduct a long series of interviews to compile enough evidence from which to draw conclusions about the adequacy of the quality system.

From an efficiency perspective, the auditor's unfamiliarity with the area being assessed causes delays in the audit process when discrepancies are uncovered. The better documented a quality system is before an independent auditor is called in, the easier and quicker the audit process. Conversely, from the effectiveness perspective, an internal assessment ensures that documentation and understanding of the quality system by the people of the organization will be at a level that makes independent auditing clean and easy. Nonconformity between the ISO 9000 standard, the quality system documentation, and employee behavior may still exist, but more than likely nonconformity will be minor, easily correctable, and will not stand in the way of registration.

This may seem like a fairly obvious point, but we have encountered more than a few department managers who believe that proceeding directly to an independent audit by an internal organization, a consultant, or a third-party registration agency is the quickest way to "find out what we need to do." In reality, a premature independent ISO 9000 audit will most assuredly lengthen the ISO 9000 registration process.

Coverage of the Assessment

Independent auditing by definition is sampling. Sampling does not critically examine everything within its universe. An independent auditor will always have a less thorough perspective than a person who works in the area being audited. An independent auditor will find specific examples of nonconformity and depending upon his or her knowledge and skill may be able to form some generalizations about the organization. However, people who work in the area being audited will invariably know whether a nonconformity is only an aberration or symptomatic of more pervasive problems.

The point again boils down to the difference between the approach of correcting nonconformities on a piecemeal basis in pursuit of ISO 9000 registration and the approach of improving the quality system in pursuit of ISO 9000 registration. Starting the ISO 9000 effort with an outside look in, the benefit the organization receives from an external auditor is a list of nonconformities to correct. Starting with a audit-ready quality system, an organization can tap an external auditor's expertise at a systematic level to make quantum improvements in the overall quality system.

Receptivity to Change

An independent audit of the organization will help an organization better understand the ISO 9000 standards and its own quality system (critical success factors for ISO 9000 registration), but not to the extent of an internal assessment. Nor does an independent audit do anything to build employee commitment to ISO 9000 (another ISO 9000 critical success factor). In fact, because the auditor's recommendations may be perceived as change being done *to* the organization rather than change being done *by* the organization, a premature independent audit may increase resistance to the ISO 9000 project.

From a cultural point of view, when an organization conducts internal assessments, discovery of a major nonconformity is an internal activity. Changes to the quality system are changes done *by*, not *to*, the organization. Employees have greater receptivity to their changes than they have to changes initiated outside the organization. They have a greater sense of commitment to those changes, and because they have learned by doing, employees have a greater understanding of both the ISO 9000 standard and their organization's quality system.

The internal assessment approach to ISO 9000 registration removes a lot of the initial fear and suspicion people associate with the discovery of problems. Few are the companies where fear does not have a presence in the corporate culture, and when one announces that areas of the company will be audited to an ISO 9000 standard, one should not be surprised if people are less than enthusiastic—especially department managers. Conducting an internal assessment of their own areas provides the people of your organization with the opportunity to discover their own problems and clean their own houses before they are scrutinized by others.

Ownership of Quality System Improvements

Closely allied to receptivity to change is the concept of ownership of quality system improvements. An external quality system audit promotes a registration focus for ISO 9000—fix nonconformities and get on with business. People may own an individual nonconformity, but no one owns quality system improvement.

As we noted earlier, part of the strategy for mustering quality purists and quality advocates into the ISO 9000 registration project hinges on your ability to leverage the ISO 9000 project as a catalyst for a long-term continuous improvement strategy. This is difficult, if not impossible, to do by attacking individual conformities within the system. The whole quality system must be examined, and systematic evaluation is best done by people who work within the system. Continuous improvement results when people take ownership not just for correcting problems, but when they take ownership of *looking for problems to correct*. An internal quality system assessment to the ISO 9000 standard is a springboard to this kind of thinking and activity.

Transferability of Knowledge

Eventually, independent auditing will become part of your quality system. To be in compliance with the ISO 9000 standard, an organization must have an independent auditing system.[1] The question is, where will those internal auditors come from? Conducting internal assessments is a good training ground for future independent internal auditors.

The experience of conducting a quality system assessment in an area in which they are familiar and comfortable provides valuable auditing experience, not just in the nuts and bolts of auditing techniques and the ISO 9000 standards, but from a human relations perspective as well. Having assessed an area in which they had responsibility—removed the beam from their own eyes, so to speak—future auditors have a better understanding of how an audit is perceived by people on the receiving side of the equation. By having done an internal assessment of their own areas, these auditors will have a deeper appreciation for how others will react to the discovery of quality system nonconformities. Having the experience of an internal assessment helps them see clearly to pull out the "motes" in other departments. Setting up a formal internal audit program that meets the requirements of ISO 9000 is discussed in Chapter 9.

STEPPING UP TO INTERNAL ASSESSMENT

The rationale for an internal assessment is that people working within a department are in the best position to understand the quality system of that department. However, in order for these people to express the functioning of the quality system in terms relevant to ISO 9000 registration, they must speak the language of ISO 9000—the language of auditing. Before proceeding with an internal assessment, you will need to provide your ISO 9000 internal assessment team with training in both the ISO 9000 standard to which you are seeking registration and in basic auditing principles.

Both a basic understanding of the ISO 9000 standard and auditing principles can be taught by a person within your organization with the proper background, one of the many ISO 9000 consulting firms, a local college or university with appropriate courses, or at one of the many ISO 9000 seminars held throughout the country. The best method depends on your organization's unique situation. Simply keep in mind that the end result of training is that your internal assessment team clearly understands the requirements of ISO 9000 and how to express those requirements in terms of auditing principles.

Experience has taught us that there is variation of interpretation of both the ISO 9000 standards and of auditing principles even among expert assessors from the same third-party registration agency, just as there can be conflicting views among jurists as to the proper interpretation of the Constitution. One assessor might deem a certain section of the ISO 9000 standard to be more important to quality than might another. An assessor's background might give him or her a greater knowledge base in one part of the standard, and consequently he or she may be unconsciously more stringent in standard interpretation in this area than might be another assessor. This is not a criticism of the professionalism of ISO 9000 registration organizations nor of their people.

Everyone has biases that are reflected in the way they interpret the ISO 9000 standards. And, if even the trained experts have biases, then certainly you can expect your internal assessment team to have individual biases toward sections of the ISO 9000 standard. Although these biases are natural, from the perspective of team dynamics, too much variation in the way your people interpret the standards can negatively impact your ISO 9000 registration effort by creating conflicts among team members.

You can minimize both the variation of interpretation and the conflict by having all your internal assessors trained by the same organization at the same time. This, however, is not always possible. For the sake of consistency and building your ISO 9000 internal assessment team into a cohesive unit, it is important to bring them together prior to the internal assessment to ensure that everyone has a common understanding of the objective, method, and expected results of your organization's internal assessment effort. You will also want to provide members of the internal assessment team with a common set of tools, for example a template[2] for reporting their findings[3] and observations,[4] to facilitate consistent reporting across the organization.

The substance of the training you provide to members of the internal assessment team is important to ensure that the internal assessment provides valuable information. However, the context of the training is important as well. Remember how daunting a task ISO 9000 registration appeared when *you* first became acquainted with it. Your internal assessment team will experience the same trepidation.

The first evaluation of a quality system, even an internal quality system assessment, is complicated by two factors. The first is psychological, the second logistical. As to the psychological, many people are reluctant to make, and consequently delay, quality system assessment because they are leery of the results. That is why it is so important in getting the ISO 9000 registration project started that you emphasize what is right about your organization's quality system and position ISO 9000 as an opportunity to enhance a functioning system. And you will find things that are right.

By focusing your initial assessment efforts on areas where you feel the organization is in or nearly in compliance with the ISO 9000 standard, you create some early success and reinforce organizational confidence. And rest assured, no matter how large a task you or members of your team perceive ISO 9000 registration to be, you will discover parts of your organization's quality system that are very much in compliance with ISO 9000 standards. Because the ISO 9000 standards address broad-based good practices, many companies discover these practices on their own—sometimes as part of a planned effort, sometimes out of sheer necessity. Such discoveries give your team and your ISO 9000 registration effort an early boost.

The confidence gained by knowing that you are already compliant with the ISO 9000 standards in some areas makes the reality that you fall short in others easier to deal with. As a driver of the ISO 9000 registration project, you must continue to remind people of areas where you are in compliance while making sure they understand that the really valuable part of assessing the quality system is understanding where your system is not in compliance with good quality practices as defined by an ISO 9000 standard. It is a blinding glimpse of the obvious, but often overlooked, that you cannot make improvements to your quality system until you know where it is deficient.

Viewed from this perspective, the knowledge of your organization's quality system weaknesses is not bad news. It is good news in that it identifies opportunities for improvement. The old saying "no news is good news" does not apply to the ISO 9000 registration project. Creating an ISO 9000-compliant quality system is an opportunity to turn weaknesses into strengths. Your team needs to understand, "bad news, not no news, is good news."

FIGURE 7–1
Two by Two Matrix Assessment Guide

		Documented System Relative to the Standard: Good	Documented System Relative to the Standard: Bad
Behavior of Employees Relative to the Documentation	Good	Documentation follows the standard and people are following the documentation.	Documentation does not follow the standard, but people are following the documentation.
	Bad	Documentation follows the standard, but people are not following the documentation.	Documentation does not follow the standard or is missing. If it is present, people are not following it.

WHAT ARE YOU REALLY ASSESSING?

Overcoming people's reluctance to do a critical examination of the organization's quality system stems partly from fear of what will be found but also has roots in simply not understanding the logistics of assessment—what is it that you are really trying to assess?

Recall from Chapter 2 that an ISO 9000-certifiable quality system has two dimensions: (1) the system as documented is capable of producing *consistent* quality, and (2) people *consistently* operate within the documented system. The relationship between the documented quality system and the behavior of people functioning within that system is illustrated in Figure 7–1. Figure 7–1 succinctly defines what ISO 9000 is really assessing and also implies the methodology for conducting an internal assessment.

Interpreting Figure 7–1, a documented quality system is "good" if it conforms to the requirements of the ISO 9000 standards, "bad" if it is not in conformance. Thus, your first task in assessing your documented quality system to an ISO 9000 standard is to determine the degree to which it conforms to the ISO 9000 standard. Along the same line of thinking, employee behavior is good if it conforms to the quality system as documented, and bad if it is inconsistent with the documented quality system. Thus, the second part of your internal quality system assessment must focus on determining if employee behavior is consistent or inconsistent with the documented quality system.

Completing an evaluation of documentation and employee behavior will help you determine which of the four quadrants of Figure 7-1 describes your situation. Then you have some decisions to make. In some cases, your evaluation will show that you need to change the quality system to be in compliance with the particular ISO 9000 standard. In other cases you will have to change employee behavior to comply with existing documentation. In some cases you may have to change both the system *and* the behavior. You can use the corrective action guide matrix in Figure 7-2 to help you make those decisions and to write a report of your assessment that includes your recommendations for actions. Each quadrant in Figure 7-2 describes the action to be taken for the corresponding quadrant in Figure 7-1. These actions will be described in more detail later in the chapter. First let's look at the steps of the internal assessment process.

ASSESSING QUALITY SYSTEM DOCUMENTATION

The first step in an internal assessment is gathering documentation that defines how a department currently does its work. Obvious sources are processes, procedures, flow charts, work instructions, training guides, and policy statements. Less obvious, but equally revealing sources, are meeting minutes, memos, checklists, organization charts, job descriptions, and project charts. Initially, collect as much as you can without preconceived concern for the usefulness of each document. Consider this initial document collection to be a brainstorming exercise; that is, don't pass judgment on the validity of any one document until you have collected everything that you possibly can. Even documents perceived to have little value may lead you to consider others of value that you may have overlooked. Having collected all the available documentation, match documents to the appropriate sections of the ISO 9000 standard to which you are seeking registration.

If your organization is typical, when you finish your document

FIGURE 7–2
Two by Two Matrix Corrective Action Guide

Behavior of Employees Relative to the Documentation		Documented System Relative to the Standard: Good	Documented System Relative to the Standard: Bad
	Good	This is the desired state. Documentation and behavior follow the standard and are consistent.	Documentation must be changed. Since people follow what is documented, compliance may easily follow.
	Bad	People's behavior must be changed to follow the documented system. Or, if behavior follows the standard, documentation may be changed.	Documentation must be changed or created. If behavior follows the standard, document what is done; otherwise behavior must also change.

collection, your work area will be piled high with stacks of documents. Organizational documentation seems to take on a life of its own, forever growing, never dying. Again, if your organization is typical, most of the documentation piled around your work area will have been created ad hoc in response to specific situations and never evaluated from a systemwide perspective. The ISO 9000 registration project is your opportunity to rectify that situation. The second step in the internal assessment process is evaluation of existing documentation. There are five key criteria you need to examine: necessity, sufficiency, compliance, accuracy, and cohesiveness.

Necessity

The first task in winnowing down the pile of documents you have collected is determining which ones are really necessary for the functioning of the business. For each document, you must determine whether or not it describes a function that is actually performed by your organization. You'll be surprised by how many documents you have collected that describe policies, processes, and procedures long out of date and no longer relevant to your business. In some cases, there will be policies, processes, and procedures still on the books that no one in the organization follows or maintains. In other cases, the documents will describe policies, processes, and procedures that are followed, but that do not add any value to the product or service your organization provides. From an ISO 9000 registration perspective, each of these cases is handled differently.

In the first case, documentation that is out of date and no longer followed should be formally discontinued. Documentation that is on the books, but not followed, will result in a finding during an ISO 9000 audit. Such situations must be corrected.

On the other hand, from an ISO 9000 registration perspective, no nonconformity occurs when a process that adds no value is documented *and* followed. Situations like this will *not* result in findings during an ISO 9000 audit. However, as discussed in Chapter 3, one of the defined results of your ISO 9000 registration project is a specific set of criteria that defines the desired characteristics of your organization's quality system. If your schedule permits, you will want to eliminate valueless policies, processes, and procedures as part of your ISO 9000 registration effort. If your schedule does not permit this kind of quality system improvement immediately, the ISO 9000 registration project still provides the opportunity to call attention to potential quality system improvements to be undertaken as part of ongoing quality system maintenance.

A good rule of thumb for determining the necessity of documentation is this—*Any document that is formally part of your organization's quality system documentation must be both kept up to date and enforced.* If you cannot identify a specific individual who is responsible for maintaining and enforcing the document, or a person who has a vested interest in maintaining and enforcing the document, the chances are the policy, process, or procedure is unnecessary to the functioning of your organization.

Sufficiency

As noted in the discussion of critical success factors in Chapter 4, closely tied to the concept of *necessity* is the concept of *sufficiency*. To have an ISO 9000-compliant quality system, you must have sufficient documentation to convince a third-party registration agency that your organization can produce products and services of *consistent* quality. It should be self-evident that the quantity and type of documentation that meets the sufficiency requirement will be different for each department within an organization and different for like functions from different organizations. It should also be self-evident that quantity alone is not the determinant of sufficiency.

The ISO 9000 standards do not specify the amount of documentation a company must have. The amount of documentation your organization needs should be guided by two requirements. First, your documented quality system must communicate the minimum requirements for producing consistent quality. Second, *all* quality system documentation must be controlled; that is, the documentation is kept current, people who need to know have the most current documentation, and out-of-date documentation is removed from circulation (see Chapter 8).

Taken together, necessary and sufficient are the guiding principles in determining the amount of documentation you need to have an ISO 9000-compliant quality system. For each policy, procedure, and policy, ask yourself, "Is it really necessary to the functioning of the business?" When you have defined all of the necessary processes, you must then look at them as a whole and ask, "Are these documents sufficient to define an ISO 9000-compliant quality system?" The three remaining key criteria help you make that judgment.

Compliance

Documentation intended to address a specific section of an ISO 9000 standard should be evaluated in terms of that section. Don't just assume, for example, that because you have a policy for the "handling, storage, packaging, and delivery" of product that you have met the criteria of ISO 9001, Section 4.15. The policy must be supported with enough documentation in the form of processes and procedures to ensure that the people of your organization will, in fact, be able to implement the policy.

In some cases you may find that your organization's documentation goes *beyond* what is required by an ISO 9000 standard and that the activities documented beyond the ISO 9000 standard do add value to your customers. This is not a cause for concern. As we saw in Figure 5–3, the ISO 9000 standards do not define the pinnacle of quality systems. The ISO 9000 standards define a minimum set of requirements that guarantee consistent quality output, not necessarily superior quality products or services. Companies that fully understand the importance of quality to the success of the organization will certainly surpass the ISO 9000 standards in many areas. Exceeding the requirements of the standards will not hurt your ISO 9000 registration effort—however, beware of creeping elegance.

In your ISO 9000 registration project plan, you described the characteristics of the quality system you wanted to have in place at the time of ISO 9000 registration. Unless there is a valid business reason to change that description and unless the impact of changes on the cost of ISO 9000 registration and the target ISO 9000 registration date are fully understood, stick to what you set out to do in your plan. You will no doubt find many places where you could improve the organization's quality system beyond what is required by ISO 9000. However, understand how any quality system improvements beyond the scope of your plan will impact the ISO 9000 registration effort before plunging ahead. In the long run, managing the ISO 9000 registration project to a successful conclusion will have more positive impact on your organization's quality efforts than ad hoc process improvements that take resources away from the ISO 9000 registration project and endanger its success.

Accuracy

Accuracy is simply summed up by saying that your quality system documentation reflects the behavior of the people who function in the quality system. If people routinely perform their jobs differently than they are described in the documentation, corrective action needs to be taken.

The requirement of accuracy drives the need to ensure that all quality system documentation is controlled in the sense that specific people within each department have responsibility to keep the documentation current and to inform the proper people of changes.

FIGURE 7–3
Example Documentation Structure

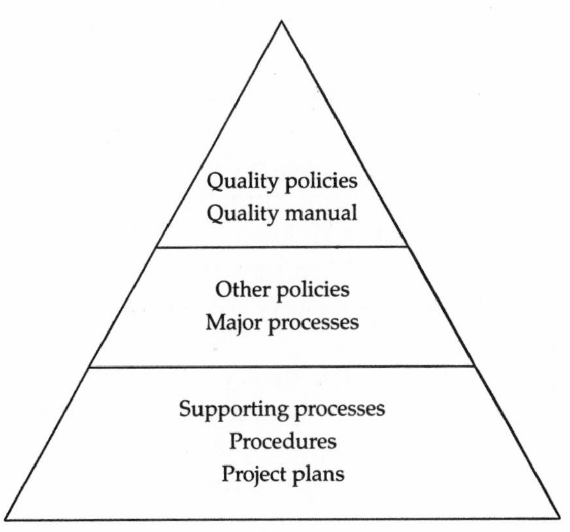

Cohesiveness

Although your evaluation of quality system documentation begins at the department level, eventually you will need to look at each document as part of a system of documentation. Figure 7–3 provides an example.

At the top of the pyramid are the organization's general quality policies. Quality policies define the basic quality values of the organization. The quality manual provides a high level implementation of the quality policies. Referenced in the quality manual are specific departmental policies and major company processes. These in turn may be supported at a work group level by supporting processes, procedures, and project plans associated with specific projects. This method of organizing documentation is discussed in more detail in Chapter 8.

ASSESSING BEHAVIOR COMPLIANCE

Once the documented quality system is defined, the next step in the internal assessment is assessing the behavior of people who work within the system. In cases where the assessor has determined that documentation complies with ISO 9000, the task is to determine if people are following the documentation. In cases where documentation does not describe a compliant system or is missing altogether, the assessor will need to evaluate the behavior of people to see if (a) they are following documentation that is inadequate, (b) they are not following the documentation, but their behavior is still not compliant with the ISO 9000 standard, or (c) they are not following documentation, but their behavior is compliant with the ISO 9000 standard. Using the corrective action matrix in Figure 7–2 helps you determine the actions you need to take to bring the organization's quality system into compliance with the ISO 9000 standard.

If your analysis falls into the upper left quadrant of the matrix, you need to take no action. The system documentation is compliant with the ISO 9000 standard and people are following the standard. This quadrant represents the strengths of your organization relative to ISO 9000.

The lower left quadrant of the matrix reflects a situation where the quality system documentation is compliant with the ISO 9000 standard but people are not following the documented policies, processes, and procedures. What do you do? The temptation is to write a memo, hold a meeting, change the compensation structure, have a public hanging, do whatever it takes to motivate people to follow the documentation. This may not be the best course of action.

Before you decide on a lower left quadrant action, you must thoroughly understand the situation. Ask yourself, "Why aren't people following the documented policies, processes, and procedures?" If it is because people are not familiar with them, then maybe the answer is to familiarize them with the documented quality system and initiate a behavior change. But what if they are not following the documented quality system because they are doing things a *better* way? If behavior does not match the ISO 9000-compliant system that is documented, that doesn't necessarily mean that the behavior must be changed. It may be that if the current behavior were documented, the quality system would comply with the ISO 9000 standard.

Certainly not all, but many, roads lead to quality. Many different approaches to meeting the requirements of ISO 9000 are equally valid. And the major point you should consider in this quadrant of decision making is *it is almost always easier to change documentation than it is to change behavior*. In determining the amount of effort required to achieve ISO 9000 registration, consider a lower left quadrant action that requires only documentation changes to be minor. If behavior changes are required, you will need to expend more effort.

The same logic applies to the lower right quadrant—the situation where the documented quality system is not in compliance with the ISO 9000 standard, but people are not following the documentation. A special case is where there is no documentation. Again, the internal assessment will need to focus on the behaviors of the people in the area. If what they *are* doing were documented, would it conform to the ISO 9000 standard? If so, with relatively little effort, you can document their activities and be in compliance with the standard. However, if in the absence of documentation, behavior is erratic, ad hoc, and inconsistent, you face a major challenge of defining and documenting an ISO 9000-compliant quality system *and* changing behavior of people to align with the documentation.

The unique case presented by the upper right quadrant is that the documented policies, processes, and procedures are not ISO 9000 compliant, yet the people are following the documentation. Depending on the degree of nonconformance, this situation requires some major effort before your organization is ready for ISO 9000 registration. You must change both the documented system and the behavior of the people.

WRITING AN INTERNAL ASSESSMENT REPORT

The internal assessment complete, the ISO 9000 representative and the internal assessment team should write up their findings in a formal *internal assessment report* for presentation to executive management. Writing the internal assessment report is one of the key actions of the ISO 9000 registration project. The finished report is a comprehensive overview of the state of the quality system in your organization. It identifies your organization's strengths and weaknesses and defines responsibility for corrective action. It moves quality out of the realm of theory and into practice.

Because the internal assessment report is the first written document resulting from the ISO 9000 registration project, it sets a tone for all that follows. The report should be above all honest—factual, relevant, and specific. Factual findings should be supported with specific evidence. Findings should be relevant to specific sections of the ISO 9000 standard, not the wish list of Quality Advocates. Findings should tie to specific nonconformities, not vague quality issues.

Writing an honest report does not mean that you should be exclusively negative. On the contrary, where your organization has strengths relative to the ISO 9000 standards, you should call these out and highlight them. It is as valuable to communicate what is right with your organization's quality system as it is to communicate about what is wrong. Don't underestimate what needs to be accomplished to achieve ISO 9000 registration, but remember, too much emphasis on the negative is detrimental to motivation to proceed.

It is also important that this report be presented to executive management *before* proceeding to take corrective action in areas where your organization is not in compliance with the standard. *Ownership of corrective action does not reside with the assessment team, but with executive management.* If the assessment team proceeds directly from assessment to corrective action, they accept de facto ownership of the quality system. Management commitment is a critical success factor for ISO 9000 registration. You should use the internal assessment process to drive home the concept of executive management ownership of the quality system. The internal assessment report is the opportunity to make executive management explicitly responsible for specific corrective actions.

A second benefit achieved from writing a formal internal assessment report is that trends across the organization become clearly visible. What might be considered a department weakness may very well be symptomatic of a larger, cross-functional, systemic issue. If you do not consolidate the results of individual department assessments, such connection may be lost. Multiple people will wind up working independently of each other on the same problem and implementing different solutions that, when they interface with each other across departmental lines, may very well make the situation worse. Certainly, independently reached solutions will not produce the most efficient or effective quality system.

A political note is also in order here. During the report writing process, interdepartmental issues are inevitable. Surfacing these issues in the context of the ISO 9000 internal assessment team will be less disruptive to the ISO 9000 registration project than immediately raising the issues at the executive level. Having gone through training together and group meetings (which you should hold periodically throughout the period of the internal assessment), by the time the internal assessment is complete, the people on your internal assessment team will be a team in practice as well as name. Internal assessment team members from conflicting organizations can address cross-departmental issues and make recommendations for proceeding that become part of the internal assessment report. Cross-functional recommendations made by the team tend to defuse issues that could cause problems if dropped into an executive session.

A third benefit of formal preparation and presentation of the internal assessment report to management is that it begins the process of building a *team commitment* to ISO 9000 registration among executives. In formal presentation of the ISO 9000 internal assessment report, you are providing executive management with a clear set of objectives that must be accomplished. Providing executive management with a clear focus stimulates action. Action is conducive to cooperation and synergy. Vague discussion does not, and can be divisive. Following presentation of the internal assessment report, we have seen managers with no stated ownership for a particular quality system weakness offer help to another executive who does have ownership. Even more surprising, we have seen that help accepted. Such activity demonstrates an executive attitude of ownership for the entire quality system, not just bits and pieces of it. Such cooperation also communicates a very powerful image to the company at large.

Every organization has a preferred method for formatting reports. There is no one right format for an internal assessment report and you should conform to your organization's report format. However, there are some key elements of an ISO 9000 internal assessment report that should be a part of your package.

The internal assessment report should clearly define the intent and scope of the internal assessment effort. It should position the internal assessment in context of the progress that has already been made toward ISO 9000 registration and what remains to be accomplished. It should give credit to those who were part of the internal assessment team. The report should clearly define the structure that is used to summarize the findings of the internal assessment. Figure 7–4 illustrates one possible format for an ISO 9000 internal assessment report.

Figure 7–4 is a typical page in the internal assessment report. It clearly identifies the ISO 9000 standard to which registration is sought, in this case ISO 9001. The page heading identifies the specific section and subsection of ISO 9001 to which the findings on this page apply. It restates the requirement of ISO 9001 and it also clarifies the intent of the requirement (see Chapter 8). Up front, the format identifies the organization's strengths in the area being assessed. It divides weaknesses into *major* and *minor* depending upon the amount of documentation that needs to be created or the degree to which behavior must be changed. A key element of the format is that the owner responsible to correct each weakness is defined by title. People may change job function, and it is important that corrective action rests with a job responsibility, not an individual, to ensure maintenance of the quality system over time.

Before presenting the internal assessment report to executive management, we recommend that members of the team discuss the results with people within their own organizations. As a main driver of the ISO 9000 registration project, you will want to follow a process much like you did in presenting the original ISO 9000 project plan. You will want to meet with key players on the executive staff prior to presenting the results to the entire executive staff. With each key player, you will want to reemphasize the *business* rationale for ISO 9000 registration, to relate the internal assessment activities to business benefits, and to obtain an initial reaction to the results of the assessment. Your ultimate objective is to have the internal assessment report understood and emotionally accepted

FIGURE 7–4
Example Internal Assessment Report

ISO 9001
4.1 Management Responsibility
4.1.1 Quality Policy

The supplier's management shall define and document its policy and objectives for, and commitment to, quality. The supplier shall ensure that this policy is understood, implemented, and maintained at all levels in the organization.

Intent

Management should demonstrate commitment visibly and actively on a continuing basis. Commitment can be demonstrated by:

- Ensuring that employees understand and implement the quality policy.
- Initiating, managing, and following up on the implementation of the quality policy including implementation of the quality system.
- Not accepting deviations from the quality policy or wasted resources in any part of the organization.

Strengths

The company has included a commitment to quality in its mission statement.

Major Weaknesses

Quality policies have been set by the quality assurance department, not by executive management.
Responsibility: president and executive staff

Minor Weaknesses

Quality policies have not been communicated to company employees.
Responsibility: vice president of corporate communications.

---

prior to its formal presentation. That way, you can use valuable meeting time developing action plans and determining resource allocations rather than handling emotionally charged reactions to the assessment.

With the completion of presentation of the internal assessment report, your organization has taken another major step toward ISO 9000 registration. The next step is correcting each instance of nonconformity found in the internal assessment and preparing for an internal *independent* audit, discussed in Chapter 9. Before we move on to the internal audit however, Chapter 8 will take a closer look at a quality system documentation structure. Chapter 8 expands on some of the ideas introduced in this chapter, and it lays the ground work for your understanding of Chapter 9.

THE NCR EXPERIENCE

We began preparation for our internal assessment by conducting a two-day training session on ISO 9000 requirements and basic auditing principles. Twelve ISO 9000 department champions received the training. The training was conducted by the ISO 9000 champion. Prior to the training the ISO 9000 champion and other members of the quality assurance organization had attended seminars conducted by educational institutions and consulting firms. Organizations already actively seeking ISO 9000 registration were benchmarked. The ISO 9000 champion had become an American Society for Quality Control (ASQC) Certified Quality Auditor (CQA).

Because our division both designs and manufactures computer products, we focused our discussion on ISO 9001: *Quality Systems—Model for Quality Assurance in Design/Development, Production, Installation, and Servicing*. However, we also spent a considerable amount of the training discussing the relationship between ISO 9001 and ISO 9004: *Quality Management and Quality System Elements—Guidelines*. We viewed ISO 9001 as the *letter of the law* and the ISO 9004 guidelines as the *spirit of the law*. When discussing ISO 9001, we looked to ISO 9004 for the *intent* of the requirement. For example, ISO 9001 mentions design reviews; ISO 9004 defines what a design review is.

We also discussed intent of the ISO 9001 requirements to our specific business situation. This was possible because the internal assessment team consisted of people from each organization in the company, including finance and human resources (a requirement set forth in our ISO 9000 registration project plan). These discussions helped us further clarify the intent of the ISO 9001 requirements as applied to our division. Understanding intent significantly aided our internal assessment and later auditing activities.

Once we felt comfortable that all the ISO 9000 department champions had a basic understanding of the ISO 9001 standard and the intent of the requirements, we moved on. Creeping elegance discussed in this chapter in connection with quality system improvements is also a danger in the training process. Certainly, you should not take any kind of training lightly, nor should you expect that you are going pluck individuals from operational organizations and in any reasonable period of time turn them into ISO 9000 experts, or for that matter, skilled quality auditors. You're not. However, you can, and that was our goal, give them a sound working knowledge of the ISO 9000 standard and basic auditing principles and techniques—enough knowledge, skill, and confidence to provide the organization with valuable insight into its readiness for ISO 9000 registration.

Internal assessment training consisted of a discussion of the principles detailed in this chapter—the concept of necessary and sufficient documentation, the relationship between the documented quality system and both the ISO 9001 standard, and the behavior of people in the company. We provided and discussed a template for preparing the final internal assessment report. The format was given to each member of the team in a standard word-processing program. Each person was assigned specific sections of the standard relevant to their departments; for example, people from engineering looked specifically at the sections of ISO 9001 having to do with design and development functions; human resources people looked at policies, processes, and procedures related to training and training records. All department champions examined how their departments controlled documentation.

Members of the internal assessment team spent six weeks assessing their own areas. They gathered information, conducted interviews, and made judgments. Each individual took a slightly different approach. Some conducted more interviews than others. Some did a more thorough job collecting documentation. We expected this and held meetings every two weeks throughout the assessment period to exchange ideas and methods and discuss findings. Because we were interested in substance and not the form of the assessment, we did not use our bi-weekly meetings to try to impose rigid auditing standards on team members. We handled cross-functional issues as they arose.

At the end of the six-week period, the internal assessment team turned in their sections of the report on a floppy disk in the format they had received. The ISO 9000 champion consolidated the various sections into a cohesive assessment report. The report was further revised so that terminology and writing style was consistent from section to section, and was organized in the format described in this chapter.

A table of contents and index were built for the final internal assessment report for easy reference by executive management. Included in the index was a list of responsibilities. Each member of the executive staff was listed by job title. For each job title, references were supplied so that the title holder could identify where to find his or her specific set of responsibilities for corrective action.

Each member of the internal assessment team reviewed the report. Their comments were discussed and incorporated as appropriate. The members of the team presented the results of the internal assessment to their respective organizations. When this was completed, the ISO 9000 champion presented the internal assessment report to the executive staff. One result of this meeting was the formation of a quality steering team made up of selected members of the executive staff including the division vice president. The specific, short-term charter of this team was to address the weaknesses raised by the management responsibility section of the ISO 9001 standard.

The internal assessment approach was very productive for us. Our department champions found the "beams" to cast out of their own departments. Later, these same department champions were used to perform independent audits and find the "motes" that remained in other departments.

Chapter Eight

Documenting the ISO 9000-Compliant Quality System

Contrary to what is sometimes claimed, the Constitution is not meant to be merely "procedural" as opposed to "substantive." In setting down the fundamental "rules of the game," the founders intended to determine in broad but definite terms the political culture and thereby the way of life of the future nation.

Thomas L. Prangle
Confronting the Constitution

It's time to put things back together again. In the previous chapter we broke apart the organization's quality system and looked at ISO 9000 documentation requirements on a department level. Intellectually, this was not a difficult task. Most of us are used to working with individual processes and procedures. Most organizations have built their quality systems from the bottom up with policies, processes, and procedures created in response to specific situations. And that documentation seems to work—and it continues to work, but only until the situation that spawned the policy, process, or procedure changes.

In today's business world, change is a given. The business climate is changing from local customers to national and international marketplaces. The employee base is diversifying. Companies are reorganizing. To meet these changes, processes and procedures undergo massive reengineering. On top of these relatively recent and radical changes in the business environment are the day to day changes every business goes through—people changing jobs, people entering or leaving the workforce, new product lines being introduced, reorganizations to meet new business demands. From the perspective of ISO 9000 registration, the question facing you is how to control your quality system documentation in the face of such change.

THE PURPOSE OF THIS CHAPTER

In this chapter, we address the question of documenting the ISO 9000-compliant quality system. This is a multi-dimensional question. In Chapter 7 we discussed two dimensions of quality system documentation. The first is the content of the documentation itself. Quality system documentation breaks down when the content fails to meet necessary and sufficient criteria for compliance with the ISO 9000 standards. A second dimension of quality system documentation discussed in Chapter 7 was its relationship to the behavior of people within the organization. The quality system breaks down if behavior does not correspond to compliant documentation. This chapter introduces a third dimension of documentation—physical and procedural control of documentation.

The ISO 9000 contractual standards require that a company establish and maintain procedures to control all documents that relate to the requirements of the standard. The standards further divide this requirement into two parts: Document Approval and Issue, and Document Changes/Modification.[1] The ISO 9000 standards address both documentation, which is the active description of your quality system, and records, which are the results of implementation of your quality system. ISO 9004 notes that a quality system should "establish, and require maintenance of, a means for identification, collection, indexing, filing, storage, maintenance, retrieval, and disposition of pertinent quality records."[2]

At first glance, ISO 9000 documentation requirements might strike many people within your organization as adding bureaucracy to the quality system and very little value. That attitude often becomes a self-fulfilling prophecy. Documentation systems growing from that attitude are devised to the letter rather than the spirit of the requirement. The resulting control systems are often so complex and burdensome that they soon fall into disuse, defeating the purpose of the ISO 9000 standards and creating a number of problems in the workplace, not the least of which are poor employee morale and inconsistent product and service quality. This chapter will help you avoid this potential pitfall by addressing both a system of documentation management and a supporting philosophy for quality system documentation.

The spirit of the documentation control requirement of ISO 9000 is really quite simple. Documentation control is intended to do two things. First, approval and issue activities are intended to ensure that an organization's quality system documentation is both necessary and sufficient. Second, change/modification procedures are intended to ensure that as documentation changes to reflect the changing activities of people working within the quality system, the modification of documentation is done accurately and in a controlled manner. In preparing quality system documentation, you should never stray far from the two principles of intent. They provide the ultimate sanity check on documentation control efforts. If a documentation control policy, process, or procedure does not contribute to one or the other principle, then it is probably an unnecessary burden on the quality system.

In this chapter, we present a structure that allows you to hold to the intent of ISO 9000 quality system documentation. We look at three key elements of a quality system documentation program that both fulfills the letter of the ISO 9000 documentation requirements and the intent:

Documentation System Structure

Documentation System Philosophy

Documentation System Management

This chapter also looks at some important quality system documents like the organization's quality policies and quality manual—their content, their structure, their preparation, and how they blend the current quality culture of the organization with the desired quality strategy. Finally, we'll examine some basic issues having to do with the physical control of documentation and provide some practical advice that applies no matter how you choose to control quality system documentation.

FIGURE 8–1
Example Documentation Structure

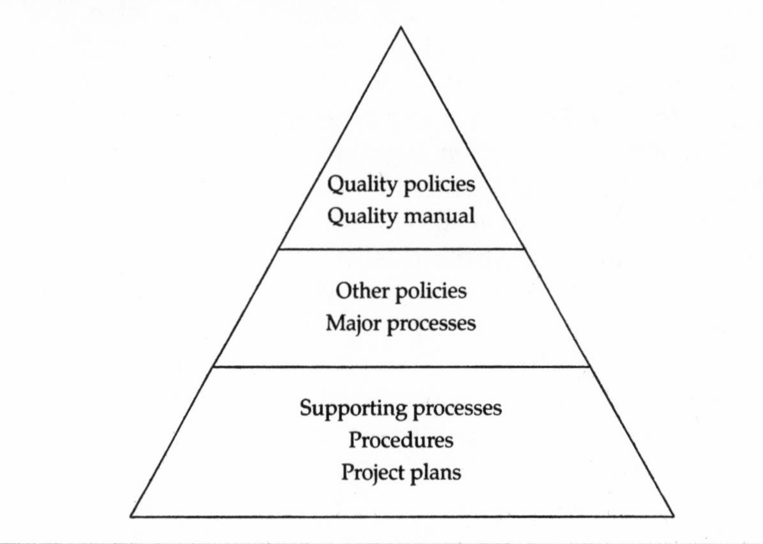

DOCUMENTATION SYSTEM STRUCTURE

In Chapter 7, we introduced a model for a documentation system that is illustrated again in Figure 8–1.

At the top of the pyramid are the organization's general quality policies. Quality policies define the basic quality values of the organization. Next is the quality manual, which provides high-level implementation of the quality policies. Referenced in the quality manual are specific departmental policies and major company processes. These in turn may be supported at the work group level by supporting processes, procedures, and project plans associated with specific projects.

The pyramidal structure of the documentation system is not accidental. It implies that working up the pyramid, each layer supports the layer above it. Working down the pyramid, each layer influences the layers below it. No layer functions independently of any other. That applies both on an operational level and on a cultural level.

On an operational level, the documentation system must provide an audit trail from top to bottom or bottom to top, depending upon where in the organization an assessor is working. For example, if your organization has a quality policy that states that the organization will maintain a quality manual with requirements for the design of computer software, then that quality manual should exist. Moreover it should have a section describing software design. In the quality manual, one would expect to find reference to a software design process (the next level down in the pyramid). An assessor would expect to find, supporting the entire structure, specific procedures defining activities that are part of the software design process.

Working up the pyramid, were the assessor to be looking at a specific software design project, he or she would expect to see reflected in that project the elements of the quality system documentation structure—that the work activities of the project follow documented procedures, that the procedures reflect the high-level software design process requirements defined in the organization's quality manual, and that the processes and procedures used to develop/design, produce, install, and service the product support the quality policies and values of the organization.

Working up and down the document system structure as described above provides operational consistency to the quality system. It ensures that when problems arise, either product or process problems, there is a top-to-bottom audit trail. Following the trail, one can determine if the problems were caused by a lapse in rigor in following the process or by a hole in the quality system, in which case the quality system must be somehow modified. There can be several reasons for the latter ranging from a specific problem with an individual employee to a systemic training issue. The point is, knowing that the problem is a breakdown between process and behavior prevents you from unnecessarily altering a perfectly good quality system every time a minor problem occurs.

In addition to operating consistency, the pyramidal structure of the quality documentation structure provides a framework for philosophical consistency of the documentation system. The philosophical basis of documentation structure is an important concept in creating documentation *that works*.

DOCUMENTATION SYSTEM PHILOSOPHY

At the top of the quality documentation system structure sits the company's quality policies. If one substitutes "quality policies" for "constitution" in the quote from Thomas Prangle that heads this chapter, one would have, in a concise statement, the underpinning for a philosophically consistent quality system documentation structure.[3] Contrary to common corporate thinking, quality policies are not meant to be only operational documents. Limiting the function of an organization's quality policies to operational issues does not address the cultural critical success factors necessary to institutionalize the ISO 9000 standards and quality system thinking into the everyday work life of the company.

Quality policies are intended to be substantive. They should be the fundamental rules that reflect the fundamental values of the organization. In broad but definite terms, the quality policies set the tone for the quality culture of an organization. Quality policies do not just define the operational present; they are the substance of the quality vision for the future.

In that sense, a company's quality policies are very much like a constitution. At the enterprise or companywide level, quality policies provide the basic framework within which specific departmental processes and procedures operate. The quality policies do not state specifically processes and procedures that must be followed (just as a constitution like the United States Constitution does not specify local ordinances); however, whatever policies and procedures are put in place at the departmental level must comply with the intent of the quality policies (just as local ordinances in the United States must be constitutionally valid).

Quality policies, then, provide a consistent mindset and a common language for decision making and selecting appropriate actions. In a quality-conscious organization, quality policies are used as both a guide for decision making and as an assessment tool for evaluating decisions after the fact for purposes of process improvement.

Carrying the constitutional approach down through the pyramid, one would expect there to be philosophical agreement between the quality policies and the quality manual and between the quality manual and departmental processes and procedures.

One would expect to see consistency between quality system documentation and behavior of the people within the organization.

For example, if a company's quality policy were to state that "when a conflict arises between quality, cost, and schedule, meeting customer expectations and doing the right thing for the customer will take precedence over all other considerations," then one would expect to see processes in place for understanding what customer expectations are, processes in place for meeting those expectations, and processes in place for handling customer problems and complaints when those expectations are not met. Further, if one were to look at records of actions taken in these cases, one would expect to see decisions made based on the needs of customers, not cost and schedule issues.

Note that this kind of approach does not violate the "business of business is business" approach to ISO 9000 registration. First and foremost, the quality policies must be accepted as reflecting sound business judgment. Recognizing that what is stated in the quality policies must eventually be carried out in practice forces the framers of the quality policies to avoid flowery expressions of the "do good and avoid evil" approach to quality, which only serves to confuse employees and create conflict between documentation and behavior, in favor of policies that can be implemented, enforced, and enthusiastically endorsed by both management and employees.

We will look at approaches to writing quality system documentation that facilitates both philosophical and operational elements later in the chapter. But first, let's look at the third key element of quality system documentation—documentation management.

DOCUMENTATION SYSTEM MANAGEMENT

Once again, cursory reading of the ISO 9000 standards may make documentation control seem like a horrendous task. Don't misunderstand—it is not easy, as examination of some of the issues will show. But the key to creating an effective documentation management system (that is, one that people can and do follow) rests in recognizing that people working within the quality system must: (1) understand what they are to do, (2) understand how they are to do it, (3) maintain a record of what was done, and (4) know to whom they should report what was done.

Those four activities are reflected in *quality documentation* and *quality records*. Quality documentation consists of those documents that inform people of what they are to do, how they are to do it, how they are to record what they did, and whom they should tell about it. Quality documents include drawings, specifications, blueprints, inspection instructions, test procedures, work instructions, operation sheets, the quality manual, operational procedures, and quality assurance procedures. The common denominator for all these documents is that they are dynamic, they change and that change must be managed to ensure that documentation is up-to-date and in the hands of the people who need it.

Quality records are the reports of "what was done." At a basic level, these reports are the source of information about how well the quality system is currently functioning. At a higher level, they are the basis for quality system improvement. Examples of quality records are inspection reports, test data, qualification reports, validation reports, audit reports, material review reports, calibration data, and quality cost reports. The common denominator for quality records is not that they change, but that they must be retained and be retrievable. The discussion of a document management system that follows applies to records as well as documentation.

As is the case with all other aspects of the ISO 9000 standards, there is no one right documentation management system. Ultimately, the system your organization adopts will depend on your company's organizational structure and culture. However, regardless of either organizational structure or corporate culture, there are two basic issues you will have to address. The first is centralized versus decentralized control of quality documentation. The second is wide distribution of quality documentation versus controlled distribution.

Centralized Versus Decentralized Documentation Control

Should your organization distribute quality documentation control responsibility throughout the organization, or should a single department like quality assurance be responsible for maintaining quality system documentation? What are the pros and cons of one method versus the other?

At the level of quality policies and the quality manual, it is fairly obvious that control of the documentation is more effectively handled within a single department like quality assurance. Because high-level documentation is applicable across all departments, it makes sense to have a single source of change management and distribution. However, understand that control of a document means incorporating and distributing changes to the document; it does not necessarily mean creation or initiation of changes to the document.

Quality assurance may own control of the quality policies and quality manual, but once the quality system concept is institutionalized in an organization, every department has the responsibility to initiate changes to the documentation based on changes in the business. Central control of the documents is only for the purpose of maintaining change management and orderly distribution.

It is below the quality manual level of the quality documentation system pyramid that the issue of centralized versus decentralized documentation control gets a little sticky. The pros of centralized documentation control are consistency of process across all organizations, economies of scale in terms of staffing, and the potential for a centralized database of quality documentation based on computer technology. The drawback is that documentation responsibility is separated from the organizations that do the work. Centralized control can make documentation seem like something imposed *on* a department, rather than something generated *by* the department. Culturally, a centralized documentation control and management system fits well in a company that has a hierarchical chain of command structure.

The alternative to a centralized control of documentation is distributed documentation control. The argument for distributed control is that it puts documentation control closest to the people who do the work. Culturally, decentralized control integrates documentation more closely with the work of the department, making people in the department much more conscious of processes and procedures and more inclined to think about process improvements.

The drawbacks, of course, are losses in the economies of scale—both the ability to employ computer technology and the ability to staff a documentation control function.

More than likely, you will find that some parts of your documentation control system will be centralized and some decentralized. It is important that you not make decisions about who controls documentation ad hoc. Fully understand the trade-off between economies of scale and putting documentation under the control of the people who actually use it before making a decision on where control belongs. And make a plan.

New computer technology and software applications are appearing almost daily. Regardless of whether documentation control rests with a single centralized source or is distributed throughout the company, a central, electronically maintained master copy is superior to paper copy distribution of documentation. Not only does it make change control easier and more accurate, but it addresses the second issue that must be considered in any documentation control scheme—wide access to versus controlled distribution of quality documentation.

Wide Access to Versus Controlled Distribution of Quality Documentation

Regardless of whether documentation control rests with a single department or is distributed throughout the company, you will have to deal with the dichotomy of wide access to quality documentation versus a tightly controlled distribution. In reality, this issue is not so much a question of confidentiality as it is a question of document control.

In today's flattening organizations, more and more people require access to documentation. As teaming becomes an accepted way of doing business, people move freely about corporations from one project to another, requiring access to new processes and procedures. Couple widespread employee movement with an environment where the processes and procedures are changing, and you have the very real potential that outdated documentation will be floating around the organization. Inevitably, some people will be using different processes and procedures than others doing the same job or supplying input or receiving output from the process. Mismatched expectations caused by mismatched processes and procedures leads to inconsistent quality.

There are manual ways to minimize such confusion. The NCR Network Products Division Quality Manual is widely distributed. However, each copy clearly carries the notation "Uncontrolled Copy" on each page. An uncontrolled copy means that the holder of the document will not be notified of changes to the document and should not rely on the contents of the document remaining accurate over time. A limited number of "Controlled" copies are distributed. These are also labeled on each page. In addition, each controlled copy is assigned to a specific person and given a serial number marked in red ink on the cover. Holders of controlled copies are automatically mailed updates. In addition, controlled copies carry a mandatory review date prior to which they must be reviewed by the document owner for currency.

When should you reissue quality system documentation? When significant changes are made to any document that is significant to the quality system, the document must be updated and distributed. However, the standard leaves to your organization to define what is a "significant" change. For example, in a dynamic environment, you might not update your company quality manual every time a change is made to a process or procedure referenced in the manual. However, you *will* want to redistribute the quality manual, or at least updated portions of it, if a major process is altered, such as automation of a previously manual process. You will want to redistribute the entire quality manual after several pages have been changed.

Mandatory review of documentation is built into the documentation management system to ensure that behavior and documentation coordination continue over time. A specific date on which a document must be reviewed makes sure all process and procedure changes are recorded, and it provides the opportunity to check that people are still following the documented process or procedure, i.e., that they have not made ad hoc changes to the way they do their jobs. If they have, you must return to the matrix analysis described in Chapter 7 and decide if you need to change their behavior or change the documentation to be consistent with the way people are doing their jobs.

Although manual documentation management meets the requirements of the ISO 9000 standard for documentation control, an electronic database system is really the ideal solution and (provided electronic access is available) virtually eliminates most distribution issues. Current documentation is maintained at a single source and is readily available. However, if employees have the ability to download and print documents, each page should still be labeled "Uncontrolled" or "Valid for date of use only" to minimize the potential that the physical copy of an out-of-date document might be referenced.

It goes without saying that documentation control is a key element for ISO 9000 registration. It is also the area most companies fall down in. When creating your ISO 9000 registration project plan, do not treat documentation control as a trivial exercise. Plan to spend a significant amount of time preparing documentation control people for ISO 9000 registration.

PREPARING QUALITY SYSTEM DOCUMENTATION

There's good news and bad news awaiting you when you begin building a quality system documentation structure. The good news is you have a lot of documentation in place. The bad news is you have a lot of documentation in place.

In Chapter 7 we discussed the necessary and sufficient criteria of quality system documentation. We also discussed cohesiveness, that is, does the documentation fit together both operationally and philosophically. If you were starting from scratch in building a quality system, cohesiveness would be relatively easy to build into your system. However, because you are starting with a mass of existing documentation, there will inevitably be both operational and philosophical conflicts between existing policies, processes, and procedures within your organization.

Lack of cohesiveness becomes acute as you move up the pyramid in Figure 8–1. It is not unlikely that two distinct departments will have different but equally ISO 9000-compliant sets of processes and procedures that will be difficult to integrate at a cross-functional level of the quality system documentation pyramid.

The task facing you when this situation occurs is to arrive at a solution acceptable to both parties. Assuming both departments have ISO 9000-compliant processes, it is best not to pit one against the other in a win-lose scenario. Nor is compromise a solution. Compromise inevitably is a lose-lose situation. Both sides give up something and neither is happy with the solution. The best approach from both a tactical and strategic approach is seeking a consensus solution. Bring the parties together and look for an alternative solution, perhaps one combining the best of each competing process, but more than likely a whole new way of doing things that is strategically in keeping with your organization's quality vision. In this way, you address the requirements of ISO 9000 while moving the organization toward a higher level quality system.

Preparing Quality Policies

Key to driving consensus-based solutions is having a well thought out and well accepted set of quality policies. A quality policy may be as simple as a few statements that define the quality values of your organization. A quality policy may also be a more comprehensive document that details specific actions and requirements expected of the organization.

Rule number one in preparing quality policies is start with what you've got. It is a mistake to think that you will change the culture of your company by rewriting the organization's quality policies. To establish any kind of credibility for your quality policies, they must have connection to the reality of the corporate culture. Certainly you can expand that vision, but there must be a connection to the existing corporate values (see the NCR example at the end of this chapter).

The second rule of quality policy development is to involve executive management in the process of formulating quality policy. Your leverage with management on this issue is that the ISO 9000 standard clearly states that defining and documenting quality policy is management's responsibility.[4] The real benefit of having management involved is that the quality policies become their policies. Over time a commitment is built to the policies. This commitment can be increased by making management not only responsible for writing the quality policies, but also for training their staffs in the policies. This method of quality policy dissemination is discussed in detail in Chapter 3. The point is, the more involved management is in the formulation of the quality policies, the more rapidly they will become an accepted part of the business fabric.

The third rule is don't think that formal acceptance or even training in the quality policies constitute commitment. They do not. On the flip side of the coin, don't buy the notion that cultural change takes time and there is nothing you can do to speed the process. Not true. Once the quality policies are prepared, take every opportunity to use them "constitutionally." When raising quality issues, associate them with specific quality policies. Remember, your goal is not to drive a particular solution, but to drive the framework of the discussion.

In the example cited previously, where doing what's right for the customer comes into conflict with cost and/or schedule issues, your objective is to use the quality policies to focus the issue to a debate about what is right for the customer. Don't use the quality policies to force a specific agenda. That tactic only meets with resistance and portrays the quality policies as bureaucratic rules rather than a constitutional framework. Position the quality policies as a guideline. Trust the people responsible to choose the action.

This kind of trust is not always easy for Quality Advocates and Quality Purists to accept. In the example above, schedule versus quality, Quality Advocates and Quality Purists may cite the policies as absolute authority for the position that a product that does not meet all predetermined quality standards should not be shipped to a customer. In point of fact, the policies may indicate just the opposite. If the customer's immediate need for the product was great *and* the customer was made aware of the product's shortcoming *and* there were remedial actions that could be taken to ensure the customer's requirements were met, then it makes no sense not to ship the product. The important point from your perspective is that the "ship or don't ship" argument is ultimately decided based on customer requirements and expectations.

Preparing the Quality Manual

Like a quality policy document, there is no one right format or methodology for preparing a quality manual. However, there are some general principles that make preparation go more smoothly and help ensure that the finished product is an accurate reflection of the way your company operates.

Up front, like most of your quality system documentation, *preparing* your quality manual will have more value to your organization than the finished document itself. Preparing the quality manual will be an eye-opener for your company. When your quality manual is complete, you will have a comprehensive picture of how your organization really operates. For many organizations, completion of the quality manual provides the first look at how all the processes and procedures of the organization fit together. Almost immediately, people begin to see avenues for improvement.

To achieve that kind of revelation, however, the quality manual must be both comprehensive and accurate. The only way to achieve those two characteristics is by a companywide preparation effort. A quality manual cannot be written by executive management, by the quality assurance organization, by human resources, or by any other functional department in the company, and accurately reflect how people behave across the company. A specific department like quality assurance may be responsible for pulling together the pieces and resolving conflicts, but initial input and final review of the quality manual must rest with line departments that do the work described in the document.

Preparing individual sections of the organization's quality manual is a primary function of the ISO 9000 department champions. Using the Internal Assessment Report as a guide, these individuals develop the sections of the quality manual pertinent to their areas. In group meetings and individual meetings between ISO 9000 department champions, cross-functional issues are resolved. A single-voice document is prepared in which consistent language and a consistent written format are used. The completed document is reviewed by the ISO 9000 department champions and endorsed by appropriate levels of management before it becomes the organization's official quality manual.

It is important to realize that out of necessity, ISO 9000 department champions interact with many people when pulling together their sections of the quality manual. In this way, both the quality system concept and the ISO 9000 concept are given wide exposure in the organization.

There is no one standard for how a quality manual should be formatted. However, if one thinks of the third-party assessors as customers, it logically follows that the quality manual should be laid out in a manner that makes it easy for them to understand your quality system, and, incidentally, this is probably the best format for your own organization to understand its quality system. Unless you have a compelling reason not to, we recommend that your quality manual format corresponds one-to-one with the sections of the ISO 9000 standard to which you are seeking registration. Each page should clearly identify the section and subsection of the standard being addressed. In addition, each page should be numbered and carry the date and revision level of the document.

Beyond those basics the amount of information included in the quality manual will depend upon each organization's documentation philosophy. However, we recommend that information should include the following: a policy statement, an applicability statement, a requirements statement, and a reference statement. Figure 8–2 shows an example quality manual format illustrating this information.

Policy statement. The policy statement is a brief overview statement of how your organization addresses the intent of the relevant section of the ISO 9000 standard. It is written in simple, declarative sentences. For example, addressing Section 4.6.4 of the ISO 9001 standard for verification of purchased product, a policy statement might read, "Product acceptability requirements, test conditions, and reference standards are included in the specifications, drawings, or purchase orders issued by the company. Purchased products are verified at either the company or at its suppliers."

From this statement, a third-party assessor learns several things about your company. He or she will know where to look for product acceptability requirements and what to look for in verification reports.

Applicability statement. This is a statement of the scope of the above policy. It tells the third-party assessor which departments within the organization are responsible and have the author-

FIGURE 8–2
Example Quality Manual Format

Widget Company Quality Manual Revision 03, April 27, 1994 Page 16 of 45
4.6 Purchasing
4.6.4 Verification of Purchased Product

Policy

Product acceptability requirements, test conditions, and reference standards are included in the specifications, drawings, or purchase orders issued by the company. Purchased products are verified at either the company or at its suppliers.

Applicability

This policy applies to all products purchased by Widget Company. It pertains to the Supplier Management and Receiving Inspection departments.

Requirements

Supplier Management

1. Coordinate product acceptance activities between Receiving Inspection and suppliers.
2. Evaluate inspection data and set acceptance levels based upon supplier performance.

Receiving Inspection

1. Perform inspection testing.
2. File inspection reports with Supplier Management.

References

WID 20032—Supplier Management Process
WID 30056—Receiving Inspection Procedure

---

ity to ensure that the organization is compliant with the relevant section of the ISO 9000 standard.

Requirements statement. This section lists the specific requirements engendered by the policy statement. Continuing the example from above, the requirements of the above policy might read that the organization's supplier management group is responsible for coordinating product acceptance activities between receiving inspection and suppliers. Receiving inspection is responsible for performing inspection testing and reporting data to the supplier management group.

Requirements statements give the third-party assessor another level of detail about your organization. He or she now not only knows what your organization does, but at a high level, how you do it.

Reference statement. This section is a simple listing of the processes and procedures that those departments that are part of the scope of the requirement use to do their work. Given this information, third-party assessors now have a clear trail to follow should they elect to go into more detail in this specific area of the standard.

It is not necessary to describe processes in detail in the quality manual. In fact, to do so is not recommended as it could easily make the quality manual an unnecessarily large document. Also, because processes and procedures are constantly changing in response to new technologies and new ways of doing business, too much low-level detail would necessarily require frequent updating of the quality manual. Unless a whole process is deleted or added, it is unnecessary to change the quality manual, which leads us to a discussion of the next level of the quality system documentation structure.

Processes and Procedures

As you move below the level of the quality manual in the quality system documentation pyramid, the question of how much documentation you need becomes more acute. You are now reaching down many levels into your organization where people are more oriented to doing jobs than they are to thinking about the quality system. This is not a comment on either the intelligence or the dedication of people in the organization. It's simply a statement of fact—line people are traditionally rewarded for how many widgets they assemble or how many products they ship on time. Any task (such as documenting procedures) that detracts from that focus can be seen as excess bureaucracy.

For this reason, you must allow both time and resources for educating your organization on the need for documented processes. As stated earlier, that need must be expressed in terms relevant to the line department, not necessarily the company as a whole. You must focus your education on how documented processes will make the line person's job easier, more efficient, and more effective. It is also preferred that process documentation be spearheaded by a champion within the organization rather than from an outside department like quality assurance. This is one reason for forming a team of ISO 9000 department champions.

For purposes of documenting your quality system, you should distinguish between *processes* and *procedures*. There are many excellent sources of information about processes and process management, and it is not the intent of this book to be a tutorial on process management. However, a few words need be said about distinguishing between processes and procedures for the purpose of documenting your quality system.

Processes describe the general way in which an output is produced. Processes may span many departments within an organization, or they may be limited to a specific department within the organization. Process documents define the input and output requirements of the work activity and the metrics taken by the process.

Procedures are the specific actions performed by individuals working within a process. A process may consist of many procedures.

From a documentation standpoint, we recommend documenting processes at a high level of detail—enough so that an individual working within a process knows what the inputs to the process are, what procedures must be followed, and what the expected output is. A process document need not detail specific procedures. Again, the object of quality system documentation is to insulate higher-level documentation from minor changes in supporting documents. You do not want to revise and distribute new processes every time a minor change is made to a procedure that supports it.

A change in a procedure involves a relatively small part of the organization. When a procedure changes, changing the documentation, distributing the change, and monitoring the behavior are relatively simple tasks controlled at the department level.

Procedures or instruction sheets are the final link between documentation and behavior. Having followed your quality system documentation structure from policy to procedure, a third-party assessor will use procedure documents to determine if behavior is consistent with the documented system.

Once a company's ISO 9000-compliant quality system documentation is in place and people are following it, you have an ISO 9000-compliant quality system. You can then move from the gaining compliance phase of your project to the ensuring continuing compliance phase. Ensuring continuing compliance of the quality system, including the use of independent auditing to do so, is the subject of Chapter 9.

THE NCR EXPERIENCE

When we first looked at our existing quality system documentation in the context of ISO 9000 registration in early 1991, we found good news and bad news. The good news was NCR had implemented process management around 1987 and our organization had been documenting processes and using process management for several years. The bad news was our organization had been documenting processes and using process management for years.

At one point, our division had over 1300 documented processes, and we were trying to manage every last one of them—an impossible task. There was a growing dissatisfaction within the organization that process management was adding bureaucracy but creating little value. Although efforts were being made to consolidate processes, there was uncertainty about the way to proceed and the criteria for process consolidation.

The ISO 9000 standards provided the tools we needed. The ISO 9000 registration project provided a companywide focus for eliminating unnecessary processes, consolidating processes across the company, creating processes where the system was insufficient, and collapsing processes into procedures. We defined the quality system documentation pyramid for our organization, and we began structuring our current documentation.

We also used the ISO 9000 registration project as an opportunity to clearly establish a division quality vision through the quality policies. NCR's Corporate Quality Assurance group issued quality policies, but in general the Network Products Division was unfamiliar with them. Even if the policies had been familiar to us, they would have necessarily had only minor relevance as they were written from the perspective of a worldwide company providing a wide range of products and services.

We took the existing NCR quality policies and defined the relevance of each NCR statement to our division. In this manner, we defined our requirements based on the existing NCR policy. As we have repeatedly stated, it was the exercise of doing this that held the real benefit. Revision of the quality policies was done by the quality steering team, made up of members of the executive staff. When the policies were complete, the executive staff discussed them with their staffs, who in turn discussed the quality policies with their staffs. The result was dissemination of the quality policies with relevance to each and every organization.

In a preface to the quality policies, we clearly positioned them as a constitution and provided guidance for their implementation. Employees received a condensed version of the policies in the form of a card that could be carried with them at all times.

We used the department champion approach in creating our quality manual. A person from each major organization in the company was responsible for writing the sections that pertained to his or her organization. Quality assurance provided a template for them to follow, similar to Figure 8–2, and was also responsible for consolidating and preparing the final document.

By the time of registration, we had eliminated nonvalue-add processes and consolidated several smaller processes into larger ones. What remained of the 1300 processes were around 150 processes, 300 manufacturing procedures and another 100 procedures that covered the rest of the company. More importantly, this lower level documentation was now tied together by the quality manual into a cohesive quality system that implemented the quality policies.

Chapter Nine

Ensuring Continuing ISO 9000 Compliance of the Quality System

On the contrary, Watson, you can see everything. You fail, however, to reason from what you see. You are too timid in drawing your inferences.

Sir Arthur Conan Doyle
Sherlock Holmes—The Adventure of the Blue Carbuncle

Sherlock Holmes was one of a kind. He did not just see—he reasoned from what he saw. Unlike his chronicler, Dr. Watson, he was not timid in drawing inferences, and perhaps more than any other reason, it was this lack of timidity that made his deductions so infallibly accurate. Unfortunately, most of us are more akin to a Dr. Watson than a Sherlock Holmes. When we observe situations, our timidity to break away from our biases limits our ability to infer all possible conclusions from what we see. We fail to realize that although a discovered truth may be obvious, what is immediately obvious is not always the truth.

And what does a Sherlock Holmes view of ISO 9000 show us? Elementary, my dear Watson. Elementary.

In previous chapters we have seen that an ISO 9000-compliant quality system is a documented system that is capable of delivering consistent quality products and/or services *and* in which people consistently function in accordance with the documented system. The obvious method for ensuring that both quality system documentation and the relationship between documentation and behavior remains ISO 9000 compliant is by observing behavior and evaluating documentation. Auditing is the formal process for doing just that.

However, as Holmes noted, just being able to see everything is not enough. Merely observing and evaluating is not enough to ensure that your organization's quality system remains compliant with the ISO 9000 standard. The results of audits must be reviewed, deductions drawn, actions taken based on those deductions—either actions targeted at improvement of an already compliant system and/or actions targeted at correcting deficiencies that heretofore had not been uncovered. In the corporate world, accomplishing that task requires management commitment and support.

At this point, the Dr. Watson in us wants to smile in satisfaction and say something like "Capital, Holmes. Brilliant, old boy." Such a comment would elicit only a sly smile from the Baker Street detective. Holmes would immediately see it as the timid response, for a quality system that relies solely on auditing to inspect quality into the business is no more an acceptable practice than is inspecting quality into products and services. Auditing followed by corrective action is reactive. A truly effective quality system is one that is self-correcting, that is, it is engineered such that information flowing through documented and consistently followed processes cause corrections to be made to the system independent of auditing. Rather than being a tool for ensuring compliance, auditing becomes a tool for ensuring that the self-correcting features of the quality system are working.

THE PURPOSE OF THIS CHAPTER

This chapter covers three main elements of ensuring continuing ISO 9000 compliance: (1) setting up an internal audit program; (2) maintaining management commitment; and (3) making the system self-correcting.

A basic requirement of the ISO 9000 standard is that an organization have in place a systematic internal auditing program. In other words, a third-party registration organization will want to see evidence that the documentation and functioning of the quality system is periodically reviewed in a formal manner, that observations and findings are recorded, that action plans are made, and that those actions are followed up and completed.

Recognizing the wisdom of the ISO 9000 requirement for an internal auditing system, this chapter presents a systematic view of internal auditing: assigning ownership of the auditing system, documenting your internal audit system, creating audit forms, and staffing your internal audit system. However, auditing is but one element of ensuring the continuing ISO 9000 compliant of your quality system. This chapter also addresses the key cultural element of maintaining management commitment to the ISO 9000 process and using both auditing and management commitment to make the quality system self-correcting. In this environment, the primary function of auditing is not looking for noncompliance, but evaluating the self-correcting features of the quality system.

Having first addressed independently the roles of auditing and management commitment to ensuring continuing ISO 9000 compliance, we conclude the chapter by examining how auditing and management commitment function in a self-correcting environment.

SETTING UP AN INTERNAL AUDIT PROGRAM

You will no doubt note some similarities between information in this chapter and Chapter 7, which deals with conducting an internal assessment of your organization's quality system. Indeed, much of what was said about conducting an internal assessment can be applied to internal auditing. What differs is not so much the methodology as the context. Although some people use the terms *audit* and *assessment* interchangeably, we view each in a different context. We refer to an audit, be it an internal audit conducted by people from your organization but outside of the department being audited or an audit conducted by a third party, as a formal, independent review of a quality system. We consider an assessment as a less formal review of a quality system for the intent of improvement.

An obvious question—and one you will no doubt hear at some point in your ISO 9000 registration project—"Why do we have to dedicate resources to internal audits?" It would seem, questioners will reason, that individuals within a department should be able to monitor their own activities and maintain compliance through internal assessments. To a large degree, that is true. Indeed, the innate understanding people have of their own departments was what prompted us in Chapter 7 to endorse an internal assessment as an early step on the path to ISO 9000 registration. However, once a department has conducted an internal assessment and feels that it is ready for ISO 9000 registration, there will be the tendency to believe that all deficiencies have been eliminated. The knowledge of their organization that enables people to make improvements to the quality system also acts like a pair of blinders. People see the obvious, but do not always see the truth. We have seen many real-life examples of this; an example from our experience makes the point clear.

In an engineering department, employees were aware that quality issues were referred to the management staff meeting for resolution. They assumed that referred issues were resolved in an orderly and timely fashion. An independent auditor, looking for continuity of action items from staff meeting to staff meeting, found no traceability of open action items from one meeting to the next. Issues were raised and left to the discretion and good habits of the management attendees of the meeting to resolve. There was no record of the assignment of action items, of their status from meeting to meeting, or of their closure or completion. Upon digging deeper, the independent auditor found issues that had been lost between meetings. There were issues that no manager remembered taking responsibility for, yet that employees thought were being addressed. Clearly, as the audit exposed, perception differed from reality.

By the way, even understanding that you may be too close to issues to see them clearly is no guarantee that you can avoid overlooking details. We found this to be true in the development of our quality manual. Assuming we were too familiar with the material in the quality manual, we were very conscious of looking for details we might have missed. We wrote, reviewed, rewrote, and re-reviewed over and over until we thought we had it perfect. Then we handed the quality manual to someone with an independent viewpoint who found 17 problems in less than an hour! All the problems were obvious once pointed out to us, but because of familiarity and despite all our efforts at objectivity, we completely missed them. Experiences like these made clear to us the value of the ISO 9000 standard that requires that "audits of the quality system, processes, and/or product shall be carried out by personnel independent of those having direct responsibility for the work being performed."[1]

The place to start in setting up an internal audit program is with ownership of the auditing system.

Assigning Ownership of the Auditing System

Regardless of the third-party registration agency you select to work with, your internal audit system will be one of the most closely scrutinized parts of your quality system, not just during the initial registration audit, but at subsequent maintenance audits as well. The functioning of your audit system is a key indicator to third-party auditors of the state of your quality system as a whole.

As such, you should devote sufficient resources to ensuring that your internal auditing program is properly implemented. For most companies, this means that there will be resources dedicated to the audit process. Just how many resources are dedicated depends on the size of the organization and the complexity of the quality process, but at the minimum, it is safe to say there will be at least a single individual who has ownership of the internal audit program. "Ownership" implies that this person should be familiar, if not expert, in internal auditing procedures in general and have very specific understanding of the ISO 9000 standards. Part of the obligations of ownership is continuing education in both these areas.

If you have a person in your organization with auditing skills, then you probably have a ready-made candidate to set up your auditing program. If not, and you can hire someone with the skills and knowledge, the option is well worth considering in light of the total resources your organization will be devoting to ISO 9000. You may also look to consulting organizations for help in setting up your internal audit process. If you elect this route, rely heavily on the consulting firm to help you set up your audit process, but also develop people within your organization to maintain the process once it is in place. Colleges and universities as well as consulting firms provide audit training. Maintaining a database of auditing training classes is a sound idea.

In addition to formal training, there are many good literature resources that describe the quality system auditing function, starting with the ISO 9000 standards themselves. ISO 9001 Section 4.17 describes requirements for quality system auditing. In addition, many governments or standard organizations have developed auditing standards that are helpful. For example, the International Organization for Standardization has an international auditing standard: the *ISO 10011 series.* These documents are also found in the *ISO 9000 Compendium* mentioned in Chapter 2. Many countries have their own quality system auditing standards. In the United States, there is *ASQC/ANSI Q1.* Also, the US Government has published the *USGAO Government Auditing Standards,* which is an excellent source of information about auditing in general that you can tailor to your specific organization.[2]

Besides standards organization literature, many books thoroughly cover the quality systems auditing function. *Management Audits,* by Allan J. Sayle, is a very thorough book about the auditing of management systems that contains several practical examples from the author's experience.[3] *The Quality Audit,* by Charles A. Mills, uses ISO 9000 examples throughout and provides a checklist for the complete ISO 9001 standard.[4] *Quality Audits for Improved Performance,* by Dennis R. Arter, is more concise than the other two books and provides practical advice on preparing the auditing report.[5] These books and others constantly appearing provide good foundational background in quality system auditing concepts and can also supplement other knowledge or practical experience that people in your organization may already have.

The owner of your internal audit process has two primary tasks to accomplish in order to implement the process. The first is documenting the internal audit system, which consists of defining the scope and methods of the internal audit process. Typically, this definition is accomplished through an audit charter, policies, processes, procedures, forms, checklists, and the like. The second task is to ensure that there is a sufficient number of capable, trained, certified auditors to implement the internal audit process.

Documenting Your Internal Audit System

Reviewing the ISO 9000 and military standards and other literature describing quality system auditing, you should have a clear understanding of how your audit system will work. You will further clarify your thinking by preparing written documentation of the system. As was the case with the ISO 9000 registration project plan, the most value you will derive from documenting your quality system audit process will likely be found in the preparation of the documentation. Writing a charter, policies, and procedures forces you to clarify and articulate your thinking. The result is a focused internal auditing process.

Begin your effort by writing an auditing charter. A charter grants the authority for a specific group or individual to carry out a specific function or activity. Your charter should be approved by the company president or all of upper management, should grant the authority to audit, and should set down some responsibilities for both the auditors and the auditees. For example, the charter should state that the auditors have the authority to audit any aspect of the quality system, and the auditees are responsible for cooperating with the auditors and for correcting deficiencies uncovered during audits. A sample audit charter is shown in Figure 9–1.

It is also valuable to have one or more audit policies that state how often audits will be conducted, where and how long audit records will be kept, and what the required qualifications of internal quality systems auditors are. There should definitely be a process or procedure that describes how the auditors will prepare for and carry out an audit, how and when the audit report will be delivered, how and when the auditee must respond to the audit report, and who arbitrates differences of opinions between auditees and auditors.

You may not choose to draft all of these different kinds of documents (charter, policy, and procedure). Some state their authority to audit within their quality manual, and incorporate policy statements within the audit procedure. It doesn't really matter what you call the documents used to describe your audit system as long as the documentation clearly defines the authority and responsibility of both auditors and auditees. Your organization's corporate culture and the documentation structure elected for your quality system will dictate the formal documents you require. For example, if formal charters are not part of your company's culture, don't force an auditing charter upon your culture. Determine where in

FIGURE 9–1
Sample Audit Charter

SAMPLE AUDIT CHARTER

1.0 Purpose

With this charter, executive management establishes a program to review and evaluate the quality system. Such reviews will be carried out by members of quality assurance or by competent independent personnel as designated by quality assurance.

2.0 Statement of Independence

The auditors must be independent of the specific activities or areas audited.

3.0 Authority to Evaluate, Investigate, and Measure Degree of Conformance

Quality assurance will audit and evaluate all elements, aspects, and components pertaining to the quality system on a regular basis. Audits will be carried out in order to determine whether various elements within the quality management system are effective in achieving stated quality objectives. Auditors have the authority to investigate any aspect of the quality system and measure the degree of conformance to specifications. For this purpose, an appropriate audit plan will be formulated by the audit team and coordinated with the auditee.

4.0 Responsibilities in the Corrective Action Process

Quality assurance will be responsible for documenting and submitting audit reports to appropriate members of company management. The report will contain well structured and comprehensive evaluations which include:

1. The overall effectiveness of the quality management system in achieving stated quality objectives.
2. Considerations for updating the quality management system in relation to changes brought about by new technologies, quality concepts, market strategies, and social or environmental conditions.
3. Specific examples of noncompliance or deficiencies; possible reasons for such deficiencies, where evident, may be included.

Permanent changes resulting from corrective action will be recorded in work instructions, processes, product specifications, and/or the quality system. It may also be necessary to revise the procedures used to detect and eliminate potential problems.

Implementation and effectiveness of corrective actions suggested in previous audits will be assessed.

FIGURE 9–1
Sample Audit Charter (Concluded)

5.0 Responsibilities of Functions Audited to Cooperate with and Support the Audit
Each auditee will cooperate with and assist the auditor in the performance of the audit and assume responsibility for any corrective action that may be required.

your culture and documentation structure it is appropriate to define the authority to audit, and define it there.

Creating Audit Forms

Forms used to report your audits are tools that structure how your auditors will carry out their function and should be given some thought. Typical forms consist of an audit report form (Figure 9–2) and a finding form (Figure 9–3).

The audit report form contains places for information about each audit conducted, such as when and where the audit was conducted, what the scope of the audit was, who performed the audit, who was interviewed, a general summation of what was found, and a reference to any associated finding forms.

The finding form contains places for information about each individual finding, such as what was observed, who was present when it was observed, whether the corrective action requires verification, and who is responsible for the corrective action. The finding form also contains an area for the auditee to describe the planned corrective action and places for signatures and dates of the auditee when the corrective action plan is submitted and for the auditor when the corrective action plan is accepted and later verified.

Audit forms can be electronic with no need for paper if you have a system that enables this. If the forms are paper, you should have an explanation, perhaps on the back of each form, of what goes into each box on the form for the benefit of those who must use these forms. This is preferable to describing it in the procedure. Then the procedure needs only to state that each form is filled out according to the instructions on the back of the form.

FIGURE 9–2
Audit Report Form

Audit area	Audit number:
Audit area manager:	Audit type: (area, process, external)
Date auditee notified:	
Date(s) audit conducted:	Closing meeting date:
Lead auditor:	
Co-auditors:	
Basis:	
Scope:	
Checklist:	
People contacted during the audit:	
Number of findings:	
Finding identification numbers:	

FIGURE 9–2
Audit Report Form (Concluded)

Comments:
Signature: (Lead auditor)

You will find it helpful for your auditors to develop some general checklists. Checklists help auditors keep focused when they are interviewing people during an audit. In that regard, checklists are an appropriate audit tool; however, auditors must be instructed not to let the checklists become a substitute for drawing inferences from the audit. Auditors must remain flexible when evidence leads them down a path that a checklist has not anticipated. Checklists used to maintain the focus of an audit, i.e., to keep the auditors focused on the scope and purpose of a particular audit, without restricting the auditors to a particular set of predetermined questions, are extremely valuable.

Once you have documented your internal audit process, you should perform a reasonability check of what you have documented against the auditing section of the applicable ISO 9000 standard, the ISO 10011 Auditing Standard, and your company culture. The reason for checking your system against the ISO 9000 is obvious: you must be compliant with the standard to be registered. The reason for checking against the ISO 10011 Auditing Standard is that it represents an international consensus of generally acceptable criteria for quality system auditing and may eventually replace the ISO 9000 standard requirements for auditing. You are ahead of the game if you comply with ISO 10011 right from the start.

Checking against your company culture makes it as easy as possible for your auditing function to succeed. As discussed in Chapter 3, if plans are at odds with company culture, you have two

FIGURE 9–3
Audit Finding Form

Audit area:	Finding number:
Audit area manager:	Finding type:
Audit number:	
Organization:	
Finding date:	Verification required? Yes or No (*Circle One*)
Description of finding:	
Requirement:	
Lead auditor:	Co-auditor:
Observed by:	
Corrective action plan:	
Estimated Completion Date:	
Committed by:	Date commitment made:
Assigned to:	Date finding closed:

FIGURE 9–3
Audit Finding Form (Concluded)

Plan accepted by:	Date accepted:
Verification description:	
Verified by:	Verification date:

choices—change your plan, or change the culture. The closer you can make your audit function fit your culture, the easier it will be to conduct effective audits. If you have no choice but to change your culture, then at least you will be clear as to what must change and why. Education through training, company newsletters, department meetings, and the like should be targeted at the changes needed in your corporate culture to make your audit function successful.

Staffing Your Internal Audit System

Once your internal audit system is documented, you need to prepare people to implement it. This preparation cannot be completed prior to the documentation because you must not only train people in the ISO 9000 standards and general auditing techniques, but specifically to follow your auditing procedure and use your audit forms. You can't teach people to follow your documented audit system until your audit system is documented.

Members of the team that performed the internal assessments of their own work areas are good candidates for internal auditors. From having performed internal assessments of their own departments, they will have gained an appreciation for the kinds of things that might be wrong with the quality system. They will be able to transfer the knowledge learned in their own areas to other areas that they audit. They will also have a sensitivity to the fear and anxiety that some people will have when being audited. They will have gained a certain amount of humility from discovering the extent to which their own house was not in order. Also, the internal assessors have already been trained in the standard. This will make your job easier when preparing them to be auditors.

You must choose your auditing team carefully, considering candidates' behavior traits as well as skill sets. An auditor's behavior when performing audits determines the characteristics of the audit experience. Consequently, you want people on the audit team who have excellent human relations skills. All the analytical skills in the world will not compensate for an auditor whose actions during an audit degrade, belittle, or intimidate those being audited. The purpose of the audit is not to intimidate the auditees, but to help them discover where to make useful improvements to the quality system. You want auditors who are cordially inquisitive, who can dig and probe without offending auditees, who are looking for facts, not faults, who can be assertive without being aggressive, who can disagree without being disagreeable, and who can make judgments without being judgmental.

There is an old joke about auditors that goes: "Arguing with a QA auditor is like wrestling with a pig in the mud—after awhile you begin to realize that the pig enjoys it." What do auditors who love to argue and pigs who love to mud wrestle have in common? Neither belongs on an audit team. One quick way to undermine the effectiveness of your audit program is to make the auditing experience unpleasant for the auditees.

People who do not possess appropriate auditing traits naturally must be educated in appropriate auditing behavior. Auditor training should not just cover the ISO 9000 standards and operational items like filling out an audit report; it should also cover methods of questioning, kinds of questions to ask and avoid, and behavioral skills to exhibit.

Auditors must also realize that there is no one best method of compliance. The methods used in an auditor's own department may work fine there, but are not the standard that is being audited against. They are a response to the standard, but there are other equally valid responses. Internal auditors must realize that the solution they helped implement in their own work area is not the only viable solution. For example, if an auditor's department logs corrective actions into an electronic logbook, he or she must not raise a finding against a department for using a physical logbook for the same purpose.

We have purposely discussed the behavioral aspects of training for auditors first because behavioral training is often overlooked when setting up an internal auditing process. It is important to recognize the critical role developing a proper attitude in your auditors plays in the success of your internal audit program. Nonetheless, we would be remiss if we didn't equally stress the importance of ensuring that your internal auditors are well versed in auditing principles in general and auditing to the ISO 9000 standards in particular.

If you recruit your internal assessors as auditors, you will have already trained them on the ISO 9000 standards. Nonetheless, during your auditing training, you should review the ISO 9000 standards to ensure that all your auditors are in general agreement about how to interpret the various sections. If you have others who are joining your internal assessors as auditors, you should have a separate longer session on the ISO 9000 standards for the uninitiated. Then you can combine the two groups for the common overview and behavior training.

Training should also cover your organization's audit procedure and the responsibilities of the auditors, lead auditors, audit manager, and auditees. Each auditor or lead auditor must clearly understand his or her role during the audit. You should also go over the forms and checklists to be used.

Portions, or all, of the audit training may be conducted by an internal expert or by an outside consultant. You may have some or all of your auditors trained outside the company. With the externally trained people, you must still cover the ground rules for audits within your company, e.g., your procedure, forms, and expected behaviors. At the end of your training, you want to have auditors who will consistently follow your procedure, use your forms, apply the ISO 9000 standards, and as much as possible raise the same findings as any other auditor on your team in the same situation.

A part of the training will be observation. Newly trained auditors will need some guidance and feedback, especially during their first audits. This feedback may be provided by your internal audit expert or a consultant. The guidance and feedback is on-the-job training, an extension of the classroom training.

We recommend that all internal auditors be internally certified. You may set the criteria for this certification at a level of sophistication that you feel is appropriate for your organization. The ISO 9000 standards do not specifically state that formal internal auditor certification is required, only that you "assign trained personnel for verification activities,"[6] and auditing is mentioned as a verification activity. For example, you may require that to become certified each auditor must take your internal auditor training class (or be trained externally in an approved course) and conduct one audit under the supervision of an internally certified lead auditor. Whether you chose to certify your internal auditors or not, be sure that their audit training is recorded in your company training records as verification that they have the skills required to conduct internal audits as required by the ISO 9000 standard: "personnel performing specific assigned tasks shall be qualified on the basis of appropriate education, training, and/or experience, as required. Appropriate records of training shall be maintained."[7]

MAINTAINING MANAGEMENT COMMITMENT

It is a basic requirement of the ISO 9000 standards that management be involved with the quality system. They must define and communicate the company's quality policy, define the organizational structure including responsibilities and authorities of individuals working within the organization, and ensure that defined positions are staffed with competent personnel. They must also periodically review the effectiveness of the quality system. These are the first requirements listed in the standards and fall under the major heading of "Management Responsibility." Beyond what the standard requires, management commitment is a critical success factor for registration and for continuing compliance.

Commitment means active involvement. In Chapter 4 we described the manifestation of active involvement as visible behaviors, i.e., specific actions that management takes that both contribute to the ISO 9000 registration effort and at the same time are visible to employees who become encouraged, if not inspired, by the example being set. You should not take management commitment or any other critical success factor for granted. Neither should you stand in the background, wringing your hands and whining to all who will listen that you can only be successful when management decides to become actively involved in the ISO 9000 project. Management commitment is not a given. It does not happen by fiat. You must plan for it and cause it to happen.

Planning for management commitment was introduced in Chapter 4. It is mentioned again here because management commitment plays as important a role in ensuring continuing ISO 9000 compliance as it does to gaining registration in the first place. The two operative ideas are *gain* and *retain.* As an ISO 9000 project leader or team member, you must prepare and execute a plan to gain management commitment to an ISO 9000 compliant quality system as necessary for registration. You must also prepare and execute a plan to retain management commitment to the ISO 9000-compliant quality system after registration. The desired commitment results from planning activities that management must execute, which when executed will demonstrate their commitment.

Whatever forum was used by executive management to address overall quality system issues prior to ISO 9000 registration, such as establishing quality policy, should be continued after registration. For example, if executive management formed a quality steering team for the purpose of defining the quality policy or policies and addressing resource requirements for the project, this team should continue to meet. Perhaps the meetings will not be as frequent. They may occur weekly prior to registration and bimonthly, or even monthly, afterwards. The point is, the quality steering team should continue to meet. Continue to use this forum to go beyond the requirements of the ISO 9000 standard. It is a part of your quality system infrastructure, put in place during the ISO 9000 registration effort, that can be used to move your organization onward to total quality management principles.

In Chapter 5, we talked about a secondary agenda in the management presentation of the ISO 9000 project plan. One item on that agenda was creating an environment for continuous quality improvement. Oftentimes, the ISO 9000 registration project becomes a vehicle for other changes to the quality system that, strictly speaking, are not necessary for ISO 9000 registration. Such changes advance the quality system beyond the strict requirements of the ISO 9000 standards. An ISO 9000–compliant quality system is a giant step from no system at all, but is several giant leaps and bounds from quality systems deployed in world class companies. The communication vehicles, teams, forums, and other infrastructures of the ISO 9000 project can continue to be used to move the company forward after registration.

However, even if your company does not wish to improve its quality system beyond compliance to the ISO 9000 standards, there is still a need for a forum like the executive management quality steering team. The standards themselves change. Minor revisions to the 1987 standards have already occurred, and more significant changes to the standards are planned for distribution before the end of the decade. These changes will require a rethinking of how a company's quality system stacks up against the changed standards.

More frequently than the ISO 9000 standards change, a company's quality system will change to address other varying business factors, such as the use of electronic versus physical documentation, changing requirements of the marketplace in which the company does business, and changes in governmental regulations. As each of these changes is proposed, the company needs to evaluate from the top down how such changes are to be implemented and what these changes mean to the company's quality policy and to the further compliance of its quality system to the ISO 9000 standards.

The quality steering team forum mentioned above is the place for *proactive* response—planned changes to the quality system brought about by changes in the work environment, marketplace, government regulation, or the ISO 9000 standards themselves. The forum for *reactive* response is the management review. The ISO 9000 standards require that a company's management periodically review the quality system for "suitability and effectiveness."[8] Internal and external quality system audit findings, product or service quality metrics, and customer feedback from surveys or complaints all feed into this forum. The purpose of management reviews is to highlight chronic problem areas and trends and assign actions to ensure that remedial and corrective action is taken.

ISO 8402 defines "preventive action" as, "an action taken to eliminate the causes of a potential nonconformity, defect, or other undesirable situation in order to prevent *occurrence*" and "corrective action" as, "an action taken to eliminate the causes of a potential nonconformity, defect, or other undesirable situation in order to prevent *recurrence*."[9] Preventive action is taken before there is a problem; corrective action is taken afterward. Preventive action is taken in proactive response forums like quality steering teams. Corrective action is taken in reactive response forums like management review meetings. Once a problem has been found, action is taken to eliminate its root cause so it does not occur again. We use the term "remedial action" to mean action taken to fix an immediate problem, and this type of action may also be taken in reactive response forums.

For example, if a customer complains that a product was damaged beyond use in shipment, a remedial action would be to ship the customer another product. If the root cause of the problem was that the company's procedure for shipping that product called for a package that was insufficiently sturdy, then a corrective action would be to change the procedure to require a sturdier package. If the procedure had been reviewed and changed to use the proper packaging prior to any shipments, this would constitute preventive action.

For continuing ISO 9000 compliance, management must be involved in both proactive and reactive forums, and their roles should be clearly defined. In the proactive forum, management's role is to develop and deploy the company's values. Management will continue to improve and communicate to the employees the values of the company as they did with the quality policy. They will also instigate, approve, and provide resources for other projects and programs that will help deploy the values. An example of this is to decide that working in teams is a company value and then approving a training program focused at teaching and encouraging employees to work in teams.

In the reactive forum, management's role is to evaluate the current system and provide resources for correcting its deficiencies.

Management's role is not to plan new programs and make new thrusts, but to evaluate if current programs are working. They should assign responsibility for and provide resources for correcting areas of the quality system that are obviously not working. An example of this is the approval of a training program focused on teaching employees to perform functions whose omission has resulted in quality problems.

Although in both of these examples training was decided upon as the solution, in the first case it was a proactive choice, while in the second it was a reactive choice. The combination of proactive advancement of the quality system followed by reactive correction is akin to a space program satellite launch. The main rocket boosters that launch the satellite from the launching pad provide proactive advancement, i.e., the satellite atop the rocket is propelled into space according to a carefully laid-out plan. The small engines on the satellite that allow it to make course alterations as it travels in its orbit provide reactive correction.

When someone is named to a management position, they do not automatically acquire *a priori* the complete set of knowledge and skills to do the job. Even if they did, when you create a new forum in which to operate, you must not assume that they know more about that forum than you do! The ISO 9000 project must communicate to management their proactive and reactive responsibilities, the forums in which these responsibilities are carried out, and the role that management plays in these forums. The ISO 9000 project manager who assumes that it is sufficient to call a meeting and the attending managers will take to it like ducks to water, knowing and performing their roles in perfect harmony, will be amazed at how little gets accomplished in so great an amount of time.

Rather, when you create a forum, take time at the first meeting to explain the purpose of the forum, where it fits into the system, and what the roles and responsibilities of those participating in the forum are. You should use the first few meetings to devise a formal charter statement. It works best if you as the expert create a charter and then let the members of the forum alter and improve upon it. It is important to establish the ground rules before conducting the business of the forum. When everyone knows why they are participating in the meetings and what is expected of them, meetings will run more smoothly and be more productive than if people have to guess why they are there. Through the productive use of the proactive and reactive forums, you can maintain management commitment to (active involvement with) the quality system and help ensure its continuing ISO 9000 compliance.

MAKING THE SYSTEM SELF-CORRECTING

Of the three main elements of ensuring continuing ISO 9000 compliance, making the quality system self-correcting is the one most often overlooked. Auditing is important and management commitment essential, but a self-corrective system is a delight because of the company resources it saves.

In the previous section we talked a great deal about management's role in the reactive forum of the management review. This role is to ensure that the quality system is working and to correct any deficiencies. The reactive role can be formidable and time-consuming, requiring several management review meetings a year if the system breaks easily and relies solely on this forum for correction. Besides, a system that relies solely on its management reviews for correction would be a great drain on valuable company resources.

The managers' typical role in the management review meetings is to take responsibility for problems that require resources from their part of the company. They then return to their departments, delegate responsibility for corrective actions to those closest to the problems, track progress made toward correction, often in departmental staff meetings, and assure that the corrective actions are taken. Do you really want your company vice presidents wrestling with the problem of why a box of parts made it through incoming inspection without being verified? The answer to this question is no. You address the question by building self-correction into your quality system.

The action of establishing the self-corrective system and integrating it into the day-to-day business of the company is a proactive effort that tinkers with the infrastructure of the quality system. Self-correction is based on a policy that when there is a problem in the quality system, the owner of the problem takes both remedial and corrective action. In many cases, the owner of the problem is the owner of the procedure or process where the problem originated. It is then this person's responsibility for taking remedial and corrective action.

In some cases, the problem occurs at the boundary between procedures or processes. If the boundary is owned by one person, such as when it is the boundary between two procedures owned by the same person, then that person is responsible for taking remedial and corrective action. When the boundary is between procedures owned by two different people, ownership is not so clear. If the two procedures are within the same division of the company, such as manufacturing or engineering, ownership can be defined at the lowest level of management in that division that is common to both procedure owners. For example, if the problem occurred at the boundary of procedures owned by the manager of software development and the manager of acceptance testing, the owner of the problem would be the director of engineering to whom both of the managers reported. The two procedure owners could escalate the problem to the director of engineering, perhaps in a staff meeting, so that remedial and corrective action could be assigned to an appropriate person or team.

If the two procedures are owned by people within different divisions of the company, e.g., customer services and marketing, the lowest level of management common to both procedure owners would be the company president. You could escalate this problem all the way up to the president's staff meeting for the assignment to an appropriate person or team, but this is as inefficient as having the president sign for the purchase of paper clips. Instead, the problem could be escalated to the quality assurance function, which would take responsibility for assembling a cross-functional team to address the problem.

Whether the two procedure owners are in the same division or not, a better solution is to have the two owners work the remedial and corrective action out between themselves or assemble a team to address it without escalating it at all. Whatever approach is taken, the approach needs to be clearly defined as a part of the quality system, and more importantly, must become a part of the company culture.

Rather than putting a drain on company resources by having executive management review all problems and assign responsibility for remedial and corrective action, there is a more appropriate and efficient use of their time. In the proactive forum, they could define a policy that requires remedial and corrective action to be taken by the owner of the process or procedure where the problem originated, or jointly by the owners of the processes or procedures that comprise a boundary where the problem occurred. An individual, or more likely a cross-functional team, could then be assigned to implement a methodology to carry out this policy.

Such implementation may involve a set of forms or an electronic system for logging such problems, and a companywide procedure for taking remedial and corrective action including the use of the logging function. The logging function helps those working on the problem as they clearly define the problem, determine the root cause, and record the planned steps for resolution and any actions required by specific individuals. As actions are assigned and taken, the logging function is used to assure that all required actions are carried out. After the fact, the logging function is the record of what was done to resolve the problem.

Deploying such a methodology into the culture requires communication. This communication may take many forms, such as a memo from the executive staff, an article in the company newsletter, training sessions on the use of the corrective action procedure and the logging system, or discussions at department meetings. Any or all of these or other forms of communication may be used. The purpose of this communication is to convey the value, purpose, and methodology of the corrective action system being deployed by the company.

Once such a self-correcting methodology is in place, the reactive forum becomes a review of how well the self-correcting system is working. Instead of reviewing each and every problem with the system as a whole, trends in problem correction, and exceptional problems that the self-correcting system did not handle well or at all, are reviewed. Rather than involving executive management in the resolutions of all problems with the quality system, their time is used more productively in fine-tuning the self-correcting part of the system so that the vast majority of problems are corrected by the quality system itself.

By the time you have addressed the issues described in this chapter, you have done as much for your quality system as you can internally. It is time to have your quality system reviewed from outside the company. A safe way to do this is by inviting a third-party assessment agency to conduct a preregistration assessment. Preparing for a preregistration assessment is the topic of Chapter 10.

THE NCR EXPERIENCE

We established an understanding of quality system auditing very early in our registration effort. In fact, we were learning about auditing months before we actually prepared an ISO 9000 registration plan. We were among the first few companies in our region to be registered to the ISO 9000 standards. Today, you can find dozens of competent and experienced consultants to assist you. At the time we established our internal audit program, we could find no external expertise conveniently available to help us. We established our internal audit program by drawing upon resources within our own company.

We learned the standard from the National Standards Authority of Ireland at a seminar in Boston. We combined our knowledge and experience of auditing with our understanding of the standard and established our internal audit program, staffed with one full-time lead auditor and 10 internally trained part-time auditors who had full-time jobs doing something else. We also relied heavily on the books about auditing mentioned earlier in this chapter, both for our own understanding and in preparing training for our internal auditors.

Our full-time auditor became our ISO 9000 auditing expert, eventually acquiring certified lead auditor status. He performed most of the audits and was the caretaker of our auditing function. The part-time auditors simply conducted audits as required. We have subsequently deployed auditing into the company business units and have eliminated the single-focused lead auditor function.

We established an audit charter, similar to the example shown in Figure 9–1, and an audit process. We also developed general checklists and audit report forms. These materials were used in our internal auditor training classes. Each internal auditor was certified by taking our class, conducting an audit under the tutelage of another certified internal auditor, and passing a proficiency exam. The majority of our internal auditors were the department champions that had led their own areas to become compliant with the standards. Our auditor training very heavily stressed the human side of auditing and we worked with our auditors to ensure that they presented themselves amiably.

We established the leadership role for our management from the first management review meeting, which we held after the internal assessment. The ownership of each finding from the internal assessment was assigned to a member of the executive staff. Even today, each finding from the external audits of our registration agency is assigned to a member of the executive staff. Our quality steering team, comprised of executive management, has continued to meet long after ISO 9000 registration. This forum was used to establish a customer satisfaction survey program conducted by volunteer employees, a quality recognition program, and other functions beyond the scope of our ISO 9000 registration.

Closed Loop Corrective Action (CLCA) is a term built into the process management concept taught throughout NCR Corporation. This idea is built into our customer complaint handling system, our manufacturing problem solving efforts, and other process related functions. CLCA has essentially the same definition as the term corrective action, defined earlier in the chapter. The closed loop idea is that you fix the process by eliminating the root cause of a problem, so that the problem will not reoccur. The idea originated in closed loop feedback systems, which by nature are self-correcting. Hence, CLCA at NCR is the self-correcting mechanism of our quality system.

SECTION

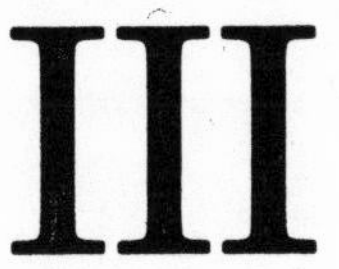

III

THE ISO 9000 REGISTRATION PROCESS

Chapter Ten

Preparing for a Preregistration Assessment by a Third Party

If you're a bird, be an early early bird—but if you're a worm sleep late.

Shel Silverstein
Early Bird

Some time ago, the pilot of a small aircraft took off from an airport, only to discover that some of the airplane's control surfaces were externally locked in place. Control surfaces are the movable external sections of the aircraft that allow it to maneuver up and down, right or left, or to bank in a turn. The most common aircraft control surfaces are the elevator, the rudder, and the ailerons. These control surfaces are sometimes locked in place with pins or vises when an aircraft is parked to protect them from being whipped about in strong winds. With some innovation and the production of prodigious portions of perspiration the pilot was able to nurse the aircraft, not gracefully, but successfully, back down to the ground. The conclusion, though a happy one in this case, could have been fatal.

This situation need never have occurred. Every pilot is taught to conduct a preflight assessment of the air worthiness of an aircraft prior to flying it. At a minimum, the free movement of the control surfaces should be checked along with other important items like engine performance, and proper instrument functioning. In the above case, the pilot skipped the preflight assessment. There are literally hundreds of incidents in the annals of flight accidents and mishaps where pilots have skipped the preflight assessment with disastrous or fatal results.

The preregistration assessment of a quality system by an independent third party is similar to the preflight assessment of an aircraft. The main purpose of a preflight assessment is for the pilot to judge whether an aircraft is ready to fly. The main purpose of a preregistration assessment is for the third-party registration agency to judge whether your quality system is ready to fly, that is, will it be ready for the registration assessment at the time indicated on your schedule. Rather than waiting until the registration assessment to find out you are not really ready, you can be an "early early bird" and discover if your registration target date is realistic by conducting a preregistration assessment.

THE PURPOSE OF THIS CHAPTER

We are strong believers in the value of a preregistration assessment. In this chapter we explain the rationale for that position, why we believe that having a preregistration assessment of your organization's quality system is a valuable exercise. We look at what a preregistration assessment is and is not and what you should expect to gain from one. We talk about the things that your organization will need to do to prepare for (and get the most out of) a preregistration assessment. An important aspect of this chapter is communication to the organization, both before and after the preregistration assessment is held.

PREREGISTRATION ASSESSMENT—WHAT IS IT REALLY?

A preregistration assessment is typically a scaled-down assessment, performed by the third-party registration agency, prior to the registration assessment. For example, if the registration assessment takes 12 assessor-days, the preregistration assessment may take only 2 assessor-days. Because fewer assessors participate for fewer days in a preregistration assessment, a smaller portion of the quality system is assessed. During the preregistration assessment, the assessors evaluate your quality system and give you a report of their findings. They do *not* assume ownership of your quality system and propose solutions to the problems found. Neither do they prescribe courses of action for you to take.

The last two points are important because there is considerable debate about preregistration assessments. Some argue that they are too expensive to be valuable. Others argue that it is unethical for registration agencies to conduct them because in so doing they are acting as consultants—a violation of their independent role during a registration assessment. Let's look at each of the objections in more detail.

Too expensive? You must weigh the price your registration agency will charge you against the perceived risk you are taking by going directly to the registration assessment with no external look at your quality system. Some registration agencies do not like to conduct preregistration assessments and charge a premium for them. You should consider the fee for this assessment as a part of your evaluation of registration agencies. For consistency, we feel it is preferable to use the same agency for your preregistration assessment and your registration assessment. Many of the benefits outlined below are predicated on the assumption that the same agency will be used for both. However, if cost is the only barrier to conducting your preregistration assessment, consider hiring a local consultant whose travel fees are less than those of your registration agency.

Unethical? It would be unethical for a registration agency to consult with you on the development of your quality system and then register that system for compliance to the ISO 9000 standards. Unfortunately, many of the arguments about the lack of ethics of preregistration assessments quote people from registered companies who have, through no more than a careless use of terminology, misrepresented the purpose of preregistration assessments. Some have used the term *consulting* to describe what their third-party assessment agency did on a preregistration assessment. Others have described it as a *guarantee* of registration. Neither of these statements is accurate when applied to reputable, accredited third-party assessment agencies. Because an organization is said to be consulting does not mean it is. If consulting consists of performing an assessment of the company's quality system, submitting a report of the findings of the assessment, and rendering an opinion on the suitability of a proposed corrective action to address a particular nonconformance, then this is no more consulting than what these agencies do on any other visit.

A preregistration assessment is a guarantee of a successful registration only in that it will help you find additional problems in your quality system that you have overlooked, which you may then correct prior to the registration assessment. In this regard, it certainly improves your chances of being registered on your first registration assessment visit. However, it is not a guarantee in the sense of a 100 percent assurance, no matter how many well-meaning, but careless, comments to the contrary are made by enthusiastic, successful ISO 9000 registration project champions. We know of several organizations that have conducted preregistration assessments only to fail their initial registration assessment, even though the same agency performed both assessments.

WHY CONDUCT A PREREGISTRATION ASSESSMENT?

If a preregistration assessment is not a guarantee of a successful registration assessment, why conduct one? Because, even if it provides no guarantee, it significantly increases your chances for success. There are seven benefits that you can gain from a preregistration assessment: 1) it determines your readiness for a registration assessment; 2) it gives you areas to improve before the registration assessment; 3) it gives you an opportunity to get feedback on areas where your confidence is low; 4) it allows you to validity-check proposed corrections to the quality system; 5) it lets you observe the assessment methodologies of the third-party agency; 6) it gives you insight into how your assessment agency views the ISO 9000 standards; and 7) it makes the project much more real to the employees of your company.

Determining your readiness for registration. As mentioned in the introduction to this chapter, the primary purpose of the preregistration assessment is to determine if you will be ready for the scheduled registration assessment. The registration agency will be able to tell by assessing your quality system and its documentation whether your quality system adequately covers the ISO 9000 standard to which you desire to be registered. If you have no internal audit system, or have not established a calibration system, you will not be ready for ISO 9001 or ISO 9002 registration in the near future. These gaping holes in the system will be obvious to you. There are more subtle indicators of failure, though, that you may miss. You may have established a documentation control system that seems functional to you, but during the preregistration assessment it may be discovered to be totally inadequate. One outcome of the preregistration assessment is to determine either that the remainder of your plan is viable, or that you have to adjust it by altering the schedule, the resources, or the work effort as described in Chapter 3.

Determining areas to improve. Any findings from the preregistration assessment will help you direct corrective action at areas that would cause you to fail the registration assessment. The results of the preregistration assessment are usually presented as a report that catalogues the findings of the assessment. This report lists those areas that require corrective action. Provided that your corrective action is adequate, you will increase your chances for success during the registration assessment. Taking corrective action on the nonconformities will also demonstrate to your assessment agency, when they return for the assessment visit, that your personnel are responsive to the discovery of problems in the system.

Feedback on areas of low confidence. As you prepare your quality system for ISO 9000 registration, you will be very confident about the compliance of some areas and not so confident about others. The preregistration assessment will give you an opportunity to hold up the areas in which you have low confidence to the scrutiny of an assessment. If the system is adequate in the areas you are unsure of, your confidence in it will increase. If it does not hold up to the assessment, your confidence in your ability to determine what is marginal will increase, and you can correct the system before the registration assessment.

Validity-checking proposed corrections. In the areas where problems are found, either because you discovered them via your own audits, or because they were found during the preregistration assessment, you will have the opportunity to ask a third-party assessor to look at the proposed solutions to those problems. What you will determine is whether the representatives of your assessment agency view your proposed solutions adequate in making your system compliant with the ISO 9000 standards.

"Aha!" say the anti-preregistrationists, "here is where you get them to consult." Not at all. You are not asking them to propose solutions, to pass judgment on whether your approach is as good as others they have seen, or to perform any other consulting activity. You are asking them to give their professional opinion as assessors on whether proposed corrections to your quality system will make it compliant with the ISO 9000 standards in areas where it is not now compliant. This approach is not only ethical, it is also wise. It makes no sense to waste company resources on a correction that will not solve the problem.

Observing the assessment methodologies of the third-party agency. It is a valuable preregistration assessment activity to observe how assessors from the third-party assessment agency conduct themselves during an assessment. What kinds of questions do they ask? Is there a pattern to how they assess? What do they consider to be objective evidence? What areas are of greatest concern to them? How do they relate to your people? How do your people relate to them? Do they look at the documentation first, or do they ask people what they do first?

Everything you can determine about how your third-party assessors actually perform an assessment is valuable to you. This information will help you take the mystery out of the registration assessment. We suggest that you train the people of your company prior to the registration assessment about how the assessment will be conducted using information gleaned during the preregistration assessment. Later in the current chapter we will discuss adjusting your own audit program based on what you learn during the preregistration assessment.

Determining how the assessment agency views the ISO 9000 standards. The ISO 9000 standards are not very wordy. The declarative portion of the most extensive of the contractual standards, ISO 9001, is only six pages long. Those six pages cover the design, production, and servicing of everything from electronic devices to lingerie, from computer software to bakery goods, and from the trucking industry to health care. Consequently, the standards are open to a certain amount of interpretation. Perhaps we would like to believe that this should not be so, but it is.

For example, one third-party agency believes that the management representative should be mentioned by name in the quality manual. Others do not care. One agency would like internal audits to be conducted with little advance notice. Others believe that an audit schedule should be published well in advance. Even within agencies there are some differences of opinion between assessors, but the agencies attempt to minimize this through training, evaluation, and consensus of assessors during the assessment visits. One benefit of the preregistration assessment is that you can learn how your third-party assessment agency views the standards. This will help you make adjustments in your quality system to accommodate your agency's interpretations. In the end, you are compliant when the agency says you are. Its interpretation of the standards is the one that counts. The sooner you learn what it is, the sooner you can adjust to it.

The project becomes real to your people. Strangely, many people seem to share the attitude, "because I know you, you can't be that great." This attitude is expressed in the maxims "familiarity breeds contempt" and "a prophet is not without honor, save in his own country." The way this attitude expresses itself in the ISO 9000 registration project is that some will not feel that you, as the project champion or as a member of the implementation team, are highly credible, because you work for the same company that they do. As if their knowing you reduces your value, somehow. When the third-party registration assessors appear and make essentially the same statements that you have made, suddenly those statements become more credible. Apart from this phenomena, the project will become more real to everyone in your company because of the preregistration assessment. Prior to this time, all of the activity has been internal, perhaps with the assistance of consultants. Now that the agency with the authority to register you to the ISO 9000 standards has come on the scene, the project takes on a new sense of urgency.

PREPARING FOR THE PREREGISTRATION ASSESSMENT

Like all of the other major events of the ISO 9000 registration project, in order to *have* a successful preregistration assessment, you must *plan to have* a successful preregistration assessment. The first two of Stephen Covey's seven basic principles of effectiveness are to be proactive and to begin with the end in mind.[1] Long before the preregistration assessment, proactively plan for it. Begin by determining what you want to gain from it. Using the list of benefits given previously in this chapter, determine how you can use the preregistration assessment to reap the most from those benefits.

Schedule the Preregistration Assessment

The most opportune time to schedule the preregistration assessment is about three to six months prior to the registration assessment. This will give you sufficient time to take corrective action on the findings of the preregistration assessment. If you have taken appropriate corrective action to the problems found in your internal assessment and independent audits, three to six months is about all the time it will take to fill in any holes found.

The exact amount of time you allot between the preregistration and registration assessments depends on factors such as the size of your organization and your estimation of its responsiveness to findings. Usually smaller organizations can react more quickly, especially if training is required. Third-party assessors need to see evidence of a system working properly before they can recommend registration. If you have major changes to make after the preregistration assessment, you can't implement these the day before the assessors arrive for the registration assessment, or there will be no evidence to see. Three to six months will probably be sufficient for most organizations to develop evidence of compliance.

Let your registration assessment agency know during your initial contact with them that you plan on conducting a preregistration assessment and the time you would like to schedule it. Get them to commit, at least verbally, that they can accommodate you. With the increase in popularity of the ISO 9000 standards and the demand being made on registration agencies, make sure you get in the queue early. Get a confirmed date from them as early as possible both for the preregistration assessment as well as the registration assessment. The third-party assessment agency will usually not confirm the registration assessment visit date until after the preregistration assessment has been completed and they have determined when you will be ready.

Get Your Own House in Order

Section II of this book gives you guidance in getting your own house in order. Before the preregistration assessment, make your quality system as compliant as you can. In Chapter 7, we made the point that it is desirable to allow a department to make itself ready prior to an independent internal audit because the department can better determine what needs to be done initially. Then the independent internal audit can be used to fine-tune the result, rather than laboriously trying to find all of the problems that the department already knows are there.

You do not have to reach a state of perfection prior to conducting the preregistration assessment. You will never reach perfection, not even before the registration assessment. Before conducting the preregistration assessment, make your initial internal assessment and correct the deficiencies found. Then conduct independent internal audits of all of the major functional areas of the company against the entire standard and correct the deficiencies found in these audits. Following this is an opportune time to conduct the preregistration assessment. It is not necessary to wait until all of the deficiencies found in the independent internal audits are corrected, but at least have corrective action plans in place. The more of these you have completed, the better, but since you often have to schedule the third-party assessors several weeks in advance, you may not have them all done.

This progression is the intent of the ISO 9000 standards. They do not proscribe a system that relies on external assessments to maintain compliance. They do proscribe a system that is self-contained and monitored by an independent internal audit program.

Plan What Will Be Assessed

In order to derive maximum benefit from the preregistration assessment, plan the agenda. This is acceptable to most registration agencies. They may have certain things they want to look at in order to determine if you will be ready for the registration assessment, but are usually quite willing to follow your guidance.

First, make sure that the entire standard is assessed. Don't just concentrate on a few major areas of the standard, but look at all of it. Any part of the standard that is not adequately addressed by your quality system will cause you to fail your registration assessment. The more the external assessors understand about how you address the standard, the better able they will be to determine your readiness for the registration assessment.

Second, to the extent that they fall within the scope of your registration, make sure that all of the major, and many of the supporting, areas of the company are assessed. You may limit the scope of your registration. For example, you may register to ISO 9001, which includes servicing, but limit the scope of the registration to service functions provided by the headquarters office, rather than including all of your field service offices in the scope. The scope must be clearly stated on your certificate of registration. You want to ensure that the areas within the scope of registration are reviewed during the preregistration assessment. For example, if you design both hardware and software products, have the assessors look at both a hardware design project and a software design project because these will follow similar but different design processes under the same area of the standard.

Third, make sure the assessors look at the areas with which you have the least confidence. These are the areas that you think are compliant with the standards, but are not absolutely sure. Maybe you have a difference of opinion among members of your implementation team of department champions, or maybe you believe your interpretation of the standard in some areas may be different from what the assessors will think. Resolve these questions during the preregistration assessment so that you will have time to correct them before the registration assessment.

Finally, we recommend that you direct the assessors to look at any area, within the scope of your registration, that has been essentially uncooperative with the ISO 9000 registration project. The purpose for doing this is not retaliatory, but practical. Any such area could cause you to fail the registration assessment. You want the problems and attitudes of that area brought to light while there is still time to fix them. Based upon the experience of several who have applied this tactic, the uncooperative area usually responds, often quite dramatically, to the scrutiny and findings of the external assessors. These areas do not want the negative publicity of becoming the sole reason for the failure of a full registration assessment.

Inform Your People about the Preregistration Assessment

Prepare the people of your organization for the preregistration assessment. In a small company, you can do this in a single meeting. In a larger company, you may not wish to hold meetings with all employees, but rather use a company newspaper, or a memo, or electronic mail. Communication is a part of your plan, so plan to communicate prior to the preregistration assessment.

The main purpose of communicating with your people is to remove the fear associated with the external assessors coming into your organization. Let your people know who this external agency is, how many assessors will be coming, when they are coming, and why. Let them know that this is an assessment of the quality *system,* not of the people who use it. Let them know that the assessors are not trying to catch anyone doing anything wrong, but are trying to determine the readiness of the system to withstand a registration assessment.

The preregistration assessment visit will set the stage for the relationship between the people of your organization and the assessors. The importance of this relationship is covered more fully in Chapter 12, but you want that relationship to be as cordial as possible. This is why you must emphasize hospitality and cordiality in the message to your people.

Tell them that the external assessors are your guests, invited there to help you improve. Inform them that the assessors may select them to answer some questions. This they should do honestly and completely. Emphasize that you want the assessors to have a clear and accurate picture of the quality system before they leave so they can point you to the areas that need correcting prior to the registration assessment.

If your people get nothing else from your communication, they should get the message: "The assessors are not here to do me any harm; they are our guests and I should treat them accordingly."

A Final Meeting

At the conclusion of the preregistration assessment, the assessors will inform you of their findings. We feel that it is best to have them present the findings to your executive management. This gives your executive management a first-hand look at the findings as they are presented by the third-party assessors and it shows the third-party assessors that your management cares about the results.

AFTER THE PREREGISTRATION ASSESSMENT

No sooner is the preregistration assessment completed than it is time to communicate again. This time you need to communicate the results of the assessment. Your executive management should hear the results of the assessment first. If they do not attend a wrap-up meeting, as suggested above, then you should present the results to them. You should give each executive manager a copy of the findings that affects his or her area and require a corrective action response within some set time, like two weeks.

You should also communicate the general results to all employees. You have raised their curiosity during the communication just prior to the arrival of the assessors—now tell them the outcome. What are the good points, where are the areas for opportunity? Will the project continue on schedule? How did we do? These are the things they want to know. To reinforce the ideas of hospitality and cordiality, you can publicly thank those who were participants in the assessment for expressing these sentiments to the assessors.

Generalize the findings by determining if each particular conformity exists in other areas besides the one in which it was found. For example, if the assessors found that action items at some particular review meeting were not traceable through to completion, see if that is the case with other review meetings. Plan and carry out corrective actions for all findings including those that have been generalized. Your intent is to eradicate from your quality system any problem found by the assessors and any other problem like it anywhere else in the system.

As the quality system is corrected, keep objective evidence showing that it now works properly. When the assessors return to perform the registration assessment, they will be able to see that you have been diligent to correct all nonconformities they found at the preregistration visit.

From your observations of the assessors' methods and findings, tune your internal auditing system. You can incorporate any good practices or techniques that you have learned from the assessors into your own program. You can also modify the program to look for the kinds of things that the assessors just found. This will help you ensure that the corrective actions are working. You should also tune your understanding of the standard to what you learned about it from the assessors. As mentioned earlier, the standard is subject to a certain amount of interpretation. It is to your advantage to make your internal auditing program interpret the standard in the same manner as the external assessors do.

The actions described above are a part of the next step in the process of becoming registered—preparing for the ISO 9000 registration assessment. These actions and many more are necessary to get ready for the focal point of the ISO 9000 registration project. Preparation for this important event is the subject of Chapter 11.

THE NCR EXPERIENCE

Being the first NCR development and production facility to become registered to the ISO 9001 standard, and one of the first companies in our region to seek registration, we had very little practical experience to draw upon to assure us that our understanding of the ISO 9000 standards was correct. The preregistration assessment experience was very beneficial, though not as beneficial as it could have been. We did not realize that we could set the agenda for the assessment, so we did not do as good a job of planning the assessment as we could have.

We did communicate with the British Standards Institution

(BSI), our third-party assessment agency, at the time of our initial contact, when we wanted to have a preregistration assessment conducted. This assessment was conducted within about one week of our original scheduled date. We also communicated to our employees, just prior to the assessment, the purpose for the assessment, when it would take place, why it was being done, and how to respond to questions. We reiterated the "you need not fear an audit" message that we had given them at the time the independent internal audit program was started, and asked them to welcome the assessors as our guests. This communication was done via a quality brief, which is a written communication from our quality steering team directly to each employee.

The preregistration assessment was conducted by one BSI assessor for two days. Both our ISO 9000 project champion and our lead auditor accompanied the BSI assessor on this visit. Because we had not set the agenda in advance for this assessment, we wasted some time putting it together in the presence of the assessor as we talked through the quality manual. In the end, the BSI assessor assessed all of the manufacturing functions, one design project, management responsibility, documentation control, responsibility and authority, training, and the internal auditing program. This agenda, put together on the run, was not as thorough and as adequate as it could have been. Still, we covered most of the functional areas including some that we were not confident about.

The assessment proved valuable in that it uncovered areas of our quality system that would not have measured up to the requirements of the ISO 9001 standard during an actual registration assessment. Without the preregistration assessment, we probably would not have made any changes to these areas prior to the actual assessments simply because we assumed that because they were working they met the ISO 9001 requirements.

For example, one area where we did not meet the requirements of ISO 9001 was design reviews. We *did* conduct design reviews, identified and assigned action items and followed up on those action items, but we had not documented the actual process by which design reviews were conducted. We overlooked this requirement in the standard because the Design Control section of ISO 9001 does not state that design reviews must be done, only that they are an example of verification. Our third-party assessor said that the Verification Resources and Personnel section of ISO 9001 requires this. Armed with this knowledge, we were able to document the process and ensure that all documentation was in place at the time of the actual registration assessment.

Another problem with our quality system at the time of the preregistration assessment was the inconsistent manner in which training records were kept. We generalized this finding and implemented a centralized repository for training records in our human resources department.

We learned that BSI assessors tend to ask people what they do first and then ask to see their procedures. We incorporated this technique into our internal audit program.

Because we did not know we could control the agenda, we did not hold a meeting with our executive management and the assessor. The assessor presented the findings to the Quality Director, the ISO 9000 Project Champion, and our Lead Auditor. We in turn communicated them to executive management the next week at our quality steering team meeting. We also communicated the results of the assessment to our employees via another quality brief.

Because we did not plan the agenda, we looked at most, but not every, area of the standard. Fortunately, we had confidence in the areas that were not addressed, and this confidence proved to be well-founded as we later passed our registration assessment on the first attempt.

The preregistration assessment was very valuable to us, because it gave us confidence that our understanding of the ISO 9000 standards was on target. It also told us that we would be ready for a registration assessment in about 3 months, which was according to our plan.

We did not have any areas that were overtly uncooperative with the project. There was one area that had not made much progress prior to the preregistration assessment, but as they realized that they could be the obvious cause of failure during the registration assessment, they got real busy getting their house in order. In fact, there was a lot more urgency placed on the project after the preregistration assessment visit because it had become much more real to everyone.

In the end, the preregistration assessment was certainly worth what it cost us. We do not believe we would have been successfully registered at our first registration assessment without it.

Chapter Eleven

Preparing for the ISO 9000 Registration Assessment

The harder you work, the luckier you get.

Gary Player
Professional golfer

An organization with which we had a cordial relationship was conducting their ISO 9000 registration project at the same time that we were. We shared information with them and they with us. Our approaches were fundamentally different and our quality manuals reflected those differences. Ours was about 50 pages in length, and besides being a road map to the underlying process and procedure documentation, it contained a policy statement for each area of the ISO 9001 standard and a brief overview of how we deployed that policy. Their quality manual was about 10 pages long and functioned as an index to the next level of documentation, which consisted of department quality manuals. Neither of us was wrong. Our choices fit our different cultures.

Our schedules for registration were nearly the same, so we carried on a friendly rivalry about which of us would be registered first. Our registration assessment was scheduled to be about five weeks ahead of theirs, so we were confident it would be us. We had planned to hold our registration assessment in the last week in June of 1991. BSI, our registration agency, could not fit an assessment into that week, but could come the first week in July. Besides being a bad time for us because of the Independence Day holiday, we had scheduled to move our manufacturing facility beginning in July. It would be impossible to assess a manufacturing facility on the move. So we rescheduled our registration assessment for six weeks later in the middle of August. Now our friends' registration assessment was scheduled ahead of ours.

Unfortunately for them, they failed their initial registration assessment. When, about two weeks later, we were successful, their response was: "You were lucky." This was not said in a joking manner. But were we? Lucky, that is? Maybe, but as pro-golfer Gary Player said, "The harder you work, the luckier you get."

THE PURPOSE OF THIS CHAPTER

An ISO 9000 registration assessment can be looked at as a two-step process—the actual assessment itself, which is the subject of Chapter 12, and preparing your organization for its ISO 9000 registration assessment, discussed in this chapter. Many organizations, and our "unlucky" counterparts were one, don't make the two-step assumption. Organizations tend to jump right from the euphoria of believing that they have finally brought their organization's quality system into compliance with ISO 9000 requirements to conducting an assessment *without taking the time to prepare the organization for the assessment process.* The result is that a lot of good work can go for naught and registration may not be achieved on the first assessment attempt.

Case in point: we had put about the same amount of effort into preparing our quality system as the organization that did not achieve registration on its first assessment. However, we worked much harder in the preparation of our people for the assessment. We told our people how the assessment would be conducted, what would happen during the assessment interviews, and how to respond to the assessors. We prepared our people to exhibit the attitudes of hospitality and cordiality mentioned in the previous chapter. Our friends did not. It contributed to their result.

They chose a newcomer to ISO registration as an assessment agency. We chose the most experienced agency in the world. One of our friendly rival's managers (not their ISO 9000 registration champion) commented after their preregistration assessment that, since their assessment agency was new to the standards, they could take advantage of their assessors' inexperience. Actually, the opposite occurred. Their less-experienced assessors raised findings in some areas that were questionable. Because our friends had not prepared their people to deal with assessors, arguments broke out, and the result was a failed assessment.

Wait a minute, you say. If the quality system is ISO 9000 compliant, why wouldn't the organization "pass" its registration assessment? This question is born of the notion that when third-party assessors visit your organization, your quality system will *speak for itself*. That is far from the case. It is the *people* of your organization who speak for your quality system. It is from your people that the third-party assessors will come to understand the relationship between your quality system documentation and the way people actually do their jobs. The true measure of your quality system will be how your people answer the assessors' questions, how they respond to requests for information, and the attitude they display toward the assessors.

This chapter helps you prepare your organization to reflect your quality system in the best possible light. This is not to imply that you can scrape and bow your way to registration with an inadequate quality system. You can't. However, you can hurt your chances for registration if your people are not properly prepared to work with the third-party registration agency conducting the assessment. You are not ready for the assessment just because your quality system is. Your people have to be ready too.

In this chapter we discuss putting the final touches on your quality system, including how to deal with any existing holes in the system at the time of registration. We also discuss in detail preparing your people for the ISO 9000 assessment—selecting and training escorts for the third-party assessors, informing management and employees of what to expect during the assessment, and sending a final message to everyone in the organization reviewing key quality system elements. Preparing for the registration assessment is hard work, but "the harder you work, the luckier you get."

PREPARING YOUR QUALITY SYSTEM FOR THE REGISTRATION ASSESSMENT

Make no mistake about it, you must have your quality system ready for the assessment. You cannot gain registration on charm and good looks alone. You should pay close attention to the following areas: 1) preregistration findings, 2) problems found internally, 3) evidence of compliance, and 4) your quality manual. In addition you should know how to handle areas of deficiency that will not be corrected prior to the registration assessment. These topics will be discussed next.

The singular focus of your ISO 9000 registration project is making your quality system compliant with the standards to effect a successful registration. This is the message of Figure 3–1. All of the resources that the project has consumed, amplified by the cultural filter, support the actions of commitment of resources, quality of effort and allocation of effort, which are directed at the project critical success factors for the purpose of making the quality system ISO 9000 compliant to reach the goal of registration. The time between the preregistration and registration assessments is the time to tie up all of the loose ends.

Correct the Preregistration Findings

It is very important to take corrective action on all preregistration assessment findings. These are the areas the assessors said you had to have corrected in order to be ready for the registration assessment. By all means, be ready.

As soon after the preregistration assessment as possible, hold a meeting with your implementation team of ISO 9000 department champions and get working on the preregistration assessment findings. If you need more resources than have been allocated, meet with your executive management and request them. Few companies will go as far as the preregistration assessment and then refuse to go further. If adequate resources are just not available, reschedule the registration assessment. As mentioned above, our registration assessment was pushed back six weeks because of a timing problem between us and our assessment agency, but we took advantage of the additional time to do a more thorough job of getting ready. To use the model given in Chapter 3, the additional time allowed us to increase the quality of our effort with a positive effect on the characteristics of the system.

One of the things that the assessors will be interested in discovering is how responsive your company is to the findings they generate. If they discover during their registration assessment that every preregistration assessment finding has been corrected, they learn something positive about your company's reaction to discovered problems. If, on the other hand, they discover a rather lax response, they may determine that your quality system does not adequately address the corrective action section of the standard. This determination could cause you to fail the registration assessment.

It bears repeating—correct every preassessment finding prior to the registration assessment.

Correct Your Internally Found Problems

Internally found problems could include those that were found during an independent internal audit. They could also include problems that occurred because a process changed, but you have not documented the change. Or there may be a problem that was discovered by the people who actually perform the work described in the procedures. There may be other sources of problem discovery as well. Whatever the source of discovery, correct the problems.

This is especially important for the findings of internal independent audits. The internal auditing function is one of particular interest to assessors because it gives them a clear view of how your organization responds when it finds problems with the quality system. Just as the assessors are interested in how your organization responds to problems they uncover, they are also interested in how it responds to problems you uncover yourself. As discussed in Chapter 9, you should make your system self-correcting. In order to have a self-correcting system, it must respond to problems found in your internal audits. The ISO 9000 standards require that you have an internal independent auditing function in place and operating. If corrective action is not taken on the findings of your internal audits, you will fail the registration assessment.

Have Evidence of Compliance

The Deming Prize, Japan's highest quality award, has as an interesting feature the requirement that while a company is being assessed to determine if it is worthy of the prize, its people must be able to produce within a set number of minutes the data that supports any particular decision they have made on behalf of the company. Although the ISO 9000 standards do not have this stringent requirement, they do require that evidence of certain events, such as reviews, verifications, tests, or audits, be accessible.

Between the preregistration and registration assessments, ensure that you have evidence of compliance for all areas of the standards. Encourage people to keep their records in order. It helps to define not only *what* records must be kept, but *where* they will be kept. For example, records of design reviews may be kept in a project notebook for each design project. Audit records may be kept in a file cabinet in the lead auditor's office. Minutes of management review meetings may be kept in the same file cabinet as audit records. Or, all of these items could be kept in electronic files on a personal computer or a network file server. Wherever they are kept, ensure that they are protected from damage or destruction.

Have your department champions make a list of each type of objective evidence and where it is found. Perform a thorough audit to ensure that each piece of evidence exists and can be located. Alternately, you could prepare a checklist based on the above list and allow each area to perform a self-assessment prior to your audit. Correct the areas where you find deficiencies. The point of this exercise is to make sure that you are ready for the assessors.

A practical benefit of this exercise is that if people have their records up-to-date and accessible, they can use them to their own ends. For example, if a design project notebook (physical or electronic) is kept up-to-date, it becomes a valuable tool in conducting a postproject review. Postproject reviews, or postmortems, are often conducted to determine what lessons from a project can enhance a subsequent project by either being repeated or avoided.

The assessors represent your customers. When they register your company to an ISO 9000 standard, they are informing your customers and potential customers that you meet the requirements of the standard. With few exceptions, your customers will rely on the validity of third-party agency assessments rather than performing one themselves. When viewed in this light, your records are also being kept by you as a requirement of your customers, i.e., to give them assurance about the operation of your quality system.

Make Your Quality Manual Current

As the other documentation in your system, your quality manual must be kept current. You may do this on a schedule, or may send out changes as they are written and approved. However you do this normally, make sure that at the time of your registration assessment, the quality manual accurately describes your quality system.

From the time that you first wrote your quality manual, your quality system has been dynamic. In fact, during the preparation for registration, it is perhaps more dynamic than it will ever be again. You are adding new procedures and getting rid of old ones. Some that you planned to add were found to be unnecessary. Your quality system changed somewhat even since the preregistration assessment. Therefore, as you bring your quality system into complete compliance with the ISO 9000 standards, update your quality manual to reflect that fact.

How to Handle Deficiencies That Have Not Been Corrected

It is late in the afternoon on the day before the registration assessment, and you are smug in the knowledge that all known deficiencies in your quality system have been searched out and destroyed, when good old Bob in Contracts calls to tell you that he has a problem: "Because we only sell the Smurfgen products in the spring, I forgot that we review the contracts for those products differently from all other products. We did not cover this in our procedures and I just received a whole batch of contracts for this product that have to be reviewed before the weekend. What do we do?"

Your smugness turns into a sour stomach as you envision the assessors wandering through Contracts writing up findings and a "good try, but try again" assessment report. Then the vision changes and you see tar and feathers and yourself being railroaded out of town—and the railway hasn't even passed through your town in 25 years.

Inevitably, though you have taken particular care to correct all deficiencies found by your internal independent quality system auditors and by the third-party assessors during the preregistration assessment, you will have missed something. There will be one or even some problems that you cannot correct prior to the arrival of the assessors. How do you handle these? What do you do about Bob?

Well, fortunately the third-party assessors will not be looking for a perfect quality system, only a compliant one. We suggest that if you have a known problem in your quality system and you can't show the assessors that you have fixed it, show them a plan for fixing it. They will be pleased to see that you have recognized and have a plan to correct the problem. Have Bob write down a description of the problem he found, what short-term action will be taken, and what he plans to do to correct the problem. Then Betty, the contract supervisor, should authorize the plan.

Bob's plan might read something like this: "Because the Smurfgen product only sells in the spring, we overlooked the necessity to document the contract review for this product line while we were preparing our department documentation. The contracts for this product are slightly different from the rest of our products, so this product requires a separate review procedure. Our plan to correct this problem is to document a Smurfgen Contract Review Procedure and train all contract reviewers on the procedure. This will be accomplished within four weeks. In the interim, only those contract reviewers that have previous experience in properly reviewing the Smurfgen contracts will review any new Smurfgen contracts. These people are Betty, Elaine, and Bob. We will notify all contract reviewers of this fact via memo."

It is not necessary to point out to the assessors that this problem exists. But if they find it, Bob can show them his corrective action plan. The assessors can verify that the plan is being carried out by asking contract reviewers how Smurfgen contracts are handled. If the response they get is, "only Betty, Elaine and Bob are allowed to review these contracts until we are all trained on the proper procedure," Bob gets high marks in the "corrective action" category. You don't have to ride the train.

PREPARING YOUR PEOPLE FOR THE REGISTRATION ASSESSMENT

As mentioned in the introduction to this chapter, the importance of preparing your people for the registration assessment should not be underestimated. In the wrap-up meeting at the conclusion of our registration assessment, the assessors remarked at how impressed they were by the people of our company. They said that everyone they talked to was cooperative with them and demonstrated ownership for and pride in their part of the quality system, while remaining openminded about the need for improvement. This was their final comment before telling us that they were recommending us for registration.

You actually begin to prepare your people for the registration assessment early in the project by informing them about the ISO 9000 standards and their importance to your company. As the processes and procedures are finalized, you prepare them further through training on the location and use of these documents. You also train them on the company quality policy.

Prior to internal auditing you train them on the purpose for audits and how quality system auditing is an evaluation of the quality system and not any particular person. Then before the preregistration assessment you reinforce the purpose for audits and encourage your people to be cordial and hospitable to the assessors.

This information is communicated in training sessions, newsletters, electronic mail, memos, and any other means available. You must determine which methods are best to use within your culture. The assessment is the focal point of all of this training. It all comes together when the assessors are present. By then, your people should know the company's quality policy, where the procedures are located that they follow on their job, where the records pertaining to their job are kept, and how their responsibilities and authority are defined. They should also know the purpose for the assessment, how they should answer questions, and how to treat the assessors.

All of this was communicated to your people at previous points in the project. Now, prior to the registration assessment, you can review this with them, and also inform them about the logistics of the assessment.

We suggest that you use a combination of formal training and a newsletter or memo. The formal training will be targeted at the assessor escorts and department managers, who can then in turn carry it to their work areas. You may also want to include your executive management in this training, with some tailoring for their needs. The newsletter or memo will be targeted at all employees.

Assessor Escorts

When the assessors are on site they require escorts to guide them from area to area. Escorts are the guides responsible for taking the assessor where they want to go and for fetching items for the assessor, such as documentation and records, when necessary. As the assessors look at organization charts and project schedules, they will ask to speak to specific individuals. They will rely on the escorts to conduct them to these people. Sometimes assessors want a single person to be their escort for the entire assessment. In a larger company, they may prefer that a person familiar with a particular functional area of the company be their escort in that area.

Because the escorts will be spending a great deal of time with the assessors, *choose your escorts carefully*. Choose people who are role models in cordiality and hospitality, friendly people who are enjoyable to be around. Eliminate from your choice anyone who is negative, abrasive, rude, argumentative, or opinionated. You want your escorts to be cooperative and helpful. A secondary characteristic is that the person understands the workings of the area in which they are escorting and who is responsible for what in that area.

Training of Escorts and Department Managers

The primary purpose of training the escorts and department managers is to prepare them for their roles during the assessment.

When the assessors are in a particular work area, the manager of the area often wishes to be present during the interviews. This is one reason they are included in the training. They are also included so they can return and give a summary of the information to the people in their department.

The content of this training is the logistics of a registration assessment and the roles and responsibilities of escorts, department managers, and company personnel being interviewed. If you are not familiar with how the registration agency conducts a registration assessment, ask them during the preregistration assessment. Most agencies do the following:

1. Conduct an opening meeting with the company to describe the purpose, scope, and logistics of the assessment.

2. Conduct a short meeting at the beginning of each subsequent day to get together with escorts and clarify where they will be assessing that day.
3. Conduct a short meeting at the end of each day to explain what was found on that day.
4. Conduct a closing meeting at the conclusion of the assessment to review the findings, observations, overall conclusions and to tell you if you will be recommended for registration.

You should tell the escorts and department managers which of these meetings you believe they should attend. The escorts should be present at all of them. The department managers should be present at the opening and closing meetings and at the meetings at the end of any day on which their department was assessed.

When they are not in these meetings, the assessors will be carrying out the assessment by interviewing company employees, reviewing records and documentation, and meeting with one another to exchange information on their findings.

After you explain the logistics of the assessment to your escorts and department managers, you should define their roles and responsibilities. First, tell them how to respond to interview questions from the assessors. This information is given for two reasons: so they will know how to answer the assessors if they are interviewed themselves and so the department managers can train their employees how to respond to assessor questions. The important elements of answering an assessor's interview question are:

1. Understand the question—ask for clarification if you don't.
2. Answer the question honestly.
3. Answer the question completely.
4. Don't answer any more than what was asked.

Point 1 is a precursor to points 2 and 3. You cannot answer a question honestly and completely unless you understand the question. Point 2 is important because the assessors cannot evaluate the quality system and help you improve it if you don't tell them the truth. Worse, if they discover through objective evidence that you are not telling the truth, they will have a very low confidence level about the effectiveness of the quality system. If something is not right and the assessors ask about it, tell them it is not right. Point 3 will help the assessors to avoid any confusion. Half answers are almost as bad as lies. Point 4 is also very important. Assessors like to follow their own threads through the system. If you volunteer that there is a problem somewhere else in the system, the assessor will be obligated to investigate it. If there really isn't a problem, because you are misinformed or because it has been fixed since you heard about it, you have just wasted the assessor's time.

Point 4 does not mean that you are trying to hide anything. If you really do know something is a problem, you still do not need to bring it up. First, since you know it is a problem, it can be fixed without having to be listed as a finding. You know it is wrong, so fix it as a part of your corrective action system. Second, auditing is sampling, just like pulling 10 bottles out of a case of 100 and inspecting them. If 10 percent of them had faulty caps, an inspection of 10 of them chosen at random may show that one is bad, leading you to believe that about 10 are bad in the whole lot. If, on the other hand, instead of choosing 10 bottles randomly, someone who knew about the problems handed you the 10 bad bottles to inspect, you might conclude that most, if not all, of the 100 were bad.

The point being made here is that assessors know that no system is perfect. In their sampling they expect to find a certain number of problems. Provided that none of these problems indicate a major breakdown of the quality system and they do not all accumulate in one area of the standard, the assessor may judge that your quality system is normal for a compliant system. They will make a judgment about the system based on the number of "faulty bottle caps" they find via audit sampling. If you inflate the number by pointing out everything that you know is wrong, they may conclude that there are several more problems than there actually are. Point 4 says to let the assessors do their job. Don't bias them unfavorably.

Once you have told the escorts and department managers how to respond if they are interviewed, you can tell them how to respond while someone else is being interviewed. Two words: BE QUIET! When assessors interview people, they want to know how those people do their jobs, not how the escort or department manager thinks they do their jobs. There is only one time when it is appropriate for an escort to speak up and that is in the case where there is a breakdown in communication. If the person is answering a different question than the one being asked, the escort can intercede to clarify the situation. For example, if the assessor asks a designer if design reviews are carried out and the designer says, "No," an escort may say, "Well, we call those design inspections." Then the designer can wax eloquent on how design inspections are done.

Finally, you can emphasize to the escorts and department managers the necessity for cordiality and hospitality. Tell them not to argue with an assessor. If there is a problem with a finding, it should not be handled in a heated argument. This will do more harm than good. Escorts should immediately attempt to defuse any situation where it looks like an argument is beginning by taking charge and saying to the employee, "We can handle this at the end of the day meeting," and then to the assessor, "Is there anything else you need to know about here?" Questionable findings should be discussed, CALMLY, by the lead assessor and your ISO 9000 management representative.[1] If the finding is wrong, the management representative can gather more evidence to show that it is. If it is not wrong, then accept it.

Training of Executive Management

Give the same training to executive management that you give to the escorts and department managers, with one additional item. Inform the executive staff about the kinds of questions they may be asked. These questions typically have to do with their responsibility for the quality system within their area of concern. How do problems get escalated?" What do they do about them? How are they involved in the review of quality, i.e., management review? How do they ensure adequate staffing for the functions performed within their area? How has the quality policy been communicated within their area? Executives should formulate answers to these questions in advance so their actual responses to assessors are concise and delivered crisply.

Training of Employees

Employees can be trained by their department managers using the same material with which they were trained. The most important parts of that training are how to answer assessor questions, avoid arguments, and be cordial and hospitable toward the assessors. The department managers can also review the location of procedures in the areas and how responsibility and authority is defined.

Final Message to Everyone

During the week before the assessors arrive, it is a good idea to review the key points of the above information with all employees. This is easily handled in a newsletter, memo, or via electronic mail sent to each employee. This final communication should cover:

1. The quality policy.
2. How responsibility and authority are defined.
3. Where procedures are found.
4. The purpose for assessments (investigation of the system, not the people).
5. How to answer interview questions.
6. How differences of opinions will be handled (no arguments).
7. The assessors as guests (cordiality and hospitality).

The delivery of this information will help make your assessment an excellent experience where your employees gain respect for the assessors and, more importantly, the assessors gain respect for your employees and your company. The process involved in undergoing the registration assessment itself is the topic of Chapter 12.

THE NCR EXPERIENCE

We paid close attention to the findings from our preregistration assessment to ensure they were corrected prior to the registration assessment. There were two concerns from the preregistration assessment that we made sure were addressed. The first was documentation of the design review process. We wrote a design review procedure and referenced it in our design process. We made sure that design teams were aware of the procedure and made sure that people documented and retained evidence that the procedure we were using was, indeed, being followed.

The second concern raised by the preregistration was the manner in which training records were kept. Our old system had managers of each functional area keep training records for that area. It was not working. Some managers had impeccable records; others had none. We addressed this by centralizing the keeping of training records in our human resources department. They already had a computerized system capable of handling the training records for all employees. We sent what training records the managers had to human resources to be entered into the system. Then we sent to each employee their own records and asked them to update the list. The system was updated with the employee corrections. At the same time, we created linkages between our accounts payable process and our training record process. Anytime an employee takes a class or a seminar that is paid for by the company, the accounts payable process forwards a notice to the training process and the training is recorded. We also made a similar connection between our training record process and our in-house resource center for courses that our employees took via satellite or microwave transmission.

The executive staff met weekly during the six weeks leading up to the registration assessment to review the status of problem correction and to apply resources where they were needed. Despite all of this effort, we still ran into a "last minute gotcha." During the ISO 9000 registration project, we transitioned from a fully integrated business unit owned by the corporation to an engineering and manufacturing plant. In the process, our marketing, sales, and services functions were absorbed into the corporate structures that perform these functions. One result of this transition was that the contract review methodology changed substantially only days before the assessment. A situation similar to the Smurfgen example given above occurred, except that instead of being true for a single product, it affected the orders for our entire product line. We handled it just like we would if the assessors were not coming. We laid out a plan to prepare our contract reviewers to follow the new methodology followed up by appropriate changes to the documented procedures and the quality manual. We were already executing this plan when the assessors arrived. The contract review area was clearly under controlled transition. There were no findings raised on contract review.

We paid a great deal of attention to preparing our people for the registration assessment. We trained our escorts and department managers on the points listed above regarding the structure of the assessment and their roles. We placed heavy emphasis on how to answer assessor questions and on being cordial and hospitable. Many of the department managers used the materials from this training to train the people of their departments.

The assessment began on a Wednesday. On Monday of assessment week we sent a quality brief to each employee that reviewed all of the items we had covered in earlier quality briefs about assessments, their responsibilities and authority, where documentation is found, and how to respond to an assessor. We also emphasized that the assessors were our guests. We had invited them to look at our quality system and help us find areas to improve, and we asked our employees to treat the assessors accordingly.

As mentioned above, the assessors were impressed with the response they received from our employees. They found our quality system to be compliant with the standards. They found that our people both demonstrated ownership for the processes they performed and were genuinely interested in any help they could receive in making those processes better. Certainly the attitude the assessors saw in our people is something that was genuine and a part of our culture. We did not create what the assessors saw through training and communication. The value of the training and communication was that it let our people know what was going to happen during the assessment, and it set the tone for the assessment.

In order to create light from electricity, there must be a bulb, a socket, wiring, and a switch appropriately connected to an electric current. In our culture all of that was already there. Through training and communication, we turned on the switch.

Chapter Twelve

Undergoing the ISO 9000 Registration Assessment

I love it when a plan comes together!

Hannibal Smith
"The 'A' Team"

Hannibal Smith was the lovable cigar-chomping leader of an eclectic, irreverent, cavalier group of modern day mavericks known as the "A" Team. Appearing weekly in the mid 1980s on NBC television, the "A" Team went outside the law to help victims of crimes, often extortion and blackmail, that the legal authorities could not or would not help. The traps for the bad guys planned by Hannibal Smith and carried out by the "A" Team were not always executed exactly as planned, but were always successful. Hannibal Smith basked in that success. During the weekly moment of truth, when good met evil, Hannibal Smith, even in the heat of battle, would lean back, light up a new cigar, and remark, "I love it when a plan comes together."

Even if your ISO 9000 champion is not as cavalier as Hannibal Smith, or the ISO 9000 project team as unconventional as Mr. T and the rest of the "A" Team, there will come a time in your ISO 9000 registration project when the plan comes together. The third-party ISO 9000 registration assessment is your organization's moment of truth.

THE PURPOSE OF THIS CHAPTER

Typically, it has been 12 to 18 months since the initial planning phase of the ISO 9000 registration project. Much planning, execution, and adjustment to the plan has occurred, and the organization is ready to measure itself against the ISO 9000 standards for real. You've made the final adjustments to the quality system, as described in Chapter 11, and you've prepared your people for the assessment process. Now is the moment of truth, the time when the plan comes together.

This chapter will take you through the steps of an ISO 9000 registration assessment. Starting with the arrival of the assessors, we discuss the logistics of the assessment and the interpersonal relationship between the people of your organization and the assessors. We discuss what to do if you achieve registration (celebrate!), and what to do if you don't.

THEY'RE HERE

On the morning of the day the assessors arrive, the ISO 9000 champion gets to work early, excited about the pending arrival of the third-party assessors. Moving papers from files onto the desk, and then back again, the champion waits for the phone call from the receptionist that announces the arrival of the assessors. The rest of the organization is anxious as well. Where will the assessors look today, with whom will they talk, what will they discover? And then the phone rings.

The first few minutes with the assessors are cordial and introductory. Usually, the names of the assessors are known in advance of their arrival. We suggest that you ask for these so you can communicate their names in advance to employees. If your company has a "welcome board" in the reception area, rather than just putting the name of the assessment agency, put up the assessors' names as well. The welcome board has nothing to do with the quality of your organization's products or services, but perception plays a big role in how assessors will react to your organization. Putting up individual names is not only a courtesy to the assessors, it communicates that your organization pays attention to detail.

During this get acquainted time, there will be some initial discussion about when lunch breaks are appropriate (when do your employees typically break for lunch), how lunches will be handled (on site, off site), when the assessment will conclude for the day (when do the shifts for your employees end), and when the final meeting will take place.

In advance of the assessors' arrival, prepare a work area for them. It should be large enough to accommodate the number of assessors that will be evaluating your organization. This number will vary. For a small organization, there may be only one assessor. For a large company, there may be a dozen. The number will depend on the size of your organization, the number of functions it performs, the standard to which you will be registered, how many locations are included within the scope of your registration, and how many days the assessors plan to spend. Again, pay attention to details. The workplace is where the assessors will place their effects, like coats and briefcases. (Are there coat racks? Is the room secure?) They will use the room to confer, reach consensus, update the assessment plan, and write the assessment report (Is the room conducive to such meetings? A white board? Flip charts? Conference table?).

After an initial cup of coffee, some light discussion about the traffic and weather, and some other discussion about the logistics of lunches and meetings, the assessors will proceed to the opening meeting.

THE OPENING MEETING

The purpose of the opening meeting is for the assessors to convey to your company the purpose of the assessment, the scope of the assessment, the logistics of the assessment, and how the recommendation for registration will be determined. The initial agenda for the assessment will also be discussed. This meeting typically takes one-half hour. It is conducted by the lead assessor.

Who attends this meeting from your organization is up to you. It can be conducted with just the lead assessor and the management representative (usually the ISO 9000 project champion).[1] We do not recommend this. We believe that it is to your advantage to have a much larger audience at this meeting. Again, thinking in terms of perception, a large audience gives the impression that ISO 9000 compliance is an organizationwide effort, and that ISO 9000 registration is important to the organization. The assessment escorts should definitely attend this opening meeting. Meeting with the assessors in advance of the assessment gives the escorts the opportunity to get to know the assessors, understand the details of the assessment process, and learn when their services will be required.

You will also want to have management from the areas that will be assessed present at this meeting. Some of these people may already be chosen as escorts for the assessment, but for those who are not, it gives them the same basic information: how and when will it happen. It also demonstrates management commitment to the quality system.

Executive management should also be present at this meeting. Some executives may be involved in the actual assessment process. In order for the assessors to know how the quality system is managed from the top of the organization, they will talk with executives. These people need to understand the assessment process every bit as much as an assembler on the factory floor.

And without being the least bit redundant, the presence of executive management at the initial meeting demonstrates their support of the quality system. We cannot emphasize enough—first impressions are important. It is better to make the point initially that your top management is interested and involved in the quality system and have the assessors confirm it later, than to begin by having them wonder about it and have to be convinced during interviews.

ORIENTATION AND COMPANY TOUR

Once the initial assessment meeting takes place, the assessors might begin conducting assessment interviews; however, in larger organizations they might first request a tour of the facilities. A facility tour tells them several things. The size of each functional unit in the company is important to the assessors. For example, how easy will it be to get around the manufacturing facility. The number of people working in each functional area is also important. Where these functional units are in relationship to one another is also of interest. For example, if an assessor is following a thread from engineering to document control to manufacturing, are these areas adjacent, or are they in separate buildings?

During the tour, the ''P'' word, perception, pops up again. The assessors will note seemingly trivial details and rightly or wrongly draw conclusions from them. Ultimately, registration to an ISO 9000 standard will rest on the soundness of your organization's quality system, but it is random impression that determines the attitude the assessor will bring to assessment process. Housekeeping is one of those details that should concern you. If the assessors see disorganization and disarray in the workplace, you may be sending a message that says the people who work in this area may have a hard time finding the tools they need to do the job. If the assessors see clutter in the incoming inspection area, they may well conclude that they need to spend a significant amount of time discerning just how it is that items are not lost track of amidst all of the clutter. Words alone will not convince them. They may question you about every item in the clutter, having you prove how you know what it is, why it is there, where it is going next, and how it will get there, until they have either proved that the clutter is indicative of an underlying problem of lack of control, or until they can prove that the clutter does not cause a problem. Even then, they may raise an observation about the clutter.

The point here again is that of first impressions. An assessor often works to the principle of *where there is smoke there is fire.* This is especially true during a registration assessment. The assessors have a short time to sample the entire quality system and cover all clauses of the standard. On subsequent surveillance assessments (discussed in detail in the next chapter), the assessors can dig deeply into a particular area of the company or standard to the exclusion of other areas. However, in the initial registration assessment, they can only sample a small part of the overall quality system to determine if your organization is worthy of registration. Necessarily, they will make some high-level judgments in order to cover as much of your organization as possible in a relatively short time.

A good first impression in an area, backed by high-level objective evidence, gives an assessor confidence that the area is in compliance with the ISO 9000 standard. A poor first impression will cause an auditor to dig deeper and to require more objective evidence.

The amount of evidence necessary to change a negative perception can be substantial.

The company tour and orientation is not an insignificant event. Assessors begin forming opinions of a company from the moment they walk in the door—or before. Prior to arrival, they began forming an impression of your organization through its quality documentation—the quality manual you sent as part of the request for a registration assessment. How the manual was organized, the content, its appearance all contributed to the assessors' impressions of your organization. The way they are greeted, the initial assessment meeting, the facility tour, all contribute to supporting or negating that initial perception. Hopefully, your documentation will send a strong positive message that will be supported when the assessors arrive on site. To ensure that it is, remember three words—details, details, details.

ASSESSOR CAUCUSES

During the assessment, the assessors will come together to share their findings and concerns with the lead assessor and with one another. As an example, one assessor, looking at design input, may discover a potential problem in documentation control and relate this to another assessor who is looking at documentation control. These caucuses usually take place in the room you have set aside for the assessors.

Knowing what the assessors are doing behind closed doors relieves some unnecessary anxiety in your organization. The first caucus usually takes place after the tour and orientation. This is when the assessors get their assignments from the lead assessor. Adjustments to the assessment schedule will take place during subsequent meetings. One assessor may be behind in one area, while another is ahead, so assignments are altered. Assessment may need to begin earlier on one day, or end later on another. Setting exact times for the duration of assessing any particular area is impractical. Complexities in the system or what is actually found in an area may cause the assessment time of any particular area to vary from plan.

The point is that your organization must remain flexible. The assessment in human resources that was planned for 1:00 PM today may not actually be done until 10:00 AM tomorrow and may take 90 minutes instead of the 60 minutes originally planned. The assessors know that your people don't just stop working to accommodate an assessment. If a key person is not available at a scheduled time, the schedule will be changed to accommodate that person. In the example above, the human resources manager may have been available at 1:00 PM, but the schedule had to be altered initially because the assessor took more time than planned in Contracts. However, when the assessor was ready at 3:00 PM, the human resources manager may have had a meeting, so they mutually agreed upon 10:00 AM the next morning.

Someone in your organization, perhaps the ISO 9000 champion, must coordinate the changes to the schedule and keep your people informed of them. These schedule changes are often negotiated over lunch or at end-of-day review meetings. Because the review meetings themselves may take place later than planned, you might have several people to inform.

A programmable phone system that can build a message list of all escorts and department managers prior to the assessment is a helpful tool. When you have to get a message out quickly to several people, you can record one message and send it to the list. Another useful tool for doing the same thing is electronic mail. Short of having these tools, you should develop a calling procedure, wherein you call five people, who are each responsible for informing several more. The first wave of these people should be those who are typically at their desks during most of the day, for example, department receptionists, secretaries, or administrative assistants.

The point is, you need to think about how you will communicate during the assessment in order to keep things running as smoothly as possible. You don't want an assessor waiting for a ride to the manufacturing facility because no one knew that he or she needed one.

ASSESSMENT INTERVIEWS

The bulk of the work of any assessment is done during interviews with people who work within the system. During interviews, the assessors are determining if people know what their responsibilities are and what authority they have to accomplish their work. The assessors will ask people to describe or demonstrate how their jobs are done. They will ask to see the documented procedures that people follow and compare them to what people indicate they do on the job.

Assessors are constantly in search of objective evidence that documented procedures are followed. Objective evidence consists of records, meeting minutes, memos, reports, filled-out forms, filled-in log books, stickers applied, stamps applied, and other tangible indications that appear as the result of following procedures.

During employee interviews, assessors take copious notes. These notes help them remember what they have seen and heard during the interviews. The notes are used to substantiate nonconformity or observations made during the interviews. When nonconformity is found, an assessor describes the finding to the employee and the escort. This follows the principle of no surprises.

Assessors want you to know when they suspect there is a problem. If the finding is not accurate, the person being interviewed has an opportunity to present evidence to the contrary. For example, if an assessor is shown reports of raw data and states that a nonconformity will be raised indicating that the data is not actionable, the person being interviewed can show the assessor an analysis of the data from which actions are taken.

HOW TO HANDLE DIFFERENCES OF OPINION

The immediate mention of a finding enables the interviewee to respond so that the assessor is sure the finding is accurate. At no time, however, should the person being interviewed be argumentative. To calmly provide evidence that supports or dispels a proposed finding is an introduction of fact. This is different than disputing whether a finding is significant or a nonconformity. For example, it may be true that instruments used to take certain measurements are not calibrated. This is either a fact, or it is not. Unless you can produce records that show the instruments are calibrated, the assessor can accurately state there is no evidence that the instruments are calibrated. A problem arises if the assessor and the person being interviewed have a difference of opinion about whether the uncalibrated instruments are used to make significant determinations of the quality of a product, not verified elsewhere.

In a situation like this, the person being interviewed must realize that it is the quality system that is being judged, not the person. This is true, even if the person being interviewed is the manager who decided that the instruments need not be calibrated. An argument at this point will not resolve the difference.

Arguments are emotionally charged, and reason and fact are often ignored. The objective becomes win-lose, I win–you lose, during an argument. Assessors do not respond kindly to having their professional opinion attacked.

A better way to handle a difference of opinion of this nature is to have your management representative discuss it with the lead assessor. For the example above, gather objective evidence that shows that what you view with uncalibrated instruments at this point is verified with calibrated instruments later in the process. Have your ISO 9000 champion present this to the lead auditor. If there is no such objective evidence, you still may claim that what is being measured is only the presence or absence of a condition, such as voltage or current, not the magnitude or preciseness of the condition. If it is logical that preciseness is not required at the point of measurement, a calm discussion will gain you more favor than a heated debate.

ROLE OF ESCORTS

The primary role of an escort during an assessment is to guide an assessor through the company. A secondary, but no less important role is to be a stress relief valve. Being interviewed is stressful. Some people respond better than others. A person may be quite competent on the job, but an emotional wreck if he or she has to answer questions about it.

If a person being interviewed is exhibiting the effects of stress during an interview, the escort can call a time out, take the assessor aside, and explain that a break might be helpful. This is particularly true if an argument is about to erupt. In that case, a break might be suggested, and the escort can take the person being interviewed aside and calm him or her down, explaining that the situation will be handled by your management representative.

As the assessor is taking copious notes, so should the escort. Any relevant information about nonconformity should be recorded. Later, after the assessors leave, their report will contain a description of nonconformity and observations, but their notes will go with them. If your escorts have taken notes, you will have more detailed information than provided by the assessment report. The detailed information will be helpful in determining the exact intent of a finding or observation, which will facilitate finding the root cause of problems, and taking the proper corrective action.

Another role an escort can play is to intervene when there is a miscommunication between the assessor and person being interviewed. For example, if the assessor asks a person one question, and the person answers another, an escort can point out the disparity. Assessors try to understand the job functions performed by the people they interview. However, they do not always completely understand where one person's responsibilities end and another's begin. An assessor may ask a person a question that the person is not qualified to answer, but in trying to be helpful, the person attempts to answer it anyway. Here an escort can point out that someone else is responsible for the function in question.

The role of escort is a very important one. Escorts must be cordial, friendly, and helpful. They must also be knowledgeable about the areas in which they are escorting so they can detect miscommunications and questions being asked of the wrong person. Finally, they must be skilled at intervening in stressful situations and defusing potential arguments. *Choose your escorts carefully and train them thoroughly for their roles.* They will spend more time with the assessors than anyone else. The influence that they can have on the success of the assessment cannot be underestimated.

END OF DAY REVIEW MEETINGS

As mentioned previously, one of the tenets of quality system auditing is the element of no surprises. Assessors do not make all of their observations secretly only to blow you away at the closing meeting or in the assessment report. They call attention to nonconformity as it is found. The main purpose of end of the day review meetings is to further assure that there are no surprises.

These meetings are usually 30 to 60 minutes in length, depending upon how much discussion takes place. In a typical meeting, the lead assessor or the individual assessors will review the findings of the day's assessment. Findings of nonconformity and observations are reviewed.

The attendees at this meeting should be the escorts and managers from the areas that were assessed that day. Not only can you review findings, but you have an opportunity to correct error. If a nonconformity has been raised based on what you consider to be shaky evidence, you have a chance to set it straight.

For example, we mentioned earlier that the assessors do not know with precision who has responsibility for what. If they ask someone a question about whether a particular function is performed and that person authoritatively says no, the assessor may raise an observation or nonconformity based upon that answer. If indeed the function is being performed by someone else, you may show objective evidence that it is, and the assessor must consider it. A problem like this should be corrected on the spot by the escort, but if it isn't, the end of day meeting gives you that opportunity.

Another opportunity that the end of day meeting gives you is to correct instances of minor nonconformity prior to the assessors' leaving. It is usually not a requirement of assessment agencies that you take corrective action during the assessment, but it doesn't hurt to do so. It does give the assessors the impression that you are responsive.

For any nonconformity that you cannot correct before the assessors leave (true in most cases), the end of day meetings give you an opportunity to plan tentative corrective action. Prior to the assessors' leaving, you can ask them whether they believe your plan for correction addresses the problem they found.

This immediate feedback has two benefits. First, even a day or two after the assessors leave, you may begin to wonder what was meant by a particular statement they made in the assessment report. Even though they attempt to be specific, in time statements can lose their meaning. If you have already gained concurrence that your proposed corrective action addresses the problem found, you will not be confused about how to respond.

Second, such activity also communicates to the assessors that you are responsive to problems with the quality system. Just as executive management presence at the opening meeting and good housekeeping create a good first impression, responsiveness to assessment findings supports a good continuous impression. You will not pass registration on impressions alone, but the more you do in your favor, the better the chance of a successful outcome.

Because the escorts and management of the areas assessed are present at each day's meeting, you can extend the meetings for the purpose of discussing corrective action. You do this, of course, after the assessors have departed. Once the assessors have finished presenting their findings for the day, you can bid them good evening and spend a little more time brainstorming and discussing possible corrective actions for findings of nonconformity raised for that day.

CLOSING MEETING

The closing meeting is essentially a verbal assessment report. In fact, in many cases, the lead assessor simply reads part or all of the written report. The only surprise at this meeting is whether you will be recommended for registration or not. Everything else in the report has been communicated as it was found and at the end of day meetings. Perhaps to build suspense, or simply to make sure the findings are heard, the assessors usually leave the declaration of whether you will be recommended for registration until after discussing the findings.

Had there been a major nonconformity that would have prevented registration, you would have known about it during the assessment. However, several minor instances of nonconformity, which in themselves are not major breakdowns of the quality system, can together indicate a major hole in the system. It is not until the assessors are preparing their final report that they judge whether the sum total of the findings of nonconformity indicate a major breakdown in the system.

The people from your company who should attend this final meeting are the executive management, the escorts, the ISO 9000 project team, the department managers, and anyone else who is interested. This is your company's chance to hear firsthand the results of the assessment and its outcome. Though it is too late for impressions to have any bearing on the outcome, a large turnout will indicate to you and the assessors the interest that your company has in its quality system.

WHAT TO DO IF YOU PASS

The suspense during the presentation of the report is almost too much. When you hear those words, "we are recommending you for registration," you will realize, like Hannibal Smith, that your plan has finally come together. What do you do next? CELEBRATE!!!

The project has been long and arduous and has probably involved more people in your company than any other project. They deserve to rejoice. The state of the quality system is what brought you the recommendation for registration, but it was your people who made your quality system what it is. They were the ones who wrestled with the cultural changes, wrote the procedures, improved the processes, kept the records, performed the internal audits, carried out the corrective actions, held up under the stress of the interviews, and led the assessors to believe that the quality system is coherent, consistent, controlled, and compliant. They deserve to be rewarded for their efforts.

We recommend that you make plans for your celebration prior to the assessment visit. Perhaps you should not actually make any binding contracts for hall rental or entertainment until after the closing meeting, but you should have your plan ready to execute. You usually want to celebrate immediately (the next day or early the next week) after the assessment so you will have to act quickly to make the celebration happen. The better the planning, the better the celebration will go. The ISO 9000 champion and executive management should express their sincere thanks for the efforts of the people in the company.

You should also have planned how to take immediate advantage of your registration through press releases, advertisements, marketing methods, and sales motions. Some companies have erected huge signs that capture attention. Others have staged news conferences involving government dignitaries. Do what you can to let your customers and potential customers know that you have passed the registration assessment. Be aware, however, that a recommendation for registration is not the same as being registered. Technically you are not registered until an official, or officiating body, of the third-party assessment agency accepts the recommendation of the assessors. Usually the acceptance is a mere formality, but a separate action nonetheless.

So, celebrate, advertise, and be pleased that your plan came together.

WHAT TO DO IF YOU DON'T PASS

It is disappointing if you do not pass the registration assessment. A lot of work has gone into the preparation of the quality system, and now you discover that there is more to do. But, you haven't failed. Failure would have been to do nothing at all—to leave the quality system the way it was when you first began your ISO 9000 registration effort. Those who have tried and failed are not failures at all compared to those who have failed to try.

In most cases, you will have only one area that is not compliant, which when made compliant will gain you registration. Now your project can focus on this one area until it is brought into compliance. The assessment report will indicate exactly what the problem is with the area, so you can focus your efforts. Even if there is more than one area that needs attention, this is more focused than the entire quality system. The problem is not that your quality system is a failure, just that you scheduled your registration assessment prematurely.

Continue to improve the areas of deficiency and then call the assessors back when you are ready. On a second assessment for registration, you will likely have fewer assessors for less time because they only need to look at the areas of deficiency. Because you have already demonstrated that most of your quality system is compliant, now you just have to demonstrate the indicated deficiencies have been corrected.

This information should be communicated to employees in a positive manner. Naturally, there will be a letdown in your organization, and perhaps you as a driver of the ISO 9000 effort will feel worst of all. But you must put aside any feelings of disappointment and renew the enthusiasm of the organization. Don't make excuses, don't blame the assessors, and don't second guess your plan. Take the situation as it exists and start the planning process again, only this time on a smaller scale.

There's a lot of wisdom in the old adage that you have to get right back up on the horse that bucked you off. The sooner you and your organization get started on eliminating the nonconformity standing in the way of ISO 9000 registration, the quicker you'll recapture the enthusiasm of the organization.

Registration will come, just later than you originally had hoped. When it does, when your plan comes together, your celebration will be well deserved.

THE NCR EXPERIENCE

The ISO 9000 Registration Project at NCR Network Products Division was a very difficult project to manage. The project planning was done at a time when the organization was NCR Comten, a wholly owned subsidiary of NCR. During the project, the organization changed structure as its marketing, sales, and customer services departments were absorbed into the NCR parent organization. In addition, the remaining engineering and manufacturing organization weathered several reductions in the size of the workforce. We had been about 2500 employees at the beginning of the project. We were under 700 at the time of registration. During the project, we had three separate vice presidents. By the time of registration, the organization was made up of three business units that reported to a vice president in another part of the country.

As if all that was not disruptive enough to the project, just six weeks prior to the date of the assessment, we moved our manufacturing facility from one city to another. Now we not only had to demonstrate that our manufacturing processes were consistent and compliant, but were resilient enough to be so in a new facility.

We were assessed by three assessors for three days. One of the assessors spent his entire time in the manufacturing facility. The other two looked at the rest of the quality system, spending most of their time in the hardware and software engineering organizations.

Our executive management attended the opening meeting along with the escorts and managers of areas that would be assessed. We had end of day meetings with the assessors, which we extended after they left to address the findings of the day. We corrected 20 findings of nonconformity during the assessment. We had 33 additional to correct after the assessors left. When they reviewed the findings with us on the last day, we had corrective action plans for all except a few that had been found late on the last day. The escorts had taken excellent notes to help us get at the essence of each nonconformity. In addition, the escorts had performed their duties well. There were no arguments, just genuine concern about making improvement.

The closing meeting was held late on the last day of assessment, a Friday in August. Even though it was past quitting time, all of our executive management and over 20 percent of our employees attended this meeting. The suspense built as the lead assessor went through the 33 findings of nonconformity and showed a histogram distribution of the findings. As is typical, the greatest accumulation was in documentation control.

Finally, the lead assessor said that there were no major findings of nonconformity, and the distribution of findings was normal for a system which had no breakdowns in any area of the standard. He said that beyond the quality system itself, our people impressed the assessors. He said they showed an ownership for the quality system and an enthusiasm for improving it. Then he said the words we had all come to hear, "we are recommending you for registration." The room broke out in spontaneous applause.

Because we had not planned a celebration prior to the assessment, several of the ISO 9000 project team members and department managers went to a nearby establishment to lift a glass with the assessors and to plan the celebration. Fortunately, some had previous experience in planning celebrations, so the planning was done quickly.

On Monday morning, we arrived at work before 5 AM to inflate ''congratulations'' balloons and tie ribbons on them. The director of quality assurance and the members of his staff congratulated employees for their efforts on the ISO 9000 project and handed them balloons as they arrived at work. For several days, the workplace was a sea of multicolored balloons floating above cubicles. Later in the day, we had a cookout and beverage lawn party for all employees. At this gathering, the quality director and ISO 9000 champion addressed the employees and thanked them for their efforts on the project.

We were not the ''A'' Team, but the ISO Team; nonetheless, our plan had finally come together.

SECTION

IV

FINAL THOUGHTS ON ISO 9000

Chapter Thirteen

Maintaining the ISO 9000 Registered Quality System

To thrive as a corporation, you must passionately pursue the perfection of the products or services that have vaulted you to success. . . . However, to survive for the long haul, you must passionately pursue the destruction of what you have created.

Tom Peters
Liberation Management

Maintaining the ISO 9000 registered quality system is more like maintaining a vast botanical garden than it is like caring for a potted plant. A potted plant you water a bit, prune a bit, feed a bit, and you're done. Maintenance of a quality system is not like that, a few adjustments here and there from time to time. The task is more like maintaining a vast botanical garden that is always changing. Plants are moved from place to place. Some plants are removed; others are introduced. Natural predators are brought in to destroy pests. Decaying foliage is removed and composted. Keeping the garden in balance as it changes is a more appropriate metaphor for maintaining a quality system.

In today's business environment, change is the name of the game. Tom Peters' statement about long haul survival is reflective of the many companies that became good at something, stuck with it through success, and then faltered as other companies with new ideas passed them by. Competitors realize that they cannot beat a successful company in its area of strength. An effective competitive strategy is called "changing the rules of the game."[1] This strategy exploits a market leader's strength by making it a liability. For example, if the leading company in the widget market wins by having the biggest and best service organization, a competitor that can make widgets that do not need servicing can capture the market. The leading company has so much invested in its service organization, it will be slow to produce a product that will render that organization useless.

Winning companies must change to keep winning. When they change, their quality system changes. The ISO 9000-registered company must take care to assure that as its quality system changes, it remains compliant with the ISO 9000 standards.

THE PURPOSE OF THIS CHAPTER

Congratulations! Your organization has achieved ISO 9000 registration. Now what do you do to maintain the compliance of the system? The answer is more of the same. This chapter looks at two activities that you put in place in order to achieve ISO 9000 registration—proactive review of the quality system and an internal auditing process. It also discusses using the regularly scheduled surveillance assessments of the third-party registration agency to continuously improve your quality system. These concepts are tied together by looking once again at the critical success factor of institutionalizing the quality system concept within your organization.

PROACTIVE MAINTENANCE OF THE QUALITY SYSTEM

Proactive maintenance simply means that as you plan changes to the business practices of your company, you perform an evaluation of the proposed changes to ensure that you still meet the requirements of the ISO 9000 standards. Then, as you implement the changes to the way you do business, you incorporate appropriate changes in your quality system.

For example, a computer company that purchases software products from outside vendors to run on its internally developed hardware might decide to form its own software development organization. The company must then ensure that its software development process is compliant with the ISO 9001 standard. It must conduct software design reviews with the same rigor as hardware design reviews, which have already undergone the scrutiny of an ISO 9001 assessment.

This example is a parallelism. Similar to the purpose for a design review, which is an appraisal process aimed at ensuring that the output of the design complies with design requirements before you actually implement it, reviewing a proposed change to the quality system is an appraisal process aimed at ensuring that the changed system complies with the ISO 9000 requirements before you actually implement it. This same principle applies whether you are making major changes as a result of reengineering a process, or minor changes as a result of continuous improvement or corrective action.

Two requirements of the ISO 9000 standards address the responsibility of maintaining the ISO 9000-compliant quality system: the requirement for an ISO 9000 management representative[2] and the requirement for regular management reviews of the quality system.[3]

It is the responsibility of an individual, designated in the standards as the management representative, to ensure the continued compliance of the quality system to the ISO 9000 standards. It is also a requirement of the standards that executive management review the quality system on a regular basis to ensure that changes have not adversely affected quality and that the quality system is still effective.

These individuals can and should take a proactive role in planning changes to the quality system. However, no small group of individuals, even upper management, and certainly no one individual, no matter how dedicated, can monitor the myriad day-to-day details of quality system functioning. That is why there is a third requirement in the ISO standards that lends itself to maintaining a compliant quality system.

THE INTERNAL AUDIT PROGRAM

The requirement that ISO 9000-compliant companies implement an internal audit program is key to uncovering minor nonconformity in a quality system before it gets out of hand.[4] We have covered this topic extensively in Chapter 9 in connection with establishing an ISO 9000-compliant quality system, but return to it here in its role in the registered company.

In reality, the function of internal auditing does not change after a company becomes registered to an ISO 9000 standard. It continues to be a tool for determining the effectiveness of the quality system and for assessing its compliance with the standards. It is not audit purpose nor audit methodology that changes once a company becomes registered to an ISO 9000 standard. Rather, it is a matter of selection of what to audit. The wise lead internal auditor will give areas of change within the company a priority on the audit schedule.

An audit schedule is not cast in stone at the beginning of the year, never to be changed or deviated from. It is wise to document in your audit procedure a method for altering the audit schedule. It is also wise to state that areas of change will be given priority on the schedule. When business changes necessitate changes to the quality system, affected areas are placed near the front of the schedule. In that way, the audit team can review the compliance and effectiveness of changes to the quality system in a manner that will allow for the immediate correction of any problems introduced by the changes.

The management representative should review the results of internal audits, or at least should be made aware of major findings of nonconformity on an exception basis. The results of internal audits should be a regular part of the management review of the quality system. These three requirements of the standard—internal audits, a management representative, and management reviews of the quality system—work together to help ensure continued compliance with the standards.

SURVEILLANCE ASSESSMENTS (THEY'RE BACK!)

The third-party assessment agency does not just appear, perform an assessment, determine that you comply with the standards, grant you registration, and ride off into the sunset. Their reputation and credibility rides on your continued compliance with the requirements of ISO 9000. Surveillance assessments are scheduled to ensure that your organization remains compliant with the standards.

Different agencies handle surveillance assessments differently. Some perform a cursory look every six months or a year and then perform a complete assessment about every three years. Others perform a more thorough look one or two times a year and still perform a complete assessment about every three years.

The British Standards Institution performs a complete assessment of a registered company's quality system over a two-year period by conducting an in-depth assessment of a portion of the quality system on each scheduled surveillance visit. For example, they will look in depth at one-fourth of the quality system every six months. On that schedule, they do not feel the need to perform a complete assessment on any single visit.

A surveillance assessment is conducted exactly like a registration assessment. The assessment will produce a list of findings of nonconformity, for which your organization must prepare a corrective action plan. Usually one of the scheduled items is the "close down" of the findings of the previous assessment. Here you must produce evidence that you have corrected the nonconformity found on the previous visit.

There are other items which are commonly reviewed on each visit. For example, the results and functioning of the internal audit system are reviewed each visit. So is the procedure for handling customer complaints. Some agencies will review the calibration (metrology) system each time. Others like to always look at corrective action. The remaining areas are less frequently reviewed.

In Chapter 10 we mentioned that one benefit of a preregistration assessment is that it allows you to fine-tune your internal audit program to the interpretation that your third-party assessment agency puts upon the standard. One of the benefits of the surveillance assessment is that it continues to calibrate your own internal audit program.

Not only can you continue to observe the methods of the external assessors, but you can evaluate why you missed a nonconformity that they found. Sometimes it is only because your audit schedule has not recently taken you into an area that they assessed. Other times it is because there is a hole in your audit program that needs to be filled.

For example, if a surveillance assessment uncovers a significant problem in an area that you recently audited, you may discover that your audit checklist needs to be expanded. You may not be asking the right questions, or you may not be asking enough. Or perhaps you need to increase your sampling size when looking at records.

Another benefit of surveillance assessments is that they bring an external perspective to the review of the quality system. Although your internal audits are conducted by people independent of the functions they audit, there is still a parochialism that takes place. After a while you believe you understand certain things about your company. As a result you may assume things to be true that are not.

Even though internal auditors resist the temptation to make assumptions, they cannot avoid it all of the time. An external assessor does not have this parochial bias and will ask questions that seem naive to you. Often, it is those naive questions that uncover some of the biggest problems.

There is another benefit of surveillance assessments that some don't like to admit. We do not all keep our quality systems in tip top shape at all times. Sometimes it is easy to let a corrective action slip, or set aside an update to a procedure for awhile. When you know that the external assessors will return periodically, it puts an extra prod on you to get things in order. It's not that you don't keep your house in order at other times. It is just that you do a little extra special job of cleaning when you know company is coming.

INSTITUTIONALIZATION OF THE QUALITY SYSTEM CONCEPT

In Chapter 4 we discussed critical success factors for registration. Really, these are also critical success factors for continued compliance. Institutionalization of the quality system is among these. By the time registration takes place, the quality system concept is an integral part of the way you do business.

This fact makes continued compliance with the standards much easier than initial compliance. After a while, changes, which received so much cultural resistance at the time they were initially introduced, become the accepted way of doing business. Internal audits, previously described as a policing function, are now expected, if not welcomed. The corrective action methodology, which some had labeled as bureaucratic overhead, is the tool you now use to effectively fix problems. Procedures, which once were maligned as a vehicle for stifling creativity, are now relied upon to guide new people on the job and as a guide to make improvements.

We have witnessed some of those who most strongly resisted initial ISO 9000 registration efforts go through the registration effort "kicking and screaming," only to leave the company at some later time and marvel at the backward quality system of their new company—even to the point of asking if they could have some sample documentation for use on the new job. Human nature makes an interesting study.

The system you put in place to become registered to an ISO 9000 standard will mature much like the hypothetical botanical garden. But maturity is not equivalent with stagnation. Like a garden, your organization's quality system will go through cycles of refinement. If you have given thought to making the system self-correcting, as described in Chapter 9, it will continue to be a valuable intellectual asset of your organization—the basis for consistent product quality—even as your company changes in response to marketplace demands.

THE NCR EXPERIENCE

We were registered to ISO 9001 in August of 1991. Every six months since that time, BSI (our third-party assessment agency) has conducted a surveillance assessment. Their assessments have uncovered some nonconformity. The BSI surveillance assessments have been very helpful to us in improving our quality system. The assessors have noted that the quality system concept is very well accepted by NCR people.

The most dramatic example of that was our second surveillance assessment, one year after registration. The assessors showed up unannounced! The first time we knew of their coming was when we got the call from the receptionist at the front desk heralding their arrival. Even though they reserve the right to do exactly this, it is not their common practice to arrive unannounced. This particular group of assessors had been scheduled by two different schedulers—one for a registration assessment, and one for our surveillance assessment. Each scheduler believed that the other was responsible for notifying us. Neither one did.

It was a valuable experience for both us and the assessment agency. What they saw was our quality system as it ran every day, not after we did a little extra special job of cleaning because we knew company was coming. They discovered that even without special attention, our documentation was up-to-date, previous nonconformity had been corrected, and the system was working within the framework of the standard. Following this visit, they reduced the number of assessor-days they had been spending on our surveillance assessments.

The quality system has withstood some major changes in organizational structure and business direction. Beyond that, some elements of total quality management have been built on top of the foundation laid by ISO 9000. Still the quality system has been resilient and as each surveillance assessment attests, it remains compliant with the ISO 9001 standard.

Chapter Fourteen

Registering the Small Company to ISO 9000 Standards

What counts is not necessarily the size of the dog in the fight, but the size of the fight in the dog.

Dwight D. Eisenhower
President of the United States

The business benefits of ISO 9000 registration for a small company are the same as for a large company. Typically, however, the event that causes urgency in a small company is that they receive notification that they will be required to seek registration by a large company customer. Small here is defined in terms of number of employees, not in terms of customer base, revenue, profit, or other financial metric. The definition of small company is not precise. Typical examples are "no more than 500 employees,"[1] or "no more than 200 employees."[2]

As large companies clamor for ISO 9000 registration because they fear loss of sales in a world market, they have begun to use the standards as a means of supplier management. Recognizing the benefit of a consistent set of criteria by which to evaluate suppliers, large companies, some with no current plans to register to ISO 9000 themselves, have begun to require their small company suppliers to register to an ISO 9000 standard.

We have said before that we believe ISO 9000 registration should be a market-driven event. The ending date of the ISO 9000 registration project should be determined by the compelling market reason for registration. If a customer requires you to become registered, your project end date will be matched to the requirement date of that customer. But how much effort must a small company expend on the ISO 9000 registration project?

The NCR Network Products Division examples given in the preceding chapters are examples of how the principles of this book have been applied to ISO 9000 registration in a large company. But, the same market forces that drive ISO 9000 registration in multinational companies are at work in small companies as well. How do the principles of this book apply to small companies? *Equally as well as they do to large companies.*

Having achieved ISO 9000 registration for a large organization and having worked with smaller companies seeking registration, it is our conclusion that although there are some technical differences between the ISO 9000 registration projects of small and large companies, the major obstacles to ISO 9000 registration are not technical, but cultural. These cultural issues are the same for any company, no matter what its size: overcoming resistance to change, involving executive management in the project, dealing with the politics of the project, preparing the people of the company as well as the quality system for registration, and dealing with the third-party assessors.

This book addresses the cultural issues of an ISO 9000 registration project. Small companies have cultures and organizational inertia just like large companies. The ISO 9000 project champion must become as much an ISO 9000 standards expert in a small company as in a large company. The ISO 9000 registration project for a small company must be as well planned as for a large company and critical success factors must be addressed. The project cannot be accomplished by one person, so a team approach is as valid in small companies as in large companies. The concepts of assessment, independent audits, preregistration assessments, registration assessments, and surveillance assessments apply to small companies as well. The tips on preparation for external assessments by a third-party agency are useful to small companies. So although the examples in the preceding chapters show how the principles discussed have been applied to a large company, the principles apply to small companies too.

THE PURPOSE OF THIS CHAPTER

Why have a special chapter on registering the small company to ISO 9000? The answer is summed up in one word—resources.

When you are first confronted with the ISO 9000 standards, the perception of a resource-intensive activity is almost inevitable. "How are we going to get this done" appears to be an even more daunting question to the small company. In this chapter we look at the resource allocation aspects of an ISO 9000 registration effort in the small company. The chapter will help you decide whether your small company registration effort will be a full-time effort or a part-time effort.

RESOURCE EXPENDITURE ON THE SMALL COMPANY ISO 9000 REGISTRATION PROJECT

The ISO 9000 registration project can be expressed in simple terms as planning, followed by a series of assessment and corrective action activities. Figure 14–1 illustrates the simplification. As we have seen in the previous chapters, project planning is followed by internal assessment, corrective action, internal independent auditing, corrective action, the preregistration assessment, corrective action, the registration assessment, corrective action, and continuous surveillance assessments followed by corrective action. Figure 14–1 depicts the repetition of assessments and corrective actions.

It is in the assessment/corrective action cycle, and in particular the corrective action part of the cycle, that most of the ISO 9000 registration project resources are expended. Communication and training are required both to perform the assessments and to carry out the corrective action. Let's explore the resource requirements for communicating, training, assessing, and corrective action separately.

Communicating

Communication is easier in a small company than in a large one. This is especially true if the company employees are all at one location. A memo can be copied and distributed to all employees rapidly. The project champion can get around and talk to all employees in a day or two. An all employee meeting is easier to orchestrate than for a large company where no single meeting room is large enough to hold all employees.

FIGURE 14–1
Simplified ISO 9000 Registration Project Activity Chart

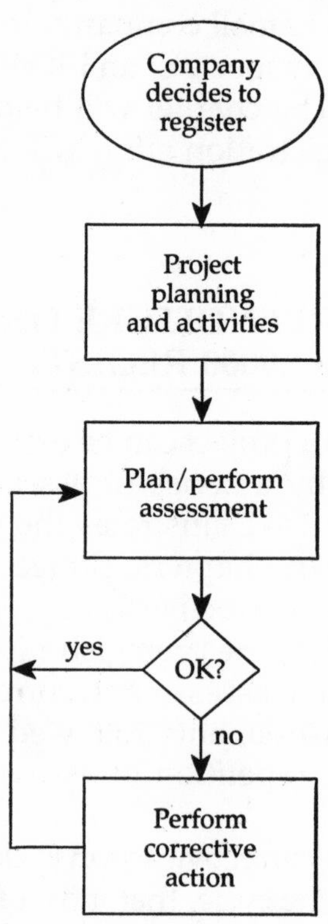

The same things need to be communicated to employees of small companies as to those of large companies. Why the project is being done, how the project is being done, who is working on it, why assessments are done, how assessments are done, and how to respond to third-party assessors are all things that employees need to hear. Memos (paper or electronic), newsletters, department meetings, and training sessions are all vehicles for communication. It is generally easier and faster to disseminate information in a small company. A paper memo can be easily copied and personally delivered by the project champion in minutes to every employee in a 40-employee company. In a 640-employee company this approach is impractical.

Though the resources required to prepare the information are about the same, the resources required to distribute it in a small company are less than in large company.

Training

Training is required in both small and large companies. In a large company, training is often handled by several individuals. The ISO 9000 project champion typically trains the project team on the ISO 9000 standards and their application to the company's business. The team members then train their own organizations. In a small company, the ISO 9000 project champion may conduct all of the awareness training for the entire company.

In the large company, the lead auditor may be someone different from the ISO 9000 project champion. The training of the internal auditors is typically done by this person. In a small company, the ISO 9000 project champion is frequently also the lead auditor, so the training of internal auditors is his or her responsibility as well.

As is true for communications, the facilitation of training in a small company is easier than in a large company. In a large company, it may take two or more training sessions just to cover one department. For a small company, the entire workforce may be covered in a couple sessions, or one all-hands session, though several smaller sessions may be preferred. The increased training responsibilities of the small company ISO 9000 project champion are offset by the reduced difficulties in training logistics. Fewer resources are expended in small companies on training than in large companies.

Assessing

In a large company, there are likely one or more dozen part-time internal auditors and it is rare that a week passes without some audit activity taking place. In a small company, there may be fewer than a half dozen part-time auditors and auditing is a monthly rather than a weekly activity.

The internal audit function of a small company is no less important than that of a large company, and the principles of Chapter 9 apply to large and small companies alike. The facilitation of the internal audit program is easier in a small company because there are fewer audits to schedule, conduct, report, and follow up on.

The same reasoning holds for the initial assessment. Fewer people means fewer functions performed, fewer functions need evaluation, and less effort must be expended in the initial assessment than for large companies.

For assessments by the third-party agency, there are fewer assessors for fewer days of assessment than for large companies. The resources required to host a third-party assessment in terms of third-party agency fees, escorting time, and lost work activity due to the assessment are also less than for large companies. In general, fewer resources are expended by the small company on all aspects of assessing than by large companies.

Corrective Action

As mentioned previously, the bulk of the resources that any company expends on an ISO 9000 registration project is in taking corrective action. This action is what makes compliance happen. Everything else in the project is an enabler for corrective action.

Corrective action is expressed in the creation and modification of quality system documentation. It is also expressed in the changes to behavior brought about by communication and training, which we have previously addressed.

Because the number of small company functions performed are fewer than large company functions, there are fewer procedures to write and correct, fewer internal audits performed, fewer items that need correcting, and therefore fewer resources expended on corrective action.

THE ISO 9000 PROJECT CHAMPION IN A SMALL COMPANY

In a large company, the champion of the ISO 9000 registration project is often a member of a quality department that is independent of all other functions of the company. Perhaps this person is the head of that organization, reporting directly to the company president or to a corporate vice president who heads a business unit of the corporation. In a small company, this situation is less likely. Many small companies do not feel they have the resources to support an independent quality organization.

The small company president may not want to increase the number of people on his or her staff, so the quality function may report to a vice president or director of a functional unit of the company. We know of one registered company where the individual responsible for the quality system reports each year to a different company vice president. In other cases, the project champion may report to the head of the design or manufacturing department. This circumstance is not surprising since it has only been in the last decade that many large companies have had quality functions that report independently to the company president.

All of this means that the ISO 9000 project champion may be an engineer, or someone with little background in quality assurance. Management of the ISO 9000 registration project may well be a part-time assignment. The impact on the project of a part-time ISO 9000 project champion will be discussed later. Besides the resource constraints a part-time ISO 9000 champion from a functional unit of the company places on the ISO 9000 registration project, it also presents other problems.

When the quality function, and in particular the management representative,[3] reports into a functional department like manufacturing rather than to the company president, it can be difficult to demonstrate how the responsibilities of that person are carried out without undue influence from the functional department manager. For example, how easy is it for the quality manager to report to the company president that a deficient product should not be shipped when the vice president of manufacturing to whom the quality manager reports is adamant about shipping it in order to fulfill revenue or schedule commitments? In such circumstances, responsibility and authority must be clearly defined and even then, it will take some convincing to make a third-party assessor believe that it really works.

When the ISO 9000 project champion reports into a functional unit of the company and not to the company president, it makes the politics of the project a little stickier. If the company president and the project leader's manager are intent on registration, the job is easier. If the company president pays little attention to the project and the project leader's manager is preoccupied with other duties, it can be very difficult to motivate one's own functional unit to change, much less the other functional units of the company. Thus the principle of targeting activities at gaining top management involvement is very important to the small company registration project.

When the organization that is lagging behind is your own, it is a bit tricky to report to the boss of your boss that your boss is the laggard. It is wise to schedule periodic reviews of the project with all of the executive management. Note that this and other activities for executive management are discussed in Chapter 4. If there are regular executive staff meetings, this review can be an agenda item at that meeting on a monthly or bimonthly basis. If the staff does not meet, you will have to schedule your own meetings. You should establish the need for reviews at the beginning of the project. Then when you have bad news to report it will not look like you called a meeting just to highlight problems.

A good way to handle the discovery of an area that is lagging behind is in contrast to areas that are progressing well. In the above example, where the department of one's own manager is not making progress, just display a chart showing how far each department has progressed. If all other departments have their documentations completed except yours, the facts will speak for themselves. The president and peers of your manager can address the issue—you are just reporting the facts. If the president and your manager's peers do not address the issue, you may need to point out that all documentation must be completed prior to some other event, such as training or internal auditing. If this still doesn't elicit a response, you may have to be courageously blunt about the potential for project slippage and ask the staff either to take some action to prevent the slippage, or to approve a new end date for the project.

The role of the ISO 9000 project champion in a small company is not significantly different from that of the champion in a large company. This person must plan, track, report on, and manage the project. In addition, he or she is the coach or facilitator for the ISO 9000 project team. In a large company, this team of department champions is often one level down from the executive staff. In a small company, it often *is* the executive staff, i.e., the managers of the functional areas of the company make up the ISO 9000 project team.

In a large company, many of the team members may be allocated full-time or three-fourths time to the project. In a small company, the functional area managers have full-time jobs already. This fact may make it difficult to keep the team focused on the ISO 9000 project, and members may miss team meetings more frequently than for the large company project team. The problem is compounded if the ISO 9000 champion is part-time as well.

The ISO 9000 registration project champion for a large or small company must become the company expert on the ISO 9000 standards and make the rest of the team the experts for their areas. In a large company, the department champions may lead subteams for their areas and delegate responsibility even further down into the organization. In a small company, less of the work is delegated but is performed directly by the team. If the team members get busy with their department responsibilities, the ISO 9000 project suffers. If a team member is falling behind in assigned project duties, the project manager should suggest that an alternate be named who can pick up responsibilities for the busy manager.

EFFECT OF ISO 9000 ON SMALL COMPANY FUNCTIONS

In Chapter 1, we generalized the effects of the ISO 9000 registration project on various company functions. These generalizations hold for large and small companies alike, with one notable exception: the newer company. First, let us make another generalization: newer companies tend to be smaller companies. Venture capitalists do not pool their money to fund upstart companies with tens of thousands of employees. Large companies like AT&T/NCR, IBM, Unisys, Control Data, and 3M have been around for decades. These all began as smaller companies and grew big.

Large, then, often means mature. Granted, many smaller companies are also mature. The generalizations in Chapter 1 about the effects of the ISO 9000 registration project on company functions were drawn from our experience with mature companies.

Most exceptions to our generalization will be found in newer, immature companies, and these are generally small companies.

In an immature company, the functional areas have not operated together long enough for the downstream manufacturing processes to have to react to over-the-wall practices of upstream processes. In such companies, the manufacturing department may not be leading the charge in quality improvement. It might be the design organization. However, a change in management can alter that situation almost overnight.

The point is that the ISO 9000 registration project champion in a small, immature company may find responsiveness in unlikely departments, while manufacturing may be one of the most difficult to deal with. The departments, manufacturing or otherwise, that respond positively to the project should be made examples of success to guide the rest of the company.

OVERALL ISO 9000 REGISTRATION PROJECT DIFFICULTY

Taking all of the above information into account, what can we conclude about the difficulty of the ISO 9000 registration project at small companies? If communicating, training, assessing, and corrective action are easier to facilitate in a smaller company, then shouldn't the project be a lot easier to facilitate as well? In many respects, yes; in some, no.

We mentioned that management of the small company ISO 9000 registration project is often a part-time responsibility. But this does not mean that the job of managing the ISO 9000 registration project is easier in a small company, only that it does not consume as much of the champion's time. In fact, part-time management of the project may be more difficult. A part-time ISO 9000 project champion may find it difficult to schedule meetings with the team of department champions, especially if they are part-time as well. Some companies get around this problem by scheduling meetings at lunch time, with lunches paid for by the project budget. A part-time ISO 9000 project champion will find his or her other responsibilities competing with the project. When there is a conflict, what will have priority? Issues such as these must be clearly addressed in the project planning and be resolved as a part of the approved project plan.

In almost all aspects of the ISO 9000 registration project, a small company will expend fewer resources to become registered than a large company. The real question is, however, does it have those resources to expend? It will document fewer processes, conduct fewer hours of training, conduct fewer internal independent audits, and be assessed by the third-party assessors for fewer assessor-days. But, will the resources expended per employee be affordable? After interviewing the project champions of both small and large companies, it is our conclusion that the resources expended per employee to gain registration by a small company are nearly equal to that of a large company.

The duration of registration projects for large and small companies alike is roughly equivalent at around 12 to 15 months. Remember the sign on the ISO 9000 war room given in the example in Chapter 2 that was altered until it became I$O 9,000,000? Underestimation of the work involved in taking a company from awareness to registration is not unique to large companies. The cultural issues of the project—the need to change behaviors and the natural resistance to that change—are found in small companies to the same extent they are found in large companies.

Communication may be faster, training may be easier to facilitate, assessing may not take as much effort, and the registration project may be managed on a part-time basis, but in a small company it still takes time for people to change their habits and become comfortable with new methods of working. It is as difficult for them as for their large company counterparts to assimilate the changes.

If you don't fall into the trap of underestimating the scope of the small company ISO 9000 registration project, it can be successful with a part-time project champion and a part-time project team. The elements of project planning in Chapter 3 and the understanding of how to address the project's critical success factors in Chapter 4 are essential to properly planning the part-time project. A good consultant can help with overall ISO 9000 training, audit training, and in setting up your documentation structure.

The duration of the project will be balanced between the market-driven needs and the availability of the part-time resources. In fact, the choice between a full-time or a part-time ISO 9000 project champion and team should be made based on the market-driven target date of the project and the resources that your company can afford to expend. There is no one right solution for everyone.

As this chapter points out, there are some technical differences between the ISO 9000 registration projects of small and large companies. However, the major obstacles to ISO 9000 registration are not technical, but cultural. These cultural issues are the same for any company, no matter what its size: overcoming resistance to change, involving executive management in the project, dealing with the politics of the project, preparing the people of the company as well as the quality system for registration, and dealing with the third-party assessors.

The previous chapters of this book help you with the cultural issues of ISO 9000 registration. With proper planning, the small company ISO 9000 registration project can be as successful and affordable as for a large company. As Dwight D. Eisenhower said, "What counts is not necessarily the size of the dog in the fight, but the size of the fight in the dog."

Chapter Fifteen

Answers to the Most Frequently Asked ISO 9000 Questions

No man can reveal to you aught but that which already lies half asleep in the dawning of your knowledge.

Kahlil Gibran
The Prophet

Because there were so few companies within the United States registered to the ISO 9000 standards at the time we became registered, once we achieved registration to ISO 9001, we gained instant popularity as a resource for companies to benchmark. We responded to scores of phone and electronic mail messages a week. (Now there is an electronic mail forum called the ISO 9000 User Group Network that we participate in. See Appendix C for more information.) We have been visited by several companies, including about a dozen people from a Malcolm Baldrige National Quality Award winner. We also spoke at several conferences, workshops, and other companies' quality events.

Ultimately, it was this desire of others to know how we did it that led to the writing of this book. As the prospect of writing the book became more real, we began collecting questions from all of the forums in which we have had the opportunity to share our experience. In this final chapter, we share with you specific questions and our answers to them. This format will help you put together answers for the inevitable questions that will arise from your organization as you move through the ISO 9000 registration process.

The questions are divided into categories. The first deals with questions about the standards themselves; the second regarding commentaries about the ISO 9000 standards; and the third with the registration process itself.

COMMONLY ASKED QUESTIONS ABOUT THE ISO 9000 STANDARDS

What is the ISO?

Some think that *ISO* is an acronym for "International Standards Organization." It is not. It is Greek for equal or uniform and is used as the prefix for words like isobar, isometric, and isothermal. ISO is the prefix of standards, like ISO 9000, published by the International Organization for Standardization. A major purpose of this organization is to develop standards that are equivalent or uniform worldwide, hence the use of term *ISO* in the name of each standard.

As mentioned in Chapter 1, the International Organization for Standardization is based in Geneva and was founded in 1946. Its purpose is to set international standards. Members are typically the standards organizations of member countries, such as the American National Standards Institute from the United States. In 1979, Technical Committee 176 was formed to create international standards for quality assurance.

Where did the ISO 9000 standards come from?

Technical Committee 176 (TC 176) of the International Organization for Standardization wrote the standards. They were initially published in 1987 and were based on the British standards BS 5750.

Why are the ISO 9000 standards necessary? Why were the standards developed?

The ISO 9000 standards were developed because of the need in a global marketplace to evaluate the quality systems of suppliers from all around the world. It is impractical for a company to perform second-party audits of suppliers that may be all over the globe, yet the control of suppliers is critical to the quality of one's own products and services. As quality became a new business focus, national and multinational standards began to appear and inconsistencies both in terminology and application of these standards abounded. Technical Committee 176 of the International Organization for Standardization was formed in 1979 to bring harmony to this area by creating international standards for quality assurance.

Who publishes the ISO 9000 standards? Where can I get copies of the ISO 9000 standards?

The International Organization for Standardization publishes the standards. You can get their documentation through the national standards organization of most countries, for example, the American National Standards Institute. We recommend that you purchase the *ISO 9000 Compendium*. It contains all of the standards, plus a glossary, several guidelines that help you apply the standards, and some vision statements about the future of the standards. You can also get the American language version of the standards from the American Society for Quality Control. For more information on how to access the ISO 9000 standards, see Appendix A.

How are the ISO 9000 standards organized?

ISO 9003 covers final inspection and test. ISO 9002 covers production and installation. ISO 9001 covers design/development, production, installation, and servicing. The other ISO documents are guidelines for either applying the standards to some particular area, like software development, for deciding which standard to register to, or for expanding on the intent of the three standards listed above. More information on this can be found in Figure 2–1.

What are the specific ISO 9000 standards to which a company can register?

ISO 9001 applies to companies that design and service what they manufacture. It also applies to software, services, and processed materials companies. ISO 9002 applies to companies that manufacture, but do not design what they manufacture. ISO 9003 applies to companies that assemble and test products designed and manufactured elsewhere. Companies that do design, service, and manufacturing may choose to register only their manufacturing function to ISO 9002, or just their inspection and test function to ISO 9003. These choices may gain registration for them, but sometimes create suspicion about the areas they chose not to register. More information on the ISO 9000 standards can be found in Chapters 1 and 2, including Figure 2–1.

Where can I get more information about ISO 9000?

Appendix A will tell you where to get ISO 9000 documents. Information in Appendix C tells you how to connect via electronic mail through the Internet to the ISO 9000 User Group Network. This network is a group of people, like yourself, connected via the Internet, who want to discuss ISO 9000 issues. Educators, consultants, government and business people are all subscribers to the network. Once connected, you are sent copies of any question, answer, notice, announcement, or pronouncement posted to the network. You can just view if you choose, or you can ask questions and receive responses from people all over the world in all kinds of industries and with all levels of experience. You can also answer the questions of others and contribute to any discussion, if you choose.

Another source of information is your local chapter of the American Society for Quality Control (ASQC) or other quality organizations. There may also be a consortium in your area of individuals from companies, consultant agencies, educational institutions, and government bodies formed for the purpose of sharing ISO 9000 information. One of the authors is currently the chairman of the ISO Quality Consortium that serves Minnesota and surrounding states. One purpose of this organization is to make information about ISO 9000 available to interested parties in the region inexpensively. The primary way of accomplishing this purpose is by conducting all-day workshops several times a year presented by people from registered companies at a nominal fee (usually $50) to attendees. The workshops are videotaped and the tapes are available for a handling fee.

Another mission of the consortium is to help in the formation of user groups of interested parties in local areas within the region, so that these people can share information among themselves. The ISO Quality Consortium has become a special interest group of the Minnesota Chapter of ASQC. For more information about the ISO Quality Consortium, you may call (612) 779-9820. There are consortiums in others parts of the United States as well.

QUESTIONS REGARDING CRITICISMS, COMPARISONS, AND THE FUTURE OF THE ISO 9000 STANDARDS

What attitudes might you encounter toward the ISO 9000 standards?

In Chapter 1, we describe four extremes. These are the quality advocate, who believes that ISO 9000 advances the quality system; the quality purist, who believes that ISO 9000 is a step backward in quality; the pragmatist, who believes that ISO 9000 may benefit the business; and the extreme pragmatist, who at best believes that ISO 9000 is a necessary evil. Most attitudes fall somewhere between these extremes, though in our experience the extremes exist as well.

What are some of the criticisms of the ISO 9000 standards? Aren't the ISO 9000 standards targeted at quality as it was in the 1970s rather than the 1990s?

The biggest criticism of the ISO 9000 standards is that they are out of date, or that they don't go far enough in their requirements. This is a common complaint of quality purists, described in Chapter 1. Some feel that ISO 9000 standards address a quality system that is very manufacturing inspection-oriented rather than a more modern total quality management approach applicable to all companies. It is more correct to say that the standards allow for this kind of quality system rather than that they require it. After all, companies that have won the US Malcolm Baldrige National Quality Award, role models of total quality management, have subsequently been registered to the ISO 9000 standards.

ISO Technical Committee 176 is aware of the deficiencies of the 1987 standard to address quality issues of the 1990s and has a vision, called Vision 2000, to update the standards accordingly.

Another complaint is that the standards are too bureaucratic or documentation heavy. This again is a case of allowing a situation rather than requiring one. The standards are surprisingly nonprescriptive. They are concerned that a quality system is under control, that is, that you can achieve the results that you plan to achieve. They are not concerned with the method you use as long as it works. This complaint will be addressed more fully in the next question.

Isn't ISO 9000 a paper chase, or at least a documentation intensive effort? Won't the ISO 9000 standards turn my company into a bureaucratic nightmare?

The ISO 9000 standards do not require mountains of paper, but you can approach it that way if you like. As mentioned in the answer to the previous question, the standards are concerned with whether your quality system is under control. A certain amount of documentation is required to do this. So is a certain amount of training. This is a communication issue. How do the people performing a job function know what to do? How you resolve this question is up to you.

Companies that address this issue by documenting hundreds of procedures for each department can become as noncompliant with the standards in a losing battle to keep the documentation up-to-date as companies that go to the other extreme of leaving workers to their own devices. One of the companies that we examined, early in our quest for understanding what the ISO 9000 standards were, took a very documentation-intensive approach. We chose to keep our documentation to a minimum, even replacing a bulging four-inch binder of procedures in the software development area with a partially-full one-inch binder. At the time we were registered, the company we examined had written hundreds of procedures, but seemed to be no closer to registration than when we first examined them. In the beginning, we went to them to learn how to approach the ISO 9000 standards; in the end, they came to us to learn how we became registered without a mountain of paper.

Often, the first effort at documenting what was not previously documented results in more documentation than is eventually needed. When a set of rules is being established where few existed before, perhaps this is necessary until the rules become institutionalized. Prior to starting the ISO 9000 registration project, we had committed the error of overdocumenting our quality system. The project, for us, was finding the right balance between amount of documentation and control of documentation as we redocumented a quality system that had moved ahead of the mountain of documents we could not keep up-to-date.

Does ISO 9000 strip engineers of their creativity?

This question expresses the fear of many engineers, hardware or software, when they first hear about ISO 9000 registration. This is especially true if there has been no specific design methodology in place prior to seeking registration, where engineers have been left to their own devices on how to perform the design function.

This is similar to an attitude that appeared when structured programming methodologies were first introduced to the production of computer software. In *Programmers and Managers,* Philip Kraft went so far as to claim that structured programming techniques were a ploy by management to de-skill the programming staff.[1]

Good designs, from the customer perspective, are not just about technical capability. They are also about other abilities like reliability, usability, installability, and maintainability. Conventional wisdom is that you only achieve all of these abilities if you have a controlled design process.

ISO 9001 only requires that you control the design, that is, that you have a methodology that you follow. No clause in the ISO 9001 standard even addresses the design function. The ISO 9001 standard addresses design input, design output, design verification, design changes, but not the design process itself. It specifically does not require that thinking be set aside. Design creativity is an integral factor of good technological capability. The requirements of the standard are targeted not so much at the technological abilities of the design, but at the other abilities.

How do the ISO 9000 standards compare to total quality management?

As mentioned in Chapter 1 and throughout the book, we believe that ISO 9000 registration is a stepping stone to total quality management. Figure 5–3 shows that a quality system that is just compliant with the ISO 9000 standards is a long way from total quality management, but it is movement in the right direction for a company with no quality system. At a recent seminar, a speaker from a Malcolm Baldrige Quality Award winning company, that has subsequently become registered to ISO 9001, remarked that if the company had it to do over, they would have preferred to get registered to ISO 9001 first.

The reason it is better to get registered first is that an ISO 9000-compliant quality system is a foundation for total quality management. It is easier to work on the foundation before putting up walls and ceilings. The foundation, in this case, is a quality system managed by the executive management of the company, with shared values in the form of a quality policy, controlled processes, an understanding that the management of suppliers is critical to the company's success, and cycles of review and improvement.

Improvement? Where do the standards say anything about improvement? Well, they don't, yet, at least not in terms of proactive improvement. But they do require corrective action, which means root cause removal be taken when a problem is discovered. Though reactive, this is one form of improvement.

The foundation is also made up of vehicles that have been put into place to make registration happen: a communication structure, an implementation team, and an executive management forum to address quality issues such as a quality steering team. Once you have a forum for executive management to address the quality system that they own, the steps toward total quality management are easier. They can now address the issues of strategic planning of quality, determining and responding to customer satisfaction, measuring processes, making proactive improvements, expanding the shared quality values to include a greater focus on the customer and a commitment to employees and to the community, and enlarging the communication system to include information for fact-based decision making.

This is exactly the path we took at NCR Network Products Division. Following the registration of our quality system to ISO 9001, our quality steering team of executive managers continued to meet and review issues like conducting a customer satisfaction survey, establishing a quality awards program, conducting surveys to determine employee satisfaction, and other elements of the structure of total quality management. Most of the work on these issues was conducted by teams of employees who reported status and results to the quality steering team.

Who was Malcolm Baldrige?

He was secretary of commerce under President Reagan. The US National Quality Award is administered under the Department of Commerce and was being formulated during Mr. Baldrige's tenure. Mr. Baldrige died in an equestrian accident and when the award was deployed it was named in his honor.

What is the future of the ISO 9000 standards?

It is intended that the standards be updated every five years. Updates to the 1987 version include the requirement for a quality manual. Previously the standards did not require this, but third-party assessors did. Some additional changes include: all clause numbers correspond to the ISO 9001 numbering scheme (4.1 through 4.20), the addition of a servicing clause in ISO 9002, the addition of a subclause on quality planning, management representative duties are more well-defined, contract review and design control have been expanded, and quality record requirements are more explicit. Also, "Purchaser Supplied Materials" has changed to "Customer Supplied Materials," "Handling, Storage, Packaging, and Delivery" also includes preservation; and the "Corrective Action" section is expanded to include preventative action. This list of changes is not comprehensive.

Several documents have been added to the original five ISO 9000 documents. These documents are guidelines for applying the standards either generically, or specifically for software companies, service companies, and processed materials companies. Figure 2-1 mentions these guidelines. The reason for the specific guidelines is because it was felt that people were clear about how to apply the standards to hardware but not to the other three areas.

ISO Technical Committee 176 has a targeted date of 1996 for implementing Vision 2000, described in the *ISO 9000 Compendium*. The committee feels that the understanding of the application of quality principles will have matured in all industries such that there will not be a need for documents describing the four different product categories: software, services, processed materials, and hardware. Their goal is to develop a single management standard (ISO 9004, updated, with appropriate new topics) and a single quality assurance requirements standard (ISO 9001, updated) with expanded guidance provided in supplementary standards as needed. The ISO 9000 standards of Vision 2000 will not express the elements of total quality management to the extent that the Malcolm Baldrige National Quality Award does, but they will take a big step in that direction.

QUESTIONS ABOUT GETTING REGISTERED

What must a firm do to comply with the standards?

The standards are not prescriptive. ISO 9001, the most comprehensive of the standards is only a little more than five pages long, excluding the introductory material. Essentially, you must show that you have each of the areas described by the standard under control. These are areas such as purchasing, training of employees, company documentation, review of contracts, company processes, test equipment, packaging, delivery, and the like. Document the rules you follow in each of the areas and provide records that show you follow the rules. The rule of thumb is: Say what you do, do what you say.

What initial problems may be encountered during the registration process? What is the most difficult thing about implementing an ISO 9000 quality system?

Corporate culture issues. People do not like to change. There are plenty of seminars on what the standards are and how they are applied. This is easy to find out. Writing a quality manual and documentation is time consuming, but not too difficult. If the only effort was documentation you could be done in about three months. Getting people to follow the documented system, to break bad habits, to form good habits of keeping records is the difficult part. The cultural issues of moving a company from unawareness to registration are the biggest issues. Dealing with the cultural issues is the foundational element of this book. Suggestions and examples are given throughout the book for dealing with the culture in all aspects of the project.

How much does ISO 9000 registration cost?

This question is difficult to answer in the general case. Large companies will spend more than small companies. Companies that already have a disciplined, well-documented system will spend less than companies of similar size that have undocumented, ad hoc methods. Companies that seek ISO 9002 registration will spend less, in general, than companies of similar size that seek ISO 9001 registration. Companies that use a registration agency from outside of their country generally pay higher registration costs (because of travel expenses) than if they used a local registration agency.

In discussing this topic with representatives from successfully registered companies, we have noted differences of approach and opinion. Some companies count only the cost paid to outside assessors. Other companies count everything spent on any quality improvement during the life of the ISO 9000 registration project. Others have reckoning methods that fall in between these. As an organization of somewhat over 600 people, we spent about 15,000 person-hours on quality improvement during the time of our registration assessment. This figure does not include activities that were performed within individual work groups in preparing and reviewing procedural documentation because we did not track these activities. The total effort was not much more than we would have spent on quality improvement anyway. Quality improvement activities in the years since registration attest to this.

Typical costs for companies in the 500 to 900 employee range, including all quality improvement activity during the project, are quoted at $300,000 to $500,000, with the cost of the assessment running $9,000 to $25,000 depending on the assessment agency chosen.

Chapters 3 and 4 will help you plan the right activities for your project. You can determine the cost of each activity by estimating the cost of the resources necessary to carry it out.

How long does it take to become registered?

This is really up to you. Chapter 3 makes the point that you should let market requirements drive your need to be registered and the time it takes you to do so. From our schedule, shown in Figure 3-3, you can see that it took us 13 months from approval of the plan until registration. This is consistent with our experience with other companies that shows that the project typically takes from nine to 18 months, with 12 to 15 months being most common. There are also exceptions. We know of one company that took about 12 months to gain ISO 9002 registration and another three years to gain ISO 9001 registration. The answer to this question for you will depend on the size of your company, the standard to which you become registered, the current level of compliance with that standard, and the urgency with which you must get registered as dictated by your marketplace.

What is the return on investment on implementing ISO 9000? What are the benefits of ISO 9000 registration?

We heard two CEOs of registered companies address this question after giving presentations on ISO 9000 from the CEO's viewpoint. They both stated that ISO 9000 registration should be part of an ongoing quality improvement effort that is inherent in the culture and not based on a desire for immediate return on investment. One felt that quality improvement does not pay an immediate return on investment and that the long-term return on investment is difficult to quantify.

Still, some have attempted to express the benefits of ISO 9000 registration. Some of those benefits have been quantified, the rest are subjective. The quantified results are expressed in terms of improvement in manufacturing yields (in one example from less than 40 percent to over 80 percent) and reduction of defects per million opportunities (in one example from 15,000 to less than 800).

They are also expressed in terms of improved test results on newly designed products and reduced customer-reported errors. These kinds of things can be expressed monetarily in terms of the reduced effort expended to rework or fix the problems.

The subjective items are more difficult to quantify monetarily. Examples of subjective items are increased cooperation between departments, a higher sense of urgency for problem ownership and resolution, and fewer problems with people not understanding their responsibilities and the procedures they need to follow.

Also, ISO 9000 registration projects tend to pick up some extra baggage as people add to the project actions that are not strictly necessary for registration, but are good, intelligent things to do. Therefore, some of the improvements are not just the result of what was done to become registered. Neither is the expense of implementing these improvements. This is why the CEOs mentioned above believe that ISO 9000 registration should be part of a broader quality improvement effort. The fact that the ISO 9000 project puts in place some elements that make the transition from ISO 9000 to total quality management easier means that some of the benefits are realized only if the ISO 9000 registration project is one step on a much longer journey.

How are issues of safety handled within an ISO 9000-compliant system?

There are two issues here: safety of employees on the job and safety of customers who use the products. Employee safety will be handled just like any other element of your quality system in documentation, training, and records. Policies will spell out general safety guidelines. Procedures will spell out particular methods of performing tasks, and proper safety equipment, tools, or attire to be used. Records will show what training has been given, that safety equipment adequacy is verified periodically, and that proper precautions have been taken. Pertinent sections of the ISO 9001 standard to address these issues are Process Control (Section 4.9), Quality Records (Section 4.16), and Training (Section 4.18).

Customer safety requirements will be documented in the product design specifications. Records of design reviews, test results, and agency safety certifications will show evidence that the safety requirements are met. Pertinent sections of the ISO 9001 standard to address these issues are Design Control (section 4.4), specifically Design Input and Design Verification, and Inspection and Testing (section 4.10). The fact that you address product safety issues within your ISO 9000 registered system does not mean that ISO 9000 registration covers product liability and safety, however. James Kolka and Gregory Scott discuss the relationship of ISO 9000 registration to EC product liability and safety in the *ISO 9000 Handbook*.[2]

Third-party assessors are chosen based on their areas of expertise. Assessors who visit your facility will be aware of general industry requirements or good practices regarding safety in your type of business and will expect to see that you have addressed these.

How do you merge corporate requirements with ISO 9000 requirements in a quality system?

A division of a large corporation that is being registered as a separate unit will face the question of the role of corporate requirements in their quality system. The policies and practices of the division are a mixture of the local and the corporate culture. Corporate policies, standards, and interfaces will influence the division's quality system.

We faced this situation when we registered our division within the NCR Corporation. Where NCR corporate policies and standards were mandatory, we adopted them wholesale. Where they were not, we viewed them as guidelines and wrote our own documents to express exactly how we implemented those corporate guidelines. In the end, our quality system reflected the mixture of NCR corporate and local cultures, but with clarity. We knew when we were following an NCR corporate standard exactly, and when we were following a local procedure based upon an NCR corporate standard.

Our quality policies are exemplary. We took the NCR corporate quality policies, reproduced them verbatim in our policy document, and in a different typeface expressed how we were implementing the corporate policy at the local level. The NCR corporate quality policies were a guideline after which we patterned our division policies. Our quality manual clearly shows that we are bound by our own implementation, not the corporate guideline.

How do you merge regulatory requirements with ISO 9000 requirements?

The answer to this question parallels the answer to the previous question on corporate requirements. The difference is that many corporate requirements can be treated as guidelines, but regulatory requirements are mandatory. You address these requirements in the appropriate places in your documented quality system. If, for example, the regulatory requirements deal with manufacturing activities, you document them in your manufacturing procedures. If the requirements deal with product characteristics, you document the requirement to incorporate them in your design procedures, and the specifics of the characteristics in your design documentation for each project. For example, a design procedure may call for a required agency test to be performed at a particular point in the process and the quality plans for each design effort will state what requirements the products must have in order to pass the agency tests.

What should I know about EEC regulations?

The European Economic Community (EEC) does *not* require blanket registration to ISO 9000 in order to do business in Europe. The EEC has targeted certain products to be regulated under recent directives for reasons of health and safety or strategic importance. The ISO 9000 standards are referenced in the regulatory requirements for these specific products.

The main thing to know is whether any new EEC directive applies to a product that your company produces. Contact the government agency in your country responsible for international trade for assistance in this effort. In the United States the Department of Commerce will help you determine if your products are regulated by the EEC.

If so, and ISO 9000 registration is a part of your compliance with an EEC directive, you must use as a third-party registration agency a notified body of the EEC, i.e., a registrar sanctioned by the EEC. No registrar outside of Europe is currently a notified body of the

EEC, but the EEC has left the door open in the future for the possibility of registration agencies outside of the EEC being granted notified body status. More information on the topic of regulated products of the EEC can be found in Chapter 1.

How do you get management buy in and support for an ISO 9000 project?

Management involvement in the ISO 9000 registration project is a critical success factor of the project as discussed in Chapter 4. You cannot wait for this involvement to happen. You must target elements of the registration plan at making it happen. One way to make it happen is to assign ownership of the responsibility to become compliant to the executive staff. If any deficiencies are found in their divisions, they are personally responsible to see that the deficiencies are corrected.

Another way to get the executive staff involved is to organize them to meet as a team responsible for formulating the quality policy. Then this team can be used to set other policies as necessary relating to release of products, corrective action, and other cross-functional issues. We even assigned this team the responsibility for disseminating the quality policies. They were not just committed; they were visibly actively involved.

Other elements of gaining management commitment are mentioned in Chapter 5.

How do third-party assessors get involved?

You hire them to audit your quality system to determine whether you say what you do and do what you say and whether you have addressed all elements of the standard. If so, they publish your name in a registry. They come back about every six months to see that you still do what you say and say what you do. For more on your relationship with the third-party assessment agency, see Chapters 10 through 13.

How do I decide how to choose a third-party registration agency?

The choice of a third-party registration agency is not an easy one. There are several things to consider. What is your reason for getting registered? Where does your company do business? What do the agencies charge for their services? How do they handle continuous surveillance assessments? Do they require recertification after a set time?

If your products are regulated by the European Economic Community and one of your reasons for getting registered is to meet these regulatory requirements, your choice of a third-party agency is limited to a notified body of the EEC. Currently only certain European third-party registration agencies are notified bodies of the EEC.

If your reasons for registration are customer driven, then your choices are broader. To date, no country requires that you be registered by a particular agency or a particular country's agency. We know of no companies that require their suppliers to be registered by a particular agency or a particular country's agency. Except within the EEC, mutual recognition of accreditation and accredited agencies between governments is not very well developed. Even within the EEC, all of the rules have not been defined.

Agencies themselves have set up memoranda of understanding (MOU) with one another to mutually accept one another's registrations. For example, with certain conditions fulfilled, the British Standards Institution (BSI) will co-register a company that has been registered by Underwriters Laboratories (UL). The applicant company applies for registration from both BSI and UL and pays the registration fees of both organizations. When the company passes the UL registration assessment, it is also granted a BSI registration. MOUs are not currently recognized by the EEC, however.

Another consideration is accreditation of registration agencies. Anyone can perform quality system assessments and grant registration. Companies may not require that their suppliers register with particular third-party agencies, but they may ask that whatever agency is used, it is accredited. Agencies are usually accredited by government or quasi-governmental accreditation bodies like the National Accreditation Council for Certifying Bodies (NACCB) in Britain. The Registrar Accreditation Board (RAB) accredits US registration bodies.

A company must be cautious in determining what their purpose for registration is and then decide which agency is best to use to fulfill that purpose.

Which accredited auditor training courses should I take?

The US Registrar Accreditation Board (RAB) rules for certification of auditors became stricter in 1993 with the RAB approval of training organizations. Many US course providers had sought accreditation from the Institute of Quality Assurance (IQA), based in London, prior to the initiation of the RAB accreditation process. IQA is recognized by the British government as an official accreditation body for course providers and lead auditors.

The IQA did not recognize RAB course accreditation and the RAB set a deadline after which it would not recognize IQA accredited courses. Other organizations accredit auditor training courses in other countries. Mutual recognition between these organizations is following the same path as mutual recognition of registration of companies to the ISO 9000 standards—it is slow in coming.

If you want to train to be a lead auditor in your company, you don't have to worry about which accredited training course to take. The main focus of auditor accreditation is on who can be an auditor for a registration agency. For example, the RAB requires that RAB-accredited registrars employ only auditors certified under the RAB's certification program.

The ISO 9000 standards do not require that your internal auditors be certified by anybody, though some assessors have written findings if the lead auditor of a company is not trained through an accredited program. In these instances, no specific accreditation was required. We think this is prescriptive and would dispute such a finding.

The internal audit function is discussed in Chapter 9.

Should we use a consultant to help us get registered?

The determination to use a consultant is a personal matter. As in choosing a registration agency, you should determine your needs before deciding whether to use a consultant, and if affirmative, which one to use. You should be clear on what you need a consultant for. Consultants can be very good at helping you structure your quality manual and documentation, performing audit training, conducting audits, and planning corrective action. They are at a disadvantage in working with your culture because even though they will interact with it, they will not work within it. Many of the cultural issues addressed in this book are not the responsibility of consultants. They provide the what, you provide the how.

There are exceptions. You may decide to hire a consultant to lead the entire project. To do so effectively, the consultant almost becomes an employee of your company. The consultant is more a contract employee than a consultant: actively involved with the project, not just giving you consultation. In that capacity, he or she will address cultural issues. This service is not usually provided by a consultant, however.

Once you are clear on what you need a consultant for, look for consultants with experience in what you need. Don't go with the cheapest one, but look at the total cost of ownership, i.e., what you get for what you pay. Paying a bit more for a consultant who has practical experience and good recommendations from satisfied registered clients is a better investment than paying less for someone who became a consultant a month ago because he or she lost his or her job.

Another thing to look for, especially if you need help in establishing an internal audit program, is accreditation. It is fairly easy today to become a certified lead assessor. Look for a consultant with these credentials.

What is the value of a preregistration assessment?

The preregistration assessment is covered in detail in Chapter 10. There are several benefits. First, it gives you an independent indication of whether you will be ready for the registration assessment according to your schedule. It is not a guarantee that you will pass the registration assessment, but it at least gives you a good indication. It also will point out areas of weakness from the third-party agency's perspective. These you can fix before the registration assessment.

Another benefit is that it allows you to learn how your third-party agency views the standard and conducts assessments. You can augment your own internal audit program with this information. It also allows your people to experience a third-party assessment prior to the registration assessment. Finally, it gives an added sense of urgency to the project, now that the third-party agency has been on the premises.

What kinds of questions do assessors ask of executive management?

Primarily the assessors want to know how executive managers are personally involved in the management of the quality system. They will want to know how each executive ensures that the people within his or her division understand the quality policy or policies and their own responsibility and authority within the quality system. The assessors will also want to know how resource utilization is determined and how adequate staffing levels are determined and fulfilled. They will want to know how planning is done to ensure that people have the appropriate skills to do their assigned tasks.

The assessors will also want to know how problems in the quality system are brought to the attention of management and how management responds to those problems. They will want to know in what forum(s) executive management reviews the effectiveness of the quality system and what they actually review. Finally, they will ask about company and division strategic planning and goals, how those goals are communicated to employees, and how executive management leads the effort to fulfill the goals.

Not all of these questions will be asked of all of executive management all of the time. They form a general representation of the kinds of questions that are asked. It is wise for your executive management to be generally aware of the sections of the ISO 9000 standards, particularly the sections that pertain to management and their own individual spheres of influence.

What kinds of things must you do to get ready for a registration assessment?

You must ready the quality system for a registration assessment. This is the goal of the registration project. Beyond that, you must get your people ready. Prepare them for what happens during the assessment. Train your escorts on their duties and responsibilities.

Address the attitudes of your people toward the assessors and the assessment. Instruct everyone in how you will handle differences of opinion with the assessors and instill the principle of not arguing. Preparation for the registration assessment is covered in detail in Chapter 11.

During the assessment itself you will have both reality and perception. Reality is what the assessors will find when they view the quality system itself. Perception is what is commonly known as first impressions. You should work at controlling both. You control reality by preparing the quality system in advance to be compliant. You control perception by giving a good first impression. The latter can be accomplished through means such as good housekeeping and good attendance at meetings during the assessment. Chapter 12 covers these concepts in more detail.

How do you phase new procedures into an ISO 9000-compliant system?

The answer to this question depends upon a couple of things, including the magnitude of the change being introduced by the new procedures and the cycle time of the process into which the procedures are being introduced. If the change is small, you may just flash-cut over to the new procedures after the appropriate training of the affected personnel.

If the change is large, you may need to validate the new procedures before implementing them. Using the Plan-Do-Check-Act Shewhart Cycle, often attributed to W. Edwards Deming who popularized it, you implement procedure changes in one area or on one project to test them out. After the trial, you make necessary modifications and then implement the new procedures globally.

If the change is being introduced into a process where the cycle time is short, such as a manufacturing process that takes only days to complete, you may just introduce the new procedures for the next run through the cycle. For an engineering process that takes months to complete, you have a more difficult problem. You could introduce the changes for any new project that begins the cycle. However, if the changes are directed primarily at the end of the cycle, you may have to wait months for them to take effect. Conversely, if you flash-cut over to the new procedures, projects which have already been several months in the process may now have new requirements placed on them that they are unable to satisfy.

For example, suppose that the testing procedures are changed to require testing to formally produced test plans. Projects that will enter the test phase in the few months following the procedural change will have already passed the phase where formal test plans should have been produced. Do you require the design teams to retroactively produce these test plans, adding initially unplanned work to the project, thereby risking a delay in delivery of the product? Or do you allow these projects to complete the cycle under the old rules perpetuating the problems that you hoped to correct with the new procedures?

These are not trivial problems to solve. Often, people whose processes have short cycle times do not appreciate the difficulty faced by those making changes to processes with long cycle times. The discussion in Chapter 3 pertaining to Figure 3–1 about project planning viewed as a system is generically applicable to all projects, not just the ISO 9000 registration project. It is a valuable guide in helping those who are faced with decisions about project disruptions such as implementing new, initially unplanned procedures. Usually some sort of phased approach is taken where projects are evaluated one by one and a decision is made based on trade offs between project delay and risks of not implementing the new procedures.

NOTES

Preface

1 Roger J. Howe, Dee Gaeddert, Maynard A. Howe, *Quality on Trial* (St. Paul, MN: West Publishing, 1992).

2 Since ISO 9001 registration was achieved, the NCR name has been changed to AT&T Global Information Solutions. However, because ISO 9001 registration was achieved as "NCR," the NCR name is used throughout the text.

Chapter 1

1 Chapter 15 contains answers to the most commonly asked questions about ISO 9000. If you have only a passing familiarity with ISO 9000 or you want to reacquaint yourself with basic ISO 9000 concepts, you may find it helpful to read Chapter 15 before finishing Chapter 1 and moving on.

2 ISO 8402:1992, *Quality Management and Quality Assurance—Vocabulary,* defines total quality management as "A management approach of an organization centered on quality, based on the participation of all its members and aiming at long term success through customer satisfaction, and benefits to the members of the organization and to society."

Chapter 2

1 Rosabeth Moss Kanter, *The Change Masters* (New York: Simon and Schuster, 1983).

2 James L. Lamprecht, *ISO 9000: Preparing for Registration* (New York: ASQC Quality Press/Marcel Dekker, 1992).

3 *The ISO 9000 Handbook,* Robert W. Peach, ed. (Fairfax, VA: CEEM Information Services, 1992).

4 Handley-Walker Company, Inc., *The Handley-Walker Guide to ISO 9000* (Valencia, CA: Handley-Walker Company, 1992).

5 Charles A. Mills, *The Quality Audit—A Management Evaluation Tool* (New York: McGraw Hill, 1989).

6 Since ISO 9001 registration was achieved, the NCR name has been changed to AT&T Global Information Solutions. However, because ISO 9001 registration was achieved as "NCR," the NCR name is used throughout the text.

Chapter 3

1 Donald L. Kanter and Philip H. Mirvis, *The Cynical Americans* (San Francisco: Jossey-Bass, 1989).

2 By "failed effort" we do not mean an effort that results in a second or even third assessment before registration. We planned for two assessments and set both cost and labor expectations right from the start. A failed effort is one that is based on unrealistic expectations and consequently disappoints those involved.

3 Much of the theory for this section is based on Porter Henry, "Manage Your Sales Force as a System," *Harvard Business Review,* March/April 1975, p. 80.

4 A "nonconformity" is the nonfulfillment of specific requirements, such as when the quality system does not comply with the ISO 9000 standards.

Chapter 4

1 See "Getting Things Done" by Maurice Hardaker and Bryan K. Ward, *Harvard Business Review,* November/December 1987, p. 112.

2 Roger J. Howe, Dee Gaeddert, Maynard A. Howe, *Quality on Trial* (St. Paul, MN: West Publishing, 1992).

3 William H. Davidow and Bro Uttal. *Total Customer Service.* (New York: Harper and Row, 1989).

4 Quality function deployment is a product development and manufacturing technique for deploying customer requirements throughout an organization's activities to ensure that the deliverable product meets those requirements. Those familiar with QFD may find it helpful to think of critical success analysis as a technique for deploying cultural requirements throughout an organization's ISO 9000 registration activities to ensure that the project is not derailed by cultural issues.

5 A discussion of the role of quality policies appears in Chapter 8.

Chapter 5

1 We use the term *subtle* rather than *hidden* because hidden agendas have a negative meaning implying that the person pursuing the hidden agenda is attempting to accomplish something in a somewhat underhanded manner. This is not what we are advocating. Having a subtle agenda is not dishonest or unethical. Pursuing a subtle agenda means that you are attempting to accomplish objectives beyond, but not contradictory to, your stated objectives.

2 Roger J. Howe, Dee Gaeddert, Maynard A. Howe, *Quality on Trial* (St. Paul, MN: West Publishing, 1992).

3 Robert Block, *The Politics of Projects* (New York: Yourdon Press, 1983).

4 Sun Tzu, *The Art of War*. Trans. by Samuel B. Griffith (London: Oxford University Press, 1963).

5 Robert Block, *The Politics of Projects* (New York: Yourdon Press, 1983).

Chapter 6

1 Richard S. Wellins, William C. Byham and Jeanne M. Wilson, *Empowered Teams: Creating Self-directed Work Groups that Improve Quality, Productivity, and Participation* (San Francisco: Jossey-Bass, 1991).

Chapter 7

1 ''The supplier shall carry out a comprehensive system of planning and documented internal quality audits to verify whether quality activities comply with planned arrangements and to determine the effectiveness of the quality system.'' ISO 9001 Section 4.17, *Internal Quality Audits.*

2 Sample reporting forms are found in Chapter 9: Ensuring Continuing ISO 9000 Compliance of the Quality System: Setting Up An Internal Audit Program.

3 A *finding* is an auditing term indicative of a nonconformity in the quality system.

4 An *observation* is an auditing term meaning a statement of fact supported by objective evidence, but not necessarily a nonconformity in the quality system.

Chapter 8

1 ISO 9001 Section 4.5, *Document Control.*

2 ISO 9004 Section 17.1, *Quality Documentation and Records, General.*

3 *Confronting the Constitution* Allan Bloom, ed. (Washington, DC: The AEI Press, 1990).

4 ''The supplier's management shall define and document its quality policy and objectives for, and commitment to, quality. The supplier shall ensure that this policy is understood, implemented, and maintained at all levels in the organization.'' ISO 9001 Section 4.1.1, *Quality Policy.*

Chapter 9

1 ISO 9001 Section 4.1.2.2, *Verification Resources and Personnel.*

2 *United States General Accounting Office Government Auditing Standards.* US Government Printing Office. 1988 revision.

3 Allan J. Sayle, *Management Audits,* 2nd Ed. (Hampshire, England: Allan J. Sayle, Ltd., 1988).

4 Charles A. Mills, *The Quality Audit—A Management Evaluation Tool* (New York: McGraw Hill, 1989).

5 Dennis R. Arter, *Quality Audits for Improved Performance.* (Milwaukee: ASQC Quality Press, 1989).

6 ISO 9001 Section 4.1.2.2, *Verification Resources and Personnel.*

7 ISO 9001 Section 4.18, *Training.*

8 ISO 9001 Section 4.1.3, *Management Review.*

9 ISO 8402:1992, *Quality Management and Quality Assurance—Vocabulary.*

Chapter 10

1 Stephen Covey, *The Seven Habits of Highly Effective People* (New York: Simon and Schuster, 1989).

Chapter 11

1 The ISO 9000 standards, e.g., ISO 9001 Section 4.1.2.3, *Management Representative,* require that there be a person, called the management representative, who has authority and responsibility for ensuring that the requirements of the standards are implemented and maintained. This person is often a company's ISO 9000 project champion.

Chapter 12

1 ISO 9001 Section 4.1.2.3, *Management Representative.*

Chapter 13

1 Michel M. Robert, ''Attack Competitors by Changing the Game Rules,'' *The Journal of Business Strategy,* September/October 1991.

2 ISO 9001 Section 4.1.2.3, *Management Representative.*

3 ISO 9001 Section 4.1.3, *Management Review.*

4 ISO 9001 Section 4.17, *Internal Quality Audits.*

Chapter 14

1 1993 Award Criteria. Malcolm Baldrige National Quality Award. "Award Eligibility Categories," p. 35. National Institute of Standards and Technology, US Department of Commerce.

2 1993 Minnesota Quality Award Application and Guidelines, "Award Categories," p. 3. Minnesota Council for Quality.

3 ISO 9001 Section 4.1.2.3, *Management Representative.*

Chapter 15

1 Philip Kraft, *Programmers and Managers.* (New York: Springer-Verlag, 1977).

2 James Kolka and Gregory Scott, "The Legal Limitations of ISO 9000 Registration and EC Product Liability and Product Safety," *The ISO 9000 Handbook*, ed. Robert W. Peach (Fairfax, VA: CEEM Information Services, 1992).

Appendix A

Where to Obtain the ISO 9000 Standards

Copies of the ISO 9000 standards, including the *ISO 9000 Compendium,* are available directly from the International Organization for Standardization. Write or call:

ISO Central Secretariat
Case postale 56
CH-1211 Geneve 20
Switzerland
Telephone: 41 22 749 01 11
Telefax: 41 22 733 34 30

The ISO documents are also available through your country's national standards organization. In the United States this is the American National Standards Institute (ANSI):

American National Standards Institute
11 West 42nd Street
13th Floor
New York, NY 10036

Individual copies of the US Q9000 (formerly Q90) series, which are equivalent to the ISO 9000 series standards, are available from the American Society for Quality Control (ASQC). Purchasing these documents from ASQC is cheaper than purchasing the ISO 9000 series from ANSI, or the ISO. Write or call:

American Society for Quality Control
300 West Wisconsin Avenue
Milwaukee, Wisconsin 53203
Telephone: (800) 248-1946

Appendix B

Critical Success Factors Related to Elements of the ISO 9000 Project Plan

Organizational Critical Success Factors for ISO 9000 Registration ("Whats") Related to Elements of the ISO 9000 Registration Project Plan ("Hows")

WHATs versus HOWs

Strong relationship:	●	9
Medium relationship:	○	3
Weak relationship:	△	1

Critical Success Factors ("Whats")	Elements of the ISO 9000 Registration Project Plan ("Hows")	1 Ownership of the ISO 9000 sections	2 Ownership of the system at the elementary level	3 Empowered department champions	4 Quality briefs	5 Training
Management active commitment to registration	1	●	○	○	△	
Adequate resources to carry out the plan	2	○	△	○		
Employee active commitment to registration	3	○	●	●	○	
Resources (employee willingness to participate)	4	○	●	●	○	
Clear and comprehensive understanding of the ISO 9000 standard	5	○	○	○	○	
Clear and comprehensive understanding of the quality system	6	○	○		○	
Understanding of the quality system concept	7				○	
Understanding of the quality documentation structure	8				○	
Communication structure	9				●	
Employee awareness of the standard and its meaning for them	10		●	△	○	
Employee awareness of the quality system	11		●	△	○	
Employee awareness of the structure and purpose of assessments	12		○	△	○	
Management awareness of the standard and its meaning for them	13	●			○	
Management awareness of the quality system	14	●			○	
Management awareness of the structure and purpose of assessments	15	○			○	
Institutionalization of the ISO 9000 quality system concept	16	●	●	△	○	
Acceptance of the quality system concept	17	●	●	△	○	
Attitude that registration results from improvement	18	△	△	△	○	
Comprehensive registration plan accepted by management/employees	19	●	●	●	○	
Importance of activities to success		73	77	42	58	
		1	2	3	4	5

		1	2	3	4	5	6	7	8	9	10	11	12	13	14	15	16	17	18	19		
6	Assessment training			○	○	●	●	○	○	○	○	○	●	△	△	△	○	○	△	○	61	6
7	Audit training			○	○	●	○	○	○	○	△	○	●	△	○	●	○	○	○		62	7
8	Escort training			●	○	○			○	○	△	○	●				○	○	△		41	8
9	Process training	△	△	△	△		●	○	○	○	△	○		△	○			○	○		36	9
10	Quality policy training (LUTI)	●				△	○	△	△	○	△	○		△	○		○	○	△		33	10
11	Benchmarks of other quality systems					△	△	○	○	○				○	○	△		△	△	△	21	11
12	Quality steering team	●	●	△		○				●				●	●	●	●	○	○	△	74	12
13	Documentation structure plan																					13
14	Quality policies	●				△	●	△	○	△	△	○		△	○		●	△	△		43	14
15	Quality manual	○	△	○	△	●	●	△	○	△	●	●	○	●	●	○	●	○	○		88	15
16	Processes/procedures	△	△	○	△		●	△	○	△	△	○		△	○		△	○	○		35	16
17	Auditor certification		○	△	△	△	△	△	△								●	○	●		30	17
18	Meetings with departments	●	●	○	○	○	○	△	△	●	●	●	●	△	△	△	○	○	○	●	89	18
19	Review meetings																					19
20	Department champions		●	○	○	●	○	○	○	●	○	○	○	△	△	△	○	○	○	○	66	20
21	Quality steering team (executive management)	●	●	△	△	●	○	○	○	●	△	△	△	●	●	●	●	●	●	○	105	21
22	Expanded management	●	●	○	○	●	○	○	△	●	○	○	○	●	●	●	●	●	●	○	115	22
23	Initial assessment plan	○	○	○	△											△	△		△	●	22	23
24	Internal assessments/audits		●	○	△	●	○	△	△	△	○	○	○	●	●	●	●	○	●		85	24
25	Pre-assessment	○	●	○	○	●	●	●	○		○	○	○	●	●	●	●	●	●	○	114	25
26	Process improvement teams		●	●	○	○	●	△		△	△	○	△				●	○	●		61	26
27	Definitions of behavior																					27
28	Management	●	●			△	○			△				●	○	○	●	○	○	△	54	28
29	Employees			●	●	△	○			△	●	○	○				●	○	○	△	54	29
30	Teams		△	●	●	△	○			○	○	○	○	○	○	○	●	○	○	△	60	30
31	Bonuses		○	○	○																9	31
32	Four-box assessment guide					△	○	●	○		△	△	●	△	△	●	○	○	○		47	32
	Critical success factor coverage	90	101	97	76	104	107	50	42	82	67	75	75	90	94	83	153	102	99	68		

Appendix C

Electronic Questions and Answers

If you are on an electronic mail system that connects to the Internet, you may send further questions to the authors at our respective network addresses:

david.huyink@network.com or

craig.westover@stpaul.ncr.com

For a richer discussion of ISO 9000 topics, there is an ISO 9000 User Group Network, to which the authors subscribe, where questions are asked and answered as a normal part of the exchange of information by the group. Questions submitted to this network are responded to by people who collectively have a diversity of experience far greater than that of the two authors alone. You can subscribe by sending a message to:

LISTSERV@VM1.NODAK.EDU

This is the network address of the list server for all special interest group networks hosted by the University of North Dakota, including the ISO9000 User Group Network. The message you send is:

SUB ISO9000 firstname lastname

Note a couple of things about the address and the message. The character after the "VM" in the address is the number one, not the letter L. The "ISO9000" in the message does not have a space between ISO and 9000. Obviously, "firstname" and "lastname" should be replaced with your first and last names. After you send this message, you will receive a response to let you know that you have been added to the list, and some information on how to get off the list at a later time if you so desire.

Once on the list for the ISO 9000 User Group Network, you may ask or respond to a question or participate in an ongoing discussion by sending a message to:

ISO9000@VM1.NODAK.EDU

This is the network address for the ISO 9000 User Group Network. You subscribe or unsubscribe to the ISO 9000 network via the *LISTSERV* address. Once a subscriber, you send messages to the network via the *ISO 9000* address.

Index

NO POSTAGE
NECESSARY
IF MAILED
IN THE
UNITED STATES

BUSINESS REPLY MAIL

FIRST-CLASS MAIL PERMIT NO. 1590 ANN ARBOR MI

POSTAGE WILL BE PAID BY THE ADDRESSEE

National Center for Manufacturing Sciences
3025 Boardwalk
Ann Arbor MI 48108-3266